When Charles II returned home he began the search for a dynastic marriage. He fixed upon the Infanta of Portugal, Catherine of Braganza, whose dowry included the possession of Tangier, Bombay and valuable trade concessions. The Portuguese had been fighting for their independence from Spain for twenty years and needed alliances to tip the scales in their favour. In return for the concessions Charles agreed to send to Portugal a regiment of horse and two of foot, which provided an excuse to ship away the remnants of the Cromwellian armies that had not been disbanded at the Restoration. The prospect of service was at first well received - "Major-General Morgan drew forth his regiment of foot consisting of 1000 proper men besides officers, and made a short speech, acquainting them that his Majesty had been graciously pleased to design them for honourable service abroad. . . Whereupon they all with great acclamations of joy, cried out ' All, all, all. . .' There were also officers and men who had remained loyal to the crown and to them Charles owed a debt of employment. Former Royalists therefore made up the balance of the regiment of horse - uncomfortable bedfellows for their former enemies.

The English and French regiments fought with courage and discipline at the series of major battles and sieges that followed, most of which have never been properly described. This is, therefore, the re-discovery of a lost episode in our military history. It was the English and French soldiers, under Schomberg's leadership, who proved the decisive factor in winning back Portugal's independence. But in return for their courage in battle, the English soldiers were rewarded with insults and want of pay. At the conclusion of peace in 1667, only 1,000 out of the 3,500 men who made up the force were left standing. 400 of these received what was effectively a death sentence: they were shipped to Tangier to join the fight against the Moors. The remainder returned to seek service in England or abroad - but places were hard to find. One veteran of the horse summed up the feelings of many - ". . . there was never a more gallant party went out of England upon any design whatever, than were that regiment of horse. . . they came into the country full of money and gallantry, and those which survived left it as full of poverty and necessity."

The author's detailed but lively text is fully supported by a range of illustrations and specially-commissioned maps.

Lieutenant General Riley's service career has been chiefly on operations. He has commanded on operations in every rank, in Northern Ireland, the Balkans and Sierra Leone, where he was one of a small number of British officers to have commanded a tri-service Joint Task Force; Iraq, where he was GOC British Forces as well as coalition commander; Senior British Military Adviser to United States Central Command; and Deputy Commander NATO ISAF Afghanistan. He was Director-General and Master of the Armouries from 2009 to 2012.

Lieutenant General Riley holds the degrees of BA (Geography) from University College London; MA (History) from the University of Leeds; and PhD (Modern History) from Cranfield University. He is a visiting professor in War Studies at King's College London, a Trustee of the Royal United Services Institute and the Chairman of the Royal Welch Fusiliers Museum and Archive Trust. He has published fifteen books of which the best known are *Napoleon as a General* (2007), *That Astonishing Infantry* (2008), *Decisive Battles* (2009), *Up to Mametz* (edited, annotated and introduced) (2010); and *A Matter of Honour* (2011). In addition he has contributed articles to a number of periodicals and compilations and is a frequent public speaker on subjects ranging from history to strategy, defence, security and international affairs. He teaches and mentors regularly in NATO and US military schools and colleges.

The Last Ironsides

A rare contemporary illustration of a harquebusier, armed with sword, carbine and pistol and dressed in helmet and buff coat. This is how the English horsemen in Portugal would have appeared in 1662, from Flaminio della Croce's, *L'essercitio della cavalleria*. (© Royal Armouries RAL. 08423)

The Last Ironsides

The English Expedition to Portugal, 1662–1668

Jonathon Riley

Foreword
by
John Childs

Helion & Company

Helion & Company Limited
26 Willow Road
Solihull
West Midlands
B91 1UE
England
Tel. 0121 705 3393
Fax 0121 711 4075
email: info@helion.co.uk
website: www.helion.co.uk
Twitter: @helionbooks
Visit our blog http://blog.helion.co.uk

Published by Helion & Company 2014. Reprinted with corrections 2015.
Reprinted in paperback 2017
Designed and typeset by Mach 3 Solutions Ltd (www.mach3solutions.co.uk)
Cover designed by James Riley
Printed by Hobbs The Printers Ltd, Totton, Hampshire

Text © Jonathon Riley 2014
Illustrations © as individually credited
Maps © Steve Waites 2014, unless otherwise credited
Cover: A contemporary illustration on tiles of the battle of Montes Claros.
(Author's collection)

ISBN 978-1-912174-10-2

British Library Cataloguing-in-Publication Data
A catalogue record for this book is available from the British Library

For details of other military history titles published by Helion & Company
Limited contact the above address, or visit our website: http://www.helion.co.uk

We always welcome receiving book proposals from prospective authors working in
military history.

Contents

List of Plates

Edward Hyde, Earl of Clarendon, engraved by Michael Loggan after Sir Peter Lely's portrait. (Author's collection)

Frederick Hermann, 1st Duke of Schomberg, engraved by Simon Gribelin after Michael Dahl's portrait It was Schomberg's abilities that brought vistory in the field in the Portuguese Restoration War. He commanded the English brigade from 1663 to 1667. (Author's collection)

Sir Robert Southwell engraved by John Smith after the portrait by Sir Godfrey Kneller. It was Southwell's mediation that brought the war between Spain and Portugal to a conclusion – although the credit was given to the Earl of Sandwich – and who secured the arrears of pay for the English brigade after a long struggle. (Author's collection)

Murrough O'Brien, 1st Earl of Inchiquin, by an unknown artist. O'Brien commanded the English brigade for the early period of its deployment to Portugal. (Author's collection)

Antonio Luis de Meneses, 1st Marquis of Marialva, by an unknown artist.

Francisco de Tuttavilla y del Tufo, Duke of San Germán, Don John of Austria's deputy during the campaign of 1663.

A contemporary sketch of Don Francisco de Mello. (Author's collection)

Luiz Vasconcellos e Souza, Conde de Castelo Melhor.

Charles II, King of England. (Soham Roots)

L'entrée du prince de Ligne à Londres, 1660 by François Duchatel. This painting shows the arrival of Jean-Charles de Watteville in early September 1660 and the environs of the Tower before the Great Fire; it was also here that on 30 September, French and Spanish soldiers fought a major street battle.

Luis de Benavides Carrillo de Toledo 3rd Marques de Caracena, by Philipp Fruytiers.

Marie-Françoise de Savoie-Nemours, Queen of Portugal by an unknown artist.

Alfonso VI, King of Portugal by an unknown artist. The King is wearing full armour in recognition that his country was at war, even though he himself never took the field.

Queen Catherine of Braganza, wife of Charles II of England, by Jacob Huysmans. (Trustees of The Queen's Royal Surrey Regiment)

Sir Richard Fanshawe, 1st Baronet, (1608–1666), by an unknown artist. Fanshawe was the English Ambassador to the court of Portugal and Spain until supplanted by Sir Robert Southwell. (Government Art Collection, 1175)

Philip IV of Spain in Hunting Attire, by Diego Velázquez.

Don John of Austria the Younger by an unknown artist.

A contemporary illustration on tiles of the battle of Montes Claros. (Author's collection)

The Parade of the Army at Tangier by Dirk Stoop (1680). This near-contemporary illustration shows the dress, equipment, Colours and organisation of a mid-seventeenth

List of Figures

List of Maps

Foreword

Despite promising in the Declaration of Breda 'to consent ... [to] the full satisfaction of all arrears due to the officers and soldiers of the army under the command of General Monck, and that they shall be received into our service, upon as good pay and conditions, as they now enjoy', Charles II decided to disband the New Model Army soon after his restoration. The parliamentary soldiers were a grave threat to the security of the new régime, while their maintenance was impossibly expensive. On 13 September 1660, he gave the royal assent to two statutes that sealed the fate of the New Model; by January 1661, it had virtually ceased to exist. Normally, a major demobilization resulted in thousands of unemployed soldiers creating a crime wave, particularly in London whence the majority gravitated but, on this occasion, the effect was less dramatic. The disbanded men received full back-pay and the majority settled quickly and smoothly into civilian life. Apprenticeship laws and certain craft guild regulations were relaxed and the king and his grandees went out of their way to provide work in the construction of houses, landscaping gardens and parkland and excavating the canal in St. James's Park. Samuel Pepys was impressed and surprised by the apparently seamless transition.

> Of all the old army now you cannot see a man begging about the street; but what? You have this captain turned a shoemaker; the lieutenant a baker; that a haberdasher; this common soldier a porter; and every man in his apron and frock &c. as if they have never done anything else.

Pepys's observation was a Londoner's pardonable exaggeration. Although the bulk of the New Model was demobilized without significant incident, not all its ex-soldiers returned meekly to civilian life. Many either volunteered for or were forced into mercenary service: 3,000 went to Russia; 6,000 were made available to the Holy Roman Empire; the Anglo-Dutch Brigade consumed 500 replacements *per annum*; and 400 garrisoned the new acquisition of Bombay.

Oliver Cromwell had dispatched a brigade of six regiments to assist the French in the capture of Dunkirk and Fort Mardyke in 1657 and the exiled Charles II had maintained seven regiments within the Spanish army. At the Restoration, these two forces were lodged in Dunkirk under the command of Sir Edward Harley. Unable to bear the expense and unwilling to harbour a nest of vipers so close to England, in 1662 Charles sold Dunkirk to Louis XIV of France for five million livres. All remaining royalist infantry was sent to England under Lord Wentworth to form a second battalion of the King's Guards. None of the old New Model units, however, was allowed to cross the Channel. Two large regiments were sold into the French army and 3,000 were dispatched to the new colony of Tangier, which had come into English possession as part of the dowry of the Portuguese princess, Catherine of Braganza, on her marriage to Charles II in 1661. The marriage treaty also included a commitment by Charles to send a brigade of 2,000 foot and 1,000 cavalry to assist in Portugal's struggle for independence from Spain, which had begun in 1640. The former was provided from still-extant battalions of the Scottish New Model while the mounted troops comprised volunteers and elements from the Dunkirk garrison. They arrived in Lisbon during August 1662 to join an international army of native Portuguese, French and Germans. Following internal discord among the senior officers, the British troops were placed under the command of the French Huguenot, Lieutenant General Herman von Schomberg, a man who was to play a significant rôle in subsequent British military history. Nevertheless, the brigade gained a fine reputation for endurance, courage and military efficiency despite neglect by the home government and discrimination from the Portuguese.

This precursor to British military involvement in Iberia during the War of the Spanish Succession and the Napoleonic Wars has received scant historiographical attention. There is no-one better qualified, both as historian and practitioner of the operational art, to fill this lacuna than General Jonathon Riley. He is an expert in early modern military history while long service in the British Army has given him broad experience and understanding of the highest levels of military command, especially in relation to coalitions. Not only has he led British units within international forces, most notably in Bosnia and Iraq, but his appointment as deputy commander of the NATO ISAF in Afghanistan provided insight into the direction of multi-national formations. He is in a unique position to appreciate the problems faced by Schomberg as operational director of the Portuguese field army and leader of the British contingent between 1662 and 1668.

Professor John Childs
University of Leeds

Acknowledgements

I would like to acknowledge with thanks for their help and patience the following people and organisations: first, to Professor John Childs who encouraged me, read and corrected the manuscripts, chastised me when needed and who with Francesca gave me so much encouragement and wonderful hospitality; there are a few historians who really understand the art of the possible on the battlefield of the past – John Childs is one of them. To Lieutenant-General Alexandre de Sousa Pinto, President of the Portuguese Commission for Military History and his staff in Lisbon, especially Colonel José Banazol, Colonel Fonseca and Lieutenant-Colonel Abilio Lousada; General Gabriel Espirito Santo; Dr Amelia Polonia of the University of Oporto; Dr Malcolm Mercer and the staff of the Royal Armouries in H.M. Tower of London; Mr Philip Abbot, Mr Stuart Ivison and the library staff of the Royal Armouries in Leeds; the staff of the National Archives, Kew; the staff of the British Library; the staff of the Bodleian Library in Oxford; the staff of the Brotherton Library at the University of Leeds; and Wienand Drenth for information on English troops in foreign service. Steve Waites, who drew all the maps to a high standard, as he has done with my last five books; Ben Scantlebury who did much primary research for me and saved me much time, trouble and loss of temper; and last but by no means least, Major Alasdair Goulden who helped me in Portugal and Spain on a detailed ground reconnaissance in January 2012. I also acknowledge Lorraine White's valuable and perceptive series of articles about the war in Iberia, using many contemporary sources in Spanish and Portuguese which I am otherwise unable to read. It is very rare indeed to find someone who has not held military command and who yet has such a ready grasp of the realities of war.

A Note on Dates

In the mid-seventeenth century, the Julian calendar was still in use in England, Scotland, Ireland, most of Germany and the Netherlands. This was ten days behind the Gregorian calendar (rising to eleven days in 1700), introduced in 1582 by Pope Gregory XIII, used in Spain and Portugal but not adopted in Great Britain until 1752. Moreover in the Julian calendar in England, the new year began on 25 March rather than on 1 January. These discrepancies have the potential to cause great confusion when trying to disentangle the dates of various campaigns and actions. I have opted to go with the dates given in the English style – the Julian calendar – throughout, although I have started the date of the New Year on 1 January.

Abbreviations

C.C.S.P.	Calendar of Clarendon State Papers
CO	Colonial Office
C.S.P.D.	Calendar of State Papers, Domestic Series
C.S.P.I.	Calendar of State Papers, Ireland
C.S.P.V.	Calendar of State Papers, Venice
H.M.C.	Historical Manuscript Commission
KB	Knight of the Most Honourable Order of the bath
KG	Knight of the Most Noble Order of the Garter
MS, MSS	Manuscript(s)
PC	Privy Council, Privy Councillor
SP	State Papers (followed by numeral denoting series)
TNA	The National Archive (formerly the Public Record Office (P.R.O.)), Kew

Prologue

The heat and drought of a Spanish summer in 1664. The siege of the little fortress and town of Valencia de Alcantara had been going on for six days and a breach had been made in the outer walls of the town. The garrison was still unshaken but the townspeople, knowing the dreadful consequences of sack, murder and pillage that would follow a successful break-in by the attackers, implored the commander to ask for terms. He would have none of it. Among the attacking force of Portuguese and allied troops, commanded by the renowned French Marshal Frederick, Duke of Schomberg, were two English regiments of foot. These regiments, the shock troops of the little allied army, were ordered to storm the breach, with the Portuguese *terzo da Armada* on their right and a French regiment on their left. At nine o'clock at night, the signal for the attack was given, and the English, according to their orders, ran like men possessed to the breach: but not a man of their allies stirred. The English fought it out above half an hour, to the admiration of all those that stood and looked on. In that short time they lost a lieutenant-colonel, a major, four captains, two lieutenants, three ensigns, nine sergeants and one hundred and fifty-eight soldiers killed. The colonel in command of the assault, leading from the front as was the absolute requirement of a senior officer in those days, was shot twice in the body; only his plate armour saved him too from death. The English pulled back, leaving their dead and with another 250 badly wounded – of whom many died of their injuries or were crippled.

Who were these men and what drove them to fight so hard in a far-off country, in a cause that our history has since forgotten? In most cases their bravery and discipline is easily explained: they were the last remnants of the old Cromwellian army, which had been disbanded after Charles II's restoration. For most of the officers and men of that army their arrears of pay and a good character were all that they received; and most needed no more. In spite of the fears of the new regime, they simply melted back into the society of the day as carpenters or cobblers, saddlers or smiths. For many men, though, military service was their life and the King's marriage to a Portuguese princess provided the chance to continue serving with their comrades. Under the terms of the treaty of marriage, Charles had to find a brigade of troops to fight for the Portuguese in their twenty-year-old war of independence from Spain. When the old Cromwellian garrison in Scotland, purged of its radical elements, was offered the chance of service abroad one regiment at least volunteered to a man, calling out 'All, all, all!' And so two regiments of foot, each a thousand strong besides their officers, were formed. Over the coming six years, in battle and siege, they would show again and again that they were indeed the last ironsides.

But there were old Royalists too, many of them despised English or Irish Catholics, men who had fought for the old king, lost their livelihood, and could not be found places in the new army at home. There were thought to be more than 5,000 officers eligible to share in the meagre compensation pot available and only three regiments of foot, two of horse and the small garrison companies of the forts and castles around the kingdom that were available to provide employment. Many therefore looked abroad: first to the great garrisons of Dunkirk and Mardyck until they were sold to France in 1663; some to the brigades employed in foreign service in France and the Low Countries; others to the overseas garrisons of the new empire: the Barbadoes, Jamaica, Bombay and Tangier. And some went to Portugal, where the brigade was to contain a regiment of horse as well as two of foot. Half this regiment had already been found from old Cromwellian soldiers but the other half was made up of Royalists, many of them gentlemen's sons. There was little love lost between the two factions until action against the Spanish provided the glue that would bind them together. One old royalist officer delighted in the restoration of the old order, telling his former enemies now in the ranks in Portugal that they were Cromwell's whelps, rebels, banished men, as good as dead – sent here for the murder of the late king.

The expedition could, under such conditions, have rapidly fallen apart; indeed it almost failed to survive its first year. But by 1668 the war had been won. The contribution of the English troops – and also the French – under the inspirational leadership of Marshal Schomberg proved decisive. The majority never saw England again. Most died in Portugal or Spain; of those who survived, 400 were handed a death sentence: service against the Moors in Tangier; others – the Catholics – had to seek service abroad with foreign monarchs. Only 500 out of more than three and a half thousand ever made it home.

1

Portugal, Spain and Europe, 1560–1660

'Portugal – I inherited it, I bought it, I conquered it.'

The modern history of Portugal – and the history of Portugal as a modern European state – begins with her war of independence from Spain. It seemed at the outset an unequal contest, for the population of Portugal in 1640 was a mere 2 million – compared with 5 million in England, 19 million in France and perhaps 22 million in the European territories of the Habsburg empire; it was the Portuguese empire overseas, built by the enormous drive for exploration of the Portuguese navigators, that made the country comparatively so wealthy for its size, population and economic potential and that made it possible to challenge the superpower of the day. From the middle of the fifteenth century, the Portuguese had explored and opened the eastern coasts of South America and the western coasts of southern Africa, establishing trade and the exchange of slaves, goods and practices between them. They reached India by sea, having rounded and colonized the Cape of Good Hope, opening a direct sea lane from Europe to Asia. They pushed on to Indonesia, China and Japan, founding a mercantile empire based on an almost insatiable European demand for spices, especially pepper, but also silk and porcelain. They built fortresses, bases and trading stations to secure their sea lanes: at Mombasa in East Africa, Goa in India, Macau in China and Nagasaki in Japan. For 100 years, there was no-one to rival them.

According to one source in 1627, there were as few as 5,000 Portuguese fighting men in Asia to protect this mercantile empire, some 3,500 of whom were stationed in the fleets of the western coast of India. A mere 300 manned the Persian Gulf fleet and only 200 the Malaccan. There were small permanent garrisons of troops in Ceylon (800 men), Malacca (100) and Mozambique (100) on the east African coast, with an unknown force at Macau.[1] The numerical weakness of Portuguese military units was compounded by their general disorganisation and indiscipline, for at this date the Portuguese had not developed the systematic professional structure of the Spanish *tercios*. By the mid-seventeenth century it was clear that the future of Portuguese overseas trade and possessions lay in the Brazils rather than Asia, for reasons that will be explored later in this chapter, but still the struggle to maintain the eastern empire diverted vital supplies and manpower from Portuguese America.

At home, from 1557 to 1562 Portugal was ruled by a Queen, Catherine. She was succeeded by the young King Sebastian, who had tried to revive the idea of a North African empire. He disappeared in the disastrous defeat by the Moors at Ksar El Kebir in 1578, which saw not only his death, but also the end of the ruling House of Aviz.

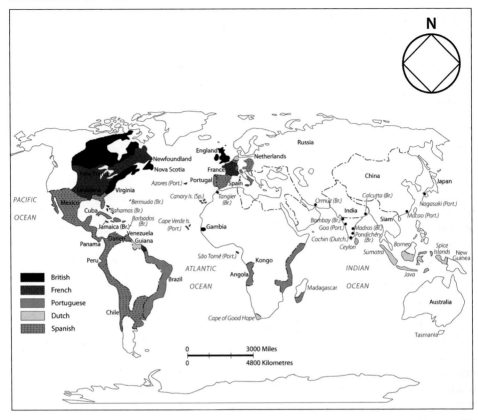

Map 1 The European Empires, c.1660.

Sebastian's successor, the Cardinal Henry of Portugal, was 70 years old at the time and his death not long afterwards precipitated a succession crisis in which the three grand-children of Manuel I (who had died in 1521) made claim to the throne: the *Infanta* Catharina, Duchess of Braganza, who was married to John, 6th Duke of Braganza; António, Prior of Crato; and Philip II of Spain. António had been acclaimed King of Portugal by the people of Santarém on July 24, 1580 and then in many cities and towns throughout the country. Some members of the Council of Governors of Portugal, who had supported Philip, escaped to Spain and declared him to be the legal successor of Henry. Philip II of Spain marched into Portugal and defeated the troops loyal to the Prior of Crato in the Battle of Alcântara. The Spanish army commanded by the Duke of Alba then marched into and occupied Lisbon and seized the contents of the treasury, while his soldiers sacked the capital. Philip is reputed to have said of Portugal: 'I inherited it, I bought it, I conquered it.'[2] He was crowned Philip I of Portugal in 1581 and recognised as king by the Cortes of Tomar; and the Portuguese House of Habsburg, also called the Philippine Dynasty, began – as did what became known as the Iberian Union. When Philip left for Madrid in 1583, he made his nephew Albert of Austria his viceroy in Lisbon. In Madrid he established a Council of Portugal to advise him on Portuguese affairs.[3]

In 1581 the Spanish crown had pledged to respect the integrity of Portuguese institutions and although this was never completely fulfilled, the essence of the agreement was honoured. A few small Spanish garrisons were established in Portugal, but there was never a widespread military occupation. Philip II never returned to Portugal, and Philip III visited the kingdom only once during his reign of twenty-three years. Portuguese interests were less respected during these years especially, and there was a tendency to promote Spanish officials to appointments in Portugal. In general, however, the benefits of the union at first outweighed the disadvantages. The Portuguese were never required to contribute to the Spanish treasury, while the Spanish crown helped to bolster Portugal's Atlantic defences. Little could be done to halt the losses in Portuguese Asia, but the Portuguese themselves recognized that that was within neither the responsibility nor the resources of the Spanish crown; moreover the Atlantic trade with the Brazils had become far more valuable and far less dangerous. Access to the wealth of Spanish America too was valued by the Portuguese. Other benefits of Habsburg rule included a new canon of Portuguese law, the *Ordenaçoes Filipinas*, issued in 1602; and efforts to improve agriculture, including the distribution of waste land for cultivation, the protection of peasants in debt and greater powers for village councils.

Discontent with Habsburg government became much more marked, however, during the reign of Philip IV and this had three main causes: first, losses from the Dutch invasion of Brazil which Spain had done nothing to deter or prevent; secondly, efforts to exclude the Portuguese from access to Spanish America; and thirdly, attempts by the Crown to levy new taxes for imperial defence. The Spanish crown tried to accord the defence of the Brazils priority equal with that of Spanish territories in the Americas, but when the Dutch invasion of Pernambuco began in 1630, it lacked the means to drive them out: a large joint Spanish–Portuguese expedition under Portuguese command was defeated by a much smaller Dutch force off the Brazilian coast in January 1640. Since the retention and development of Brazil was now much more important than what little remained of Portuguese Asia, this mattered.

At home, a new pro-Habsburg aristocracy had been created in Portugal after 1580 by the award of new titles, but the lesser nobility became increasingly disillusioned with the status quo. As Habsburg rule wore on, they were becoming a marginalized rural class, living with their tenants on small estates, excluded from access to imperial appointments. During the 1620s, the Spanish crown raised a number of forced loans in Lisbon, provoking discontent among the mercantile class. The Count-Duke of Olivares, Prime Minister of Spain,[*] then attempted to make the Portuguese pay increased taxes for their own defence. In 1637 agricultural prices took a tumble throughout Portugal, presenting the peasantry with further problems. When higher taxes were levied, a popular revolt broke out in the royal city of Évora and it spread through most of Alentejo and the Algarve, with its effects felt as far away as the north-west. Although this revolt was soon put down by Castilian troops, it was warning of popular emotion. The growing dissatisfaction with the situation culminated in a coup d'état organized by elements among the nobility and bourgeoisie – a contrast to the popular uprising of three years

---

[*]   Gaspar de Guzmán y Pimentel Ribera y Velasco de Tovar, Count-Duke of Olivares and Duke of San Lúcar la Mayor (1587–1645), prime minister from 1621 to 1643.

before – on 1 December 1640, sixty years after the crowning of Philip I as the first of the dual monarchs. The plot was chiefly planned by three men: Antão Vaz de Almada,[*] Miguel de Almeida,[†] and João Pinto Ribeiro.[‡] They, together with a small group of armed fellow-conspirators, stormed the Royal palace in Lisbon, murdered the Secretary of State, Miguel de Vasconcelos, and imprisoned the king's cousin, Margaret of Savoy, Duchess of Mantua[§] who had been governing Portugal as vicereine in Philip's name. She, famously, tried to calm the Portuguese people during demonstrations in the Terreiro do Paço, at the time Lisbon's main square, but failed.[4]

The moment was well chosen: Philip's armies were heavily committed to fighting against France in one of the many episodes of the Thirty Years' War, while at the same time having to deal with the revolt in Catalonia which became known as the Reapers' War.[5] Olivares now demanded Portuguese assistance in putting down the revolt in Catalonia. Some 6,000 troops had already been impressed from Portugal; John, 8th Duke of Bragança – or Braganza – head of the senior family among the Portuguese nobility and nominal commander of Portugal's military forces had been ordered to Spain with a new levy of Portuguese troops, but had delayed his departure. John was the obvious national leader and the enthusiastic support of the population was immediately obvious: within a matter of hours, he was acclaimed as King John IV of Portugal and he accepted the throne that same day. On 2 December 1640, the day after the coup, John began his first acts as de facto sovereign of the country and the news spread rapidly by courier, proclamation, newspapers and word of mouth.

John took immediate steps to strengthen his position. Francisco de Lucena, secretary to the governing council of Portugal for the past 36 years, transferred his allegiance to the new king as Chief Minister and confirmed most of the existing office-holders in their posts, thus ensuring a smooth and seamless transfer of authority. On 11 December 1640, a council of war was created to prepare for military operations – for there was never any doubt that the Spanish would retaliate. Next, the king created the Junta of the Frontiers, to take charge of the border fortresses and their garrisons; the defence of Lisbon; the garrisons of all other forts and castles; and the ports. It was as well that he took these steps, for in 1641 another popular revolt broke out, harnessed by elements among the nobility and supported by the Inquisition – and indeed the Papacy – which was firmly in favour of the union with Spain. The ringleaders were arraigned for high treason and executed. Among these were Miguel Luís de Menezes,[¶] who had long been a prominent supporter of Spanish rule, but Lucena, whose son had continued to serve the Spanish government in Madrid, was also arraigned and executed in Évora.

In the Decree of 13 May 1641, John took further steps to ensure that all of the national fortresses would be strengthened and modernised and that these improvements would be paid for through regional taxes. John IV also organized his army on the lines established under the earlier Military Laws of King Sebastian and these reforms were amongst the most innovative and sweeping measures of their time. The infantry was organised on

---

*   Antão Vaz de Almada (1573–1644) was later Portuguese ambassador to London.
†   Miguel de Almeida, 4th Count of Abrantes (1575–1650).
‡   João Pinto Ribeiro (1590–1649).
§   Margaret of Savoy (1589–1655).
¶   Miguel Luís de Menezes II, 2nd Duke of Caminha (1614–1641).

similar lines to the Spanish infantry, into five regular *terzos* of 2,000 men each – those of the Armada, Lisboa, Alentejo, Algarve and the Navy; the cavalry was formed of independent companies of 100 mounted men, who were regarded as something of an elite;[6] and there was an establishment of 300 artillerymen.[7] Since the Spanish model was used, it is worth rehearsing what that meant. Throughout the Eighty Years' War with the Dutch and after, the Spanish infantry, the backbone of her army, was organised in *tercios* of about twelve companies, commanded by a *Maestro de Campo*, a rank somewhere between colonel and major-general. After 1636, the company consisted of 200 men with eleven officers and staff, thirty musketeers, sixty arquebusiers – mounted infantry or dragoons armed with a lighter weapon than the musketeers – sixty-five armoured pikemen and thirty-four un-armoured pike-men. The eleven officers and staff were a captain and his page, a lieutenant, an ensign, a sergeant, two drummers, one piper, a chaplain, a quarter-master and a barber-surgeon.[8] In the 1580s and after, Spanish troops, especially the infantry, were always regarded as the elite fighting troops of Europe, with special pay and privileges and rich rewards. Even allowing for Spanish self-congratulation it must be acknowledged that these troops were experienced veterans, well trained and equipped. They were followed in excellence by the North Italians, English and Germans.

When John IV of Portugal set out to adapt this organization he could not rely on the range of methods for raising men that were available to the Spanish with their large European possessions. Instead, John decided on a mass levy in order to generate the numbers of troops he needed to face the powerful armies of his enemy. The king aimed to mobilize all able-bodied men in the kingdom and decreed that all men from 15 to 60 years of age were liable for obligatory military service according to the country's ancient *Ordenanzas* or ordinances. Local officials appointed from the gentry and nobility – who, in time, would become known as *Ordenanza* officers – were instructed to compile muster rolls of all able-bodied men in their districts. From these lists three classes of men were selected. The first class comprised the unmarried younger sons of families, except for those needed to work farms and the sons of widows. They were drafted into the royal service as *soldados pagos* (paid soldiers) in the regular army and they filled the ranks of the first-line units. The second class required all the exempted men and the married men able to bear arms to muster into auxiliary *terzos* of 600 men each in ten companies, organised in every district: there would be five of these *terzos* in Lisbon and twenty-five in the provinces. This militia reserve formed the second line of the army. The third class consisted of *Ordenanza* companies of 240 men each, made up of older men. These companies were largely responsible for the conduct and implementation of the recruiting system. In the event of national emergencies, however, they were to form the third line units of the army. The dual nature of the duties performed by these reserve units was usually misunderstood by English and French observers and the crucial part they played in the all-important draft system was largely ignored, possibly because there was nothing quite like it elsewhere.

King John IV's orders produced a regular army of 20,000 foot and 4,000 horse, making it one of the largest standing armies in Western Europe at the time. Mobilization of the second and third line units would swell its numbers further to more than 30,000 foot and 7,800 horse of which 16,000 were in the frontier province of Alentejo; however although generally successful by the standards of the day, most infantry units seldom rose above 600 strong and cavalry companies rarely above 80.[9] It was this extraordinary

Figure 1 An idealised representation of a company of foot soldiers in Allain Mallet's
Les traveaux de Mars, ou l'art de la Guerre. (© Royal Armouries RAL. 08482)

organisation, with its reserves, which produced the force that fought for the independence of the country from Spain. After the war, Portugal maintained its standing army and continued its selective draft system. It should be noted that Portugal, unlike nearly every other kingdom, did not have regiments of royal guards: the closest thing to a guard unit was the small company of largely ceremonial archers, armed with halberds rather than bows, which escorted the monarch and acted as his close protection. Ordinary guard duties at court and palaces in and around Lisbon were usually assumed by detachments of marines and of the 1st Artillery Regiment, which was consequently called the *Corte* Regiment. Foreigners often assumed that the senior *terzo* of the field army, that of the Armada, was a regiment of guards as it occupied the position of honour on the right of the line of battle: a fair assumption, given the usual practice of the day.

After winning several small victories early on in the war, John tried to make peace quickly – but without success. He himself was never recognised by the Spanish and the war that followed the Portuguese revolt dragged on for twenty-eight years. It has become known to history by various names, most notably as the Portuguese Restoration War, or the Acclamation War. With the bulk of what would otherwise have been overwhelming, indeed decisive, Spanish military power deployed elsewhere, and the Portuguese unable to raise an army powerful enough to invade Spain, the Restoration War consisted in the main of border skirmishes, cavalry raids and the sack of border towns, combined with occasional invasions and counter-invasions, many of them half-hearted and under-resourced. Portugal was able to finance her war effort because of her revenues from the spice trade with Asia and the sugar trade from the Brazils in spite of the Dutch war; and she received some support from the European opponents of Spain, particularly the Dutch once the war between the two countries had been concluded – as well as France and England. However, the overriding goal of Portuguese diplomacy, a formal alliance with France, continued to evade her. So too did a place in the negotiations for the European settlement of settlements, the Peace of Westphalia in 1648. With this treaty and the end of hostilities against the rebels in Catalonia in 1652, Spain was again able to direct her main effort against Portugal.

Because of these factors of dispersion and dislocation, there were only five major set-piece battles during twenty-eight years of war. Three theatres of operations were eventually opened, but most activity was focused on the northern front around Galicia and on the central front between Portuguese Alentejo and Spanish Extremadura. The southern front, where the Portuguese Algarve is contiguous with Spanish Andalusia, was a logical target for Portugal, but it was never the focus of Portuguese offensive operations until late in the war, probably because the Portuguese queen, Luisa de Guzmán,* was the sister of the Duke of Medina-Sidonia,† the leading Spanish nobleman of Andalusia. John IV died on 6 November 1654 after a reign of fifteen years and was succeeded as regent by his queen, Luisa, during the minority of their son, Alfonso VI. Not surprisingly given her parentage, Luisa began seeking an accommodation with Spain.

---

*   Luisa de Guzmán (1613–1666) was the eldest daughter of the Duke.

†   Alonzo Perez de Guzman, 7th Duke of Medina Sidonia (1550–1615) had commanded the Spanish Armada against England. His son was Juan Manuel Perez de Guzmán y Silva (1579–1636), 8th Duke; Luisa was his daughter.

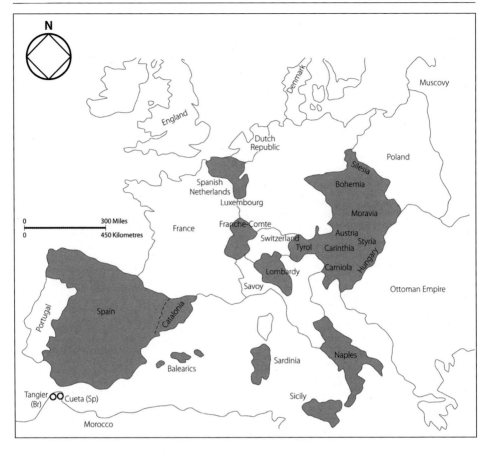

Map 2 The Extent of Habsburg Dominions in Europe, 1667.

The time seemed right for an accommodation, for even mighty Imperial Spain had been drained by her long wars and she was short of men, money and capable generals. True, Spain possessed a reputation at this time as the most formidable military power in Europe, if not the world; but with its heavy commitments elsewhere, Spain had little choice at first but to fight a defensive war in Iberia. From the 1590s onwards, the Spanish had faced a manpower crisis caused by the coincidence of maximum military pressure combined with plague in the Iberian peninsula: there were wars in Languedoc and Brittany in support of insurrections inside France; simultaneous campaigns in Lombardy, Franche-Comté, the Netherlands and at sea; and the Empire was also fighting the Turks for control of Hungary. The additional costs of fighting in Iberia were unwelcome to say the least, for by the 1650s, there were over 20,000 Spanish troops in Extremadura alone, and another 27,000 in Flanders. Between 1649 and 1654, almost 30 percent of Spanish military expenditure – around 6 million ducats[10] – was directed towards fighting Portugal, a figure that rose higher still during the major campaigns of the 1660s. Military pressures were exacerbated by natural disasters. Between 1598 and 1602, around eight percent of the population of Spain was killed by plague, exacerbated further by a sequence of failed harvests throughout the 1590s. The overall effect of plague and emigration reduced Spain's population from 8 million in the early sixteenth century to 7 million by the mid-seventeenth century – a turning-point in the demographic history of Castile in particular; land was taken out of production for lack of labour and the incentive to develop it, and Spain, although predominantly agrarian, depended on imports of foodstuffs. No wonder that this period has been characterised by historians as the decline of Imperial Spain.[11]

Military expenditure had, moreover, done little to stimulate the domestic economy: Silver from her South American mines passed through Spain like sand through a sieve to pay for troops in the Netherlands and Italy, to maintain the emperor's forces in Germany and ships at sea, and to satisfy consumption at home. The amount of precious metal brought from America and spent on Spain's military establishment quickened inflation throughout Europe, left Spaniards without sufficient specie to pay debts, and caused Spanish goods to become too overpriced to compete in international markets. Nor could American bullion alone satisfy the demands of military expenditure. Domestic production was heavily taxed, driving up prices.[12] As her supply of specie decreased in the seventeenth century, Spain was neither able to meet the cost of her military commitments nor to pay for imports of the manufactured goods that could not be produced efficiently at home. The costs of war caused Spain to be technically bankrupt on three occasions in 1607, 1627 and 1647; there were fifty mutinies over arrears of pay in the Army of Flanders between 1570 and 1607. How to export military costs was therefore a major preoccupation; the best way to do this was to extract contributions of food and money from enemy or conquered territory and especially go into winter quarters on an opponents' territory, forcing the enemy's population to bear the costs of the army.[13]

Portugal, for its part, had no need to take Spanish territory other than for bargaining purposes and it too was inclined to a defensive war. There was thus little impetus by either side to seize, maintain and exploit the initiative. Resources were too limited and governed the art of the possible. For long periods, without either men or money, neither side mounted formal campaigns and when operations were undertaken, they were often driven by remote political considerations – such as Portugal's need to impress potential allies – rather than by clear military-strategic objectives aimed at achieving a decision. In addition, given the problems of campaigning in the winter – weather, poor roads and lack of the means to supply the armies in the field – and the oppressive heat and drought of summer, most of the fighting was confined to two short campaigning seasons in the spring and autumn. More will be said of this, where appropriate to the context, in the following chapters.

*   *   *

The Portuguese Restoration War is usually considered to have fallen into three periods. The first, early, stage from 1640 to 1646 embraced several major engagements whose main effect was to demonstrate that the Portuguese could not easily be brought back under Spanish dominion. The Spanish deployed seven *tercios* to the frontier and after a period of stand-off, on 26 May 1644, a large column of Spanish troops and mercenaries, commanded by the Neapolitan Marquis of Torrecuso, was stopped at the Battle of Montijo by the Portuguese, who were led by the Brazilian-trained Matias de

Albuquerque,* one of a number of experienced Portuguese colonial officers who rose to prominence during the war. Indeed it was colonial troops, often descended from Portuguese veterans who had settled in the colonies and intermarried with local women, who proved the most formidable soldiers in the struggle against the Dutch and Spanish. The Portuguese followed up their victory by laying siege to and capturing Valencia de Alcantara in July 1644. Not long afterwards, in November 1644, Torrecuso crossed the frontier from Badajoz in a rare winter campaign to attack the Portuguese town of Elvas, which he besieged for nine days. He suffered heavy losses and was forced back across the border.

The second period ran from 1646 to 1660 and was in effect a military stalemate, characterized by small-scale raiding, while Spain concentrated on winning its other wars elsewhere in Europe. The major engagement of this period, the Battle of the Lines of Elvas was fought on 14 January 1659. Portuguese troops, under the command of Antonio Luís de Menezes, Marquis of Marialva,† son of the man who had been executed after the failed coup of 1641, and Sancho Manoel de Vilhena,‡ scored a resounding victory over the Spanish. After the conclusion of the Treaty of the Pyrenees in November 1659 the Spaniards again laid siege to Elvas, but they were driven off once more by de Menezes.

The war then became a frontier confrontation, a cycle of attrition, often between local forces composed of neighbours who knew each other well, but this familiarity did not moderate the destructive and blood-thirsty impulses of either side, of the sort that had become commonplace elsewhere during the Thirty Years' War. The harsh and merciless nature of the fighting was often exacerbated by the use of mercenaries and foreign conscripts; incidents of great cruelty were reported on both sides. Soldiers and officers, many of them mercenaries short of pay, became diverted towards plunder and desertion. The Portuguese settled old scores that had lain unsettled during the sixty years of Spanish domination; while the Spanish often took the view that their opponents were not an opposing army entitled to chivalrous treatment under the normally agreed rules of combat, but rebels. In November 1645, for example, 800 Portuguese soldiers took on a Spanish force and came off worse: seventeen escaped, 143 were taken prisoner, and 640 were killed. In 1650, it was reported of Portuguese behaviour towards Spanish captives that they:

> cut off Don Francisco de Amezquita's instrument of nature whilst he was still almost alive, they cut off Lieutenant Don Juan Cid's ears after killing him, another soldier … arrived at Ceclavin with his ears cut off, they killed an aide of the *maestro de campo* and afterwards they spiked him with pikes and spread-eagled him on a rack, and did the same to another cavalry soldier, and two cavalry ensigns and up to fourteen soldiers who were otherwise unhurt, leaving them for dead … and to a cavalry soldier who was badly wounded they threw some gunpowder on the ground and blew him up.[14]

---

* Matias de Albuquerque, 1st Count of Alegrete (1580–1647) was nicknamed 'the hero of two continents' on account of his military victories.

† Antonio Luís de Menezes, 1st Marquis of Marialva and 3rd Count of Cantanhede (1603–1675).

‡ Sancho Manoel de Vilhena, 1st Count of Vila Flor (1610–1677).

While raiding the northern Portuguese village of Moimenta in 1641, Spanish troops pillaged the place – of course – but also killed everyone they found and burned the houses with the inhabitants in them.

The third, final, period of the war, with which this book is concerned, ran from 1660 to 1668, during which time Philip IV of Spain unsuccessfully sought a decisive victory that would bring an end to hostilities while foreign intervention on the Portuguese side sought the same end.

*   *   *

Bad as the situation seemed to the Spanish government, matters were not especially rosy when seen from the point of view of Spain's most determined enemy, France. Warfare on the scale of that in progress throughout Europe in the early seventeenth century was only possible through the organisation of a centralised state. The ultimate expression of this idea was that which emerged in France during the reigns of Louis XIII and XIV. Louis XIV in particular harnessed the largest block of national population in Europe and directed its energies towards centrally directed policies and strategies, under great military captains like Turenne and de Saxe. Between the sixteenth and eighteenth centuries, the French regular army grew by a factor of fifteen.[15]

Even so, in 1640, Cardinal Richelieu, chief adviser and minister to King Louis XIII, knew all too well that France was operating militarily at the limits of her power. She was at war with Spain on three fronts: in the Pyrenees, in Flanders and in Franche-Comté, the latter two regions being Spanish territories. She also faced rebellions within France that were supported and financed by Madrid. Seen from Paris, Philip IV of Spain controlled considerable territories in Italy, where he could, whenever he chose, further stretch French resources by opening a fourth front against French-controlled Savoy, where Christine Marie of France* ruled as regent on behalf of her young son, Charles Emmanuel II, Duke of Savoy.†

Richelieu therefore decided that the best way to relieve pressure on France would be to force Philip IV to divert military resources to other theatres of war – he sought to do this by creating internal problems for the Spanish. The Portuguese revolt was a heaven-sent opportunity to do just that. To fulfil Richelieu's intention and to cement the interests of Portugal and France, a treaty of alliance between the two countries was concluded in Paris on 1 June 1641 and a large contingent of French troops was sent to serve in Portugal. The treaty endured for eighteen years, until Richelieu's successor, Cardinal Mazarin, broke it and abandoned his Portuguese and Catalan allies to sign a separate peace with Madrid.

From 1635, France managed to campaign against her enemy simultaneously on four fronts: Lombardy, Catalonia, Alsace and the Netherlands, thus keeping Spanish armies in a state of permanent overstretch throughout the Portuguese revolt. A Spanish attack into France in 1636 to relieve pressure elsewhere failed. Yet in 1643 the Captain-General

---

*   Christine Marie of France (1606–1663), sister of Louis XIII and Duchess of Savoy by marriage. At the death of her husband Victor Amadeus I in 1637, she acted as regent of Savoy.

†   Charles Emmanuel II (1634–1675) was the Duke of Savoy from 1638 to 1675 and under regency of his mother until 1663.

of the Army of Flanders, Don Francisco de Melo, Marquis of Tor de Laguna, decided to invade France: with Richelieu dead and Louis XIII in terminal decline, France seemed headed for civil war. Active intervention against France had long been an established credo; in 1558, for example, Philip II observed that 'I am well aware that it is from the Netherlands that the King of France can best be attacked and forced into peace.'[16] So rather than compromise with the Dutch and let his French enemy disintegrate, de Melo intervened: with 19,000 infantry and 8,000 cavalry he invaded France and besieged Rocroi, a small fortress that commanded the routes from Rheims and Soissons, respectively, to Paris. The French pulled together and sent a relief army of 17,000 foot and 6,000 horse under the 22-year-old Prince of Condé. In the ensuing defeat the Spanish lost 7,000 casualties and 8,000 prisoners;[17] but more than that, the invincible reputation of the Spanish army was lost. De Melo was recalled in disgrace.

French armies and the Dutch navy now cut off the Spanish Netherlands from all outside assistance. Nor had Spain anything much in the way of manpower or money to send, for the outbreak of war in the Iberian peninsula absorbed all other resources. In July 1644 Philip IV informed his ministers that peace should be concluded on all fronts as rapidly as possible, first and foremost with France: but France had no advantage to gain after Rocroi by making peace. French armies conquered Spanish towns in the south of the Netherlands and again beat the Spanish field army at Lens in August 1648. But Philip's initiatives elsewhere were not without some success, for in January 1648, a peace was at last made with the Dutch, ending the Eighty Years' War and recognising a Dutch sovereign state. In October of the same year, the Thirty Years' War was also concluded in Germany with the Peace of Westphalia. Spain ceded Alsace to France, thus severing the great Spanish Road, the corridor that connected the Spanish provinces in the Low Countries with Lombardy and allowed for the movement of troops and supplies between the two.

The French victory at Lens did not, however, stop the threatened slide into civil war in that country. In January 1649 the Fronde revolt broke out and the French government fled Paris. Presented with this opportunity to recover territory and prestige, Spain proved slow at regaining either. Some towns were recovered, but the manpower and money to invade and punish France were simply not there. As well as the Portuguese revolt, in 1647–1648 there were serious revolts in Naples and Western Sicily, which took almost a year to quell; riots inspired by near-famine conditions in Andalusia; and a virulent outbreak of plague in Valencia and western Spain. The revolt in Catalonia was still raging but without French support, the revolt was brought under control until 1652.

The Fronde was crushed in August 1653 with the recapture of Bordeaux by the forces of Louis XIV and France was once more a threat to the Empire. Then in December 1654, Protectorate England declared war, taking valuable Spanish possessions in the West Indies like Jamaica and destroying the Indies fleets of 1656 and 1657. Defeat after defeat followed in Lombardy, Catalonia, the Netherlands and Portugal. In particular, the French and English armies in the Low Countries inflicted a humiliating defeat on the Army of Flanders at the Dunes on 14 June 1658, which led to the loss of Spain's best port in the Netherlands, Dunkirk. In September 1658, faced with collapse, Philip IV sued for peace at almost any price and in May 1659 a cease-fire was agreed with France. The Treaty of the Pyrenees was signed on 7 November 1659, ending the long war. By this treaty, France gained Roussillon, Perpignan, Montmédy and other parts of Luxembourg,

Artois and other towns in Flanders, including Arras, Béthune, Gravelines and Thionville; and a new border with Spain was fixed along the Pyrenees. In addition, Spain was forced to recognize and confirm all other French gains at the Peace of Westphalia.

In exchange for Spanish territorial losses, the French king pledged to end his support for Portugal, withdraw his troops from Iberia, and renounce his claim to the county of Barcelona, which the French crown had claimed since the Catalan Revolt. The Portuguese could no longer therefore receive direct French support, although Richelieu continued covertly to provide financial subsidy and a force of 600 'volunteers'. The treaty also arranged a marriage between Louis XIV of France and Maria Theresa of Spain, the daughter of Philip IV. Maria Theresa was obliged, however, to renounce any claim to the Spanish throne, in return for a monetary settlement as part of her dowry. This settlement was never paid, a factor that eventually led to the War of Devolution in 1668. In addition, the English Protectorate government, which had sent troops to fight alongside the French in the Low Counties, received Jamaica and the great fortress and port of Dunkirk from the Spanish. But of most significance to the Portuguese was the clause by which the French recognised Philip IV of Spain as the legitimate king of Portugal.[18]

*　*　*

At the time of the Lisbon coup, the Portuguese had been at war with another major mercantile power, the Dutch, for nearly forty years. Concurrently, Spain and the Netherlands were engaged in the Eighty Years' War, the long and grinding struggle from 1568 to 1648 in which the Dutch fought for their independence. The two struggles were combined and intertwined in the Thirty Years' War after Portugal became subject to the Spanish crown. This Dutch-Portuguese War was fought almost entirely outside Europe, with the Dutch East India Company and the Dutch West India Company attacking Portugal's valuable colonial possessions from the Brazils to the Azores and Madeira, to Tangier and then the Guinea coast of West Africa, around Africa to Angola and Mozambique, to Bombay in India and into the east as far as Japan.

Though the ten-year truce, begun in 1609, between the Dutch and the Habsburg empire during their long war never applied to Asian waters, the main period of confrontation with the Dutch did not begin until the truce expired in 1619. Development of the main Dutch base at Djakarta on Java threatened the key Portuguese position of Malacca and Portuguese operations in the Moluccas were all but eliminated. Simultaneously, Dutch incursions greatly reduced the trade with China and Japan, though a Dutch attempt to seize Macau in 1622 was crushed. Between 1629 and 1636, almost 150 ships were lost to the Dutch in Asian waters alone, and this was well beyond the capacity of Portuguese ship-building to replace. The low point of Portugal's fortunes in the east came between 1625 and 1640; in only one of those years were more than three ships sent to India.

After the acclamation of John IV, this pattern of events continued unabated even though Portugal and the Dutch Republic signed a treaty of offensive and defensive alliance, otherwise known as the Treaty of The Hague, on 12 July 1641. Even though a Dutch military contingent actually served with the Portuguese army against their common enemy from 1641 to 1645,[19] the treaty was not fully respected by either party and therefore had no effect on the Portuguese colonies in the Brazils and Angola that had fallen to the Netherlands. The Dutch occupied Malacca and then São Tomé and Ano Bom on 16 October 1641, where they remained until 6 January 1649. In 1642 they occupied Portuguese Guinea. Goa was under Dutch blockade from 1637 to 1644 and the Dutch conquest of Ceylon began in 1638. All Portuguese traders and missionaries were expelled from Japan in 1639, bringing the once highly profitable Japanese trade to a complete end. On either side of the Atlantic, a crucial thirty-year struggle for control of both the Brazils and Angola was waged with the Dutch from 1624 to 1654 and the ultimate defeat of the Dutch in those two regions was due more to Portuguese colonial soldiers than to the homeland: they were not ousted from Africa (they retained the Cape Colony) until 1648 when colonial Brazilian troops under Salvador Correia de Sà* landed in Angola, recaptured the main town of Luanda and expelled the Dutch. Even so, the Dutch retained a foothold in the Brazils themselves until 1654 when colonial Brazilian troops drove the Dutch out of the great plantation colonies in Pernambuco, in north-eastern Brazil, re-establishing Portugal's South American possessions.

But as one possession was recovered, it seemed that another was lost, for as early as 1622 the trading post at Ormuz was seized by the Arab Sultan of Oman, a subject of Persia and in alliance with the English;[20] and in 1656 Portugal lost control of Colombo in Ceylon to the Dutch; within two years, the Dutch had control of the whole island. Faced with the power of Spain at home and the Dutch abroad, Portugal needed a powerful ally. If France had deserted her, there was only one other place to turn: England.

---

*   Salvador Correia de Sà (1602–1688) was Governor of Rio de Janeiro, Southern Brazil and Angola.

2

The Portuguese Marriage Treaty, 1660–1662

'the interest of Portugal and all its dominions'

The alliance between England and Portugal, often spoken of as England's oldest alliance, dates from the treaty signed at Windsor in 1386 by John I of Portugal and Edward III of England[1] – John married Edward's grand-daughter, Philippa of Lancaster. However even before then, English crusaders had fought with the Portuguese against the menace of militant, aggressive Islam in 1147. By 1660 the alliance had survived competition for maritime trade in the Indies and even the Protestant Reformation – chiefly because of the shared fear of Spanish domination of Europe. Charles I of England had negotiated potential military alliances with France, the Netherlands and Portugal, all rivals of Spain, directly before the outbreak of the Civil Wars which engulfed England in 1642.[2] But even after the English Parliamentary armies had fought and won these wars, Portugal's royal government had continued to receive and recognize English princes and nobility, and had offered protection to the royalist fleet. Not unnaturally this strained relations with the victorious Commonwealth government to the point where there was war between England and Portugal from 1652 to 1654.

Mutual fear of Spain was, however, a stronger force than short-term rivalries; peace was agreed and signed between the two countries on 10 July 1654.[3] With it, an Anglo-Portuguese treaty was signed at Westminster between John IV and Oliver Cromwell. John agreed to prevent the molestation of English traders in Portugal and its possessions; they were allowed to use their own bible and to bury their dead according to Protestant rites even though they were on Catholic soil. The main beneficial effect for John IV was the security provided by English naval power against a possible Spanish attack on Lisbon. As well as the restoration of commercial privileges for the English, Cromwell's alliance with France and their war against Spain in the Low Countries undoubtedly contributed to the successes of the Portuguese by further diverting Spanish resources, helping the Portuguese to win the important victory against the Spanish at Elvas in January 1659 – not long after the Spanish army had been defeated at the battle of the Dunes in June 1658. The Treaty of the Pyrenees, as already noted, changed the situation again and in terms of the English alliance, it coincided with the death of Olivier Cromwell. During the brief Protectorate of Richard Cromwell, the Portuguese ambassador to England had been negotiating with the Council of State, seeking permission for the King of Portugal to levy troops in England.

But being a good statesman, John IV had maintained contact and good relations with Charles I throughout the war until his execution even as he repaired relations with the Commonwealth and later the Protectorate. As early as 1644, a marriage between Charles, Prince of Wales, and a Portuguese princess had been suggested. Although at the time this was opposed by Queen Henrietta Maria, the subject was again raised in 1649 after the killing of Charles I by the Portuguese ambassador in The Hague to the new, but exiled, King Charles II: and he found a sympathetic ear.[4] The maintenance of these good relations with the exiled Charles II made for an easy resumption of normal business after the restoration of the Stuart dynasty in England, Scotland and Ireland in 1660. To the Portuguese, a firm understanding with England could compensate them for the loss of French support after the Treaty of the Pyrenees, cement commercial relations and provide security through a renewal of the ancient alliance. The way to achieve these ends would be a dynastic marriage between the new king and John IV's daughter, the *Infanta* Catherine of Braganza.

This was more than just a renewal of old ties, however – it was a matter of survival for Portugal.[5] Catherine of Braganza's godfather, Francisco de Mello, had been sent to begin the work of negotiation of the treaty with the Protectorate in 1657. On the restoration of the Portuguese ruling dynasty in 1640 he was imprisoned by order of the Count-Duke of Olivares, Prime Minister of Spain, and when released hastened to offer his sword to John IV. He travelled to England, where he spent some time at the court of Charles I. Passing over to the Netherlands, he assisted the Portuguese ambassador to equip a fleet in aid of Portugal and himself brought it safely to Lisbon in October 1641. He should further not be confused with Dom Francisco Mello Manuel da Camarra, ambassador to the Netherlands and England; nor with Dom Francesco Manuel de Mello, a cousin, envoy to Italy and England in 1663.

De Mello soon gathered a strong impression of the quality of the English army: 'There are some fine regiments of cavalry and infantry here, and they are billeted in the city as if they were Romans. Their discipline is admirable, for none of the soldiers swear or gamble, and they are promptly cashiered for doing either of these two things.'[6] After Oliver Cromwell's death in 1658, de Mello's task became more difficult in the prevailing climate of uncertainty and it was not until the final day of the Protectorate, 18 April 1660, that a treaty was signed, giving Portugal permission to recruit up to 10,000 foot and 2,000 horse and to buy arms and ammunition in England. Even while negotiating the treaty, de Mello had become aware of rumours of the restoration of the monarchy. As soon as this became a racing certainty, de Mello established communications with Charles through Sir Richard Talbot, later Duke and Earl of Tyrconnell and Charles II's Lord Lieutenant in Ireland. He also curried favour with the English merchants to such good effect that 200 of them petitioned Charles to maintain trade with Portugal; and he sounded out General George Monck with the idea of a marriage between the king and the Portuguese *Infanta*[7] once it was clear that Monck's sense of duty was moving him irrevocably towards a restored monarchy. To ensure that he had Monck's full attention, De Mello told him that the Spanish had decided, should the king be recalled to England, that they would detain him in Brussels until he had surrendered England's two most recent and valuable colonial possessions – both acquired under the Protectorate – Jamaica and Dunkirk;[8] this was subsequently confirmed by French sources.[9]

Once Charles was back in England he refused to ratify the Portuguese treaty with the Protectorate, but he began to consider the matter of marriage seriously and from it, an heir to cement his restored position. His mother, Henrietta Maria, and his cousin Louis

XIV of France were intent on turning Charles towards Catholicism – and what better way than a Catholic marriage? De Mello called on the former parliamentarian Edward Montagu, Earl of Manchester, who had been active later in Charles II's restoration, and also on the Lord Chamberlain, to press the Portuguese case. Of the *Infanta* Catherine he stressed that 'She was indeed a Catholic, and would never depart from her religion; but she had none of that meddling activity which sometimes made persons of that faith troublesome when they came into a country where another mode of worship was practised. He had "authority to make the proposition to the king, accompanied with such advantages as he thought no other power in Europe could offer".[10] De Mello became the first foreign ambassador to have audience with the restored king – and he was received very kindly.[11]

From the very beginning of his monarchy, Charles was perennially short of money and de Mello's line of approach certainly made Manchester sit up and take notice, for de Mello was granted an audience with the king the next day, praising Catherine's virtues of course but also offering £500,000 sterling, along with the assignment to the Crown of England in perpetuity, of the city and port of Tangier.[12] This, with the city of Ceuta, was all that Portugal had to show from the dreams of Prince Henry, in 1415 and later King Sebastian in 1578, of a North African empire.[13] In addition, he offered free trade with the Brazils and the East Indies – valuable commercial opportunities which Portugal had hitherto denied to all others – and finally the city, port and island of Bombay, on the west coast of India. Given Charles's empty coffers and heavy debts, he listened to the proposal with surprise and pleasure. But what would be required in return? Of course, a full and defined liberty of worship for the queen along with an income to guarantee her state; and protection for Portugal from Spain and the Netherlands.

Charles said nothing without consulting his Chancellor, Edward Hyde, Earl of Clarendon, whom he had learned to trust implicitly throughout the hard years of exile. Clarendon's daughter Anne married the Duke of York and their daughters Mary and Anne were both subsequently Queens of England. Clarendon was cautious, suggesting a Protestant wife like the daughter of the Prince of Orange. When Charles raised his mother's likely objections to this course of action, Clarendon appears to have agreed to discuss matter further with de Mello. A full meeting of Charles's Privy Council, although desiring peace with Spain, concurred that the possession of Tangier and Bombay provided such advantages that 'would enable them to give the law to all the trade of the Mediterranean.'[14] Tangier in particular was felt to be vulnerable to seizure by the Dutch, who would build a mole to protect the harbour and from there, push into the Mediterranean and down the Atlantic coast of Africa. However, in offering Tangier, 'Portugal was offering what it could not expect to retain long without help.'[15] Clarendon was by this time favourable to the Portuguese proposal and since the proposed Queen was a Catholic he asked Charles to appoint a committee of five to consider the matter: himself, Ormond, Manchester, Lord High Treasurer Thomas Wriothesley, Earl of Southampton* and Secretary of State Sir Edward Nicholas† met at Clarendon's house and came to the unanimous view that Clarendon should push forward the negotiations with de Mello.

---

*   Sir Thomas Wriothesley, 4th Earl of Southampton, KG (1607–1667) was a staunch supporter of Charles II in exile who became Lord High Treasurer after the Restoration.
†   Sir Edward Nicholas (1593–1669) was Secretary of State to Charles I and Charles II.

De Mello therefore offered to return to Portugal, inform the king and the Queen-Regent of how things stood, 'not doubting to return with full powers for the completion of the treaty.'[16] Charles sent a letter to the Queen-Regent with de Mello and one to King Alfonso declaring his wish to marry Catherine. For many in Portugal, this was help from Heaven, for they expected to be attacked soon and in the words of the Queen-Regent it was worth all their East Indian possessions.[17] She did not, for obvious reasons, think it worth the American possessions. Even so, the marriage of the *Infanta* with a Protestant monarch was deeply unpopular with those among the Portuguese nobility who favoured alliance with France: rival Anglophile and Francophile parties developed at the Portuguese court. The loss of Tangier had to be concealed for as long as possible, especially from the Menezes family which held the governorship.

While Charles was eager for the commercial and colonial advantages promised by a Portuguese alliance, and for the great dowry offered, the prospect of provoking a war with Spain by military assistance to Portugal was a serious obstacle which long delayed any decision. The Spanish ambassador Jean-Charles de Watteville* was, not surprisingly, furious – as indeed was the whole of the Spanish court, for had they not given Charles shelter while in exile; and was this how they were to be repaid? Watteville tried remonstrating with Charles and then deprecating Catherine – she was deformed, sickly, barren.[18] Charles was thoroughly dismayed and when De Mello returned, he was denied audience – for Charles was now casting around elsewhere. Enquiries were made about the two young Princesses of Parma, but it was reported by George Digby, Earl of Bristol,† that between them, they seemed to match all the descriptions that the Spanish Ambassador had laid at Catherine's door. The diarist and commentator Gilbert Burnet, Bishop of Salisbury‡ remarked that: 'Spain, in this case, was too much a party to have any great credit given to what they said; and the veneration paid to the memory of the late King, who had intended, as some affirmed, a marriage between his son and this *Infanta*, made the proposition better accepted.'[19] A betrothal in Portugal would have provided further opportunity for Spanish obstruction, since a Papal dispensation would have been required and the Papacy sided with Spain. Charles sidestepped this neatly by waiting until a proxy marriage had been concluded and then presenting a letter declaring Catherine to be his wife.[20]

The ambassadors of France and Spain, Godefroi, Count D'Estrades§ and de Watteville, were so urgent in putting their points of view on Charles's marriage, as well as intent on establishing precedence between them, that a major street battle erupted between the two factions on 30 September 1660, on and around Tower Hill.

---

*   Jean-Charles de Watteville, Prince de Ligne (1628–1699) arrived in London in September 1660 with the prime objective of preventing the Anglo-Portuguese marriage.

†   George Digby, 2nd Earl of Bristol (1612–1677) was the son of the 1st Earl and had supported Charles I and Charles II throughout the Civil Wars and in exile.

‡   Gilbert Burnet (1643–1715), Scotish theologian and Whig, left a detailed, if slanted, record of his life and times in *A History of His Own Times*.

§   Godefroi, Comte d'Estrades (1607–1686) was a French diplomatist and Marshal. In 1646 he was named ambassador extraordinary to the Netherlands and took part in the conferences at Münster that brought the Thirty Years War to a conclusion. Sent to England in 1661, he obtained the restitution of Dunkirk by purchase to France in 1662.

Charles gave orders that there should be no interference, so the garrison troops looked on:[21] 'A wild day in London – loose horses galloping, bullets striking innocent spectators who responded with brickbats, and English soldiers cheering the Spanish.'[22] Cheering them, presumably, because many of the royal guardsmen had fought with them against the French at Dunkirk only two years before. The Spanish had the best of the fight, for at least five Frenchmen were killed and another thirty wounded, but in the end the French had the best of the intrigue for the matter of the marriage was settled by a combination of factors. Louis XIV, who was anxious for any marriage that drew Charles towards the Catholic Church as well as one that diminished the power of his rival, Spain, sent word to Charles 'to express his regret that anything should have taken place to delay his marriage with "a lady of great beauty and admirable endowments, and added that he himself had formerly had serious thoughts of marrying her". He concluded by sending the Chevalier Antoine de Jacques de Bastide* with letters of credit amounting to 500,000 *livres* to relieve Charles of any pressing temporary embarrassment, as well as 300,000 *pistoles* towards the cost of the expedition to Portugal – and more if needed.[23] In the end, the French subsidy was agreed at 2,000,000 livres in three years and it was this that probably clinched the matter,[24] along with the matter of foreign possessions: giving in to Spain meant the loss of Dunkirk and Jamaica; alliance with Portugal meant keeping these and adding Bombay and Tangier. At about the same time, as Clarendon told Parliament, the privy council advised Charles 'how heart-breaking a thing it would be to his people to lose the possession of so great a trade, and those other immense advantages they had by that treaty, and that it would be judged an irrecoverable error in policy if Portugal should be suffered again to be swallowed up by Spain.'[25]

To avoid crowning an English Queen using Catholic rites, Charles's own coronation took place on 23 April 1661. He told Parliament of his intention to marry on 8 May and on 13 May de Mello wrote to the King of Portugal with the news that both houses of parliament had voted addresses of congratulation. It was another month before the marriage treaty was signed, on 23 June 1661.[26] It began by ratifying the previous treaties of 1642 and 1654 before laying out the new arrangements. Article III ceded the city and castle of Tangier to the Crown of England – not the nation or its parliament – thus saddling Charles with costs that were to prove near-ruinous over the next twenty years – with all its rights, territories and profits; it was to be taken into possession by Lord Sandwich's fleet, which would then return to Lisbon to collect the *Infanta*.

Article V detailed the financial element of the queen's dowry – 2 million *cruzadoes* (crowns), or half a million pounds sterling, in gold, silver, treasure, bills, and other merchandise. Servicing this debt burdened the Portuguese exchequer for the next half-century. Article VII laid out the right of free exercise of the Catholic religion for the queen and Article VIII her own financial allowance, an income of £30,000 a year from the English Crown which was to continue should she become a dowager.

Article XI ceded Bombay on similar terms to Tangier. Article XII gave free trade with India through the Portuguese possessions on the sub-continent; and free trade with the Brazils through the ports of Rio, Bahia and Pernambuco. Article XIV laid down that if

---

* Chevalier Antoine de Jacques de Bastide (?–1674), no other biographical details found.

Ceylon, which was now occupied by the Dutch, could be recovered, it would be divided between the two allies. To engage the commercial benefits offered by Tangier and the Indies, two companies were formed by Royal Charter, along the lines of the Dutch East and West India Companies and the earlier Virginia Company, as the basis for beginning trade and founding a new empire on both continents. While the Honourable East India Company did just that until its administrative function was wound up after the great Mutiny in 1857, Tangier became a liability that was maintained only with enormous difficulty and expense until 1680; and the Royal African Company, set up under James, Duke of York, collapsed during the Anglo-Dutch wars in the 1670s.[27]

The final articles detailed what Charles would give in return. Article XV committed the King of England to:

> take the interest of Portugal and all its dominions to heart, defending the same with his utmost power by sea and land … and that he will transport thither at his proper costs and charges two regiments of horse, each consisting of 500, and two regiments of foot, each consisting one thousand, all which shall be fully armed at the charge of the King of Great Britain, but after they are landed in Portugal they shall be paid by the King of Portugal; and in case the said regiments come to be diminished, by fight or disease, the King of Great Britain shall be obliged to fill up the number at his own charge; and that he will cause the said regiments to be transported as soon as the Lady Infanta shall arrive in England.

Article XVI provided ten ships of war from the Royal Navy, if Portugal should be invaded. Article XVII went to de Mello's earlier intelligence, laying down that Dunkirk and Jamaica should never be ceded by England to Spain; and that no separate peace would be concluded between England and Spain that did not also involve Portugal. Finally, a Secret Article bound England to provide the same scale of protection – at least in principle – to the Portuguese colonies as was being accorded to the mother country.

A by-product of this relationship was that the English soon began to dominate the trade in wine from Portugal after tensions with the French denied them Bordeaux wines. Brandy was added to the Portuguese wines to fortify them for the Atlantic voyage and so Port was born. English mediation also helped to oblige the Dutch to acknowledge formally Portuguese rule in the Brazils, in return for uncontested control of Ceylon and eight million guilders. The agreement was formalized in a new Treaty of The Hague, signed on 6 August 1661. Sir Richard Fanshawe* was dispatched as envoy to Lisbon in August 1661 to oversee the ratification of the treaty and the implementation of its terms.[28] Once the marriage was agreed, he was instructed to remain as Ambassador to the courts of both Spain and Portugal.[29] It is to his accounts that we owe much of what we know about the later history of the war and the role of the English brigade.

The provision of troops, although welcome, was not quite what the Portuguese had had in mind. Rather than be given leave to raise a foreign force in their own employ,

---

*   Sir Richard Fanshawe, 1st Baronet (1608–1666) served as a Royalist officer during the Civil Wars. He was a noted poet and translator. He served as Ambassador to the courts of Spain and Portugal from 1662 until his death in 1666. His wife's memoirs, cited in this book, are a useful source of personal detail of his life and times which supplement the bare bones of his official correspondence.

what they most wanted was that England and Portugal should fight a combined war against Spain. To this the English government was never likely to agree; but it was this clause that further delayed the treaty. This difference in attitude partially explains why it was so difficult to persuade the Portuguese to fulfil their obligation to pay the troops once they had been landed in Portugal. The difference of opinion was made even starker by Charles's belief that the transportation costs would be met by the French: Clarendon and Monck both believed in this and saw it as the best means of employing surplus troops from the Dunkirk Garrison, rather than disband them. As Clarendon said: 'he [i.e. the king] had such a body of men ready for such a service which could with *much more security* and little more charge be transported to Portugal, than be disbanded in the place where they were.'[30]

The English fleet under Edward Montagu, Earl of Sandwich,* which took possession of Tangier in January 1661 reached Lisbon in the following spring Montagu, had served Parliament as an infantry officer and later admiral. With Monck he supported the restoration of Charles II and brought the king home. Charles made him deputy to James, Duke of York, the Lord High Admiral. He had urged the acquisition of a Mediterranean base for several years both for trade and as a base of operations against the Barbary corsairs. He was in many ways therefore a natural choice as envoy. The appearance of Sandwich and his fleet caused the Spanish army, which was threatening the city, to withdraw in confusion.[31] Sandwich, who had been one of the main supporters of the treaty, then acted as the king's proxy in the nuptial ceremony in Lisbon,[32] before embarking the queen, her entourage of 250, and part of the dowry in the *Royal Charles*. The queen landed at Portsmouth, where the king met her for the first time, on 21 May 1662. Although various accounts say that he found her attractive, Burnet was more spiteful – probably on account of her religion:

> the Archbishop of Canterbury came to perform the office; but the Queen was so bigoted that she would neither say a word nor bear the sight of him. So the King said over his part hastily, and the Archbishop pronounced them married; but they were afterwards married again by the Lord D'Aubigny according to the Roman ritual. She was a woman of mean appearance and of no agreeable temper, and therefore the King had no great consideration for her; and though at first he did observed some decencies, and did not visit his mistress openly, yet he soon grew weary of that restraint.[33]

As to the dowry, Sandwich told Clarendon that he had spent 200,000 crowns from the money with the fleet; that he had the equivalent of 400,000 crowns in money, sugars, plate, jewels and other merchandise on board, with another 800,000 in bills of exchange, to be paid two months after the marriage took place.[34] As the Portuguese crown equated to about five shillings, this made a total of £350,000; it is uncertain that the balance was ever paid.[35] But having made the match and signed the treaty, Charles now had to find the troops to fulfil his end of the bargain.

---

* Edward Montagu, 1st Earl of Sandwich KG (1625–1672).

3

Raising the English Brigade, 1661–1662

'So Honourable an Expedition'

'I will not go on my travels again' is a quotation often attributed to Charles II. In it, there is often a note of reserve, as if he believed that the sort of confrontation that had ruined his father had to be avoided at any cost. That may be so, but there is also an underlying threat in that same idea, for Charles was painfully aware that it had been the want of a reliable, professional army that had allowed the rebellion under his father to prosper. France, Spain and Sweden were the first states to form standing armies, but after Peace of Westphalia in 1648 the trend intensified. As France became the dominant power in Europe, so Louis XIV expressed this power through military force; others followed.[1] Moreover, as well as increasing the number of native Frenchmen in his armies, Louis also solidified the use of foreign contingents – more of which later in this chapter. Because of the high incidence of desertion and inefficiency among the poorest classes of native troops, foreign soldiers provided a stiffening of professional expertise.[2] One French source remarked that 'Les victoires de Louis XIV seront souvent dues autant a des soldats d'autres nations qu'a des soldats français.'[3]

Charles II had considered the issue of a standing army from the beginning of his reign, however popular dislike of the army was marked and he had to act carefully, for the general feeling was that a standing army was a threat to the people's liberties. Titus Oates was quoted as saying that 'In peace there is nothing for an army to subdue but Magna Carta.'[4] Neither could the old army of Parliament, with its mix of loyalties to the Protectorate or Parliament and its marked tone of republicanism, be taken wholesale into the service of the new regime even after Monck had purged it of its more extreme elements.[5] Nor did the Privy Purse allow for the maintenance of other than the Royal garrisons, the companies of the foot guards and the regiments of life and horse guards: parliament would have to vote money for more than these.

Although, therefore, Charles was determined to have a new, professional army, the old one loyal to the republic had first to be disbanded: he was not taken in by the shouts of acclamation at the Blackheath review for the faces of the soldiers were said to have shown that they 'were drawn thither to a service they were not delighted in.'[6] An Act of Parliament was quickly passed to pay off the troops,[7] for to keep such a body under arms would have posed a continual threat to the new monarchy and its institutions. Ironically, it fell to former Royalist turned Cromwellian commander, architect of the Restoration and now the Captain-General, Lieutenant-General George Monck, Duke of Albermarle, to oversee the disbandment and thus do away with his own power base.

All arrears of pay, plus an extra week's money, required the staggering sum of £850,000. By way of comparison, the entire exchequer income of England and Wales for the year 1660 was £1,185,000 with another £143,000 for Scotland and £207,000 for Ireland. A huge slice of this was expended anyway on maintaining the armies: £638,000 per year for the army in England, £148,000 for Scotland, £104,000 for Ireland, £54,000 for the Jamaica garrison and £77,000 for the garrisons of Dunkirk and Mardyck.[8] The additional money required was raised by an unpopular poll tax. The rapid disbandment which released large numbers of republicans into the country was soon causing concern: on 19 May 1661 a Proclamation had to be issued in advance of the king's coronation, 'ordering all cashiered officers and soldiers of the late Army to depart on or before that date, and not come within twenty miles of London or Westminster till May 20th'.[9] Not that events bore out these fears, for as Bishop Burnet wrote of the old army, 'they were certainly the bravest, the best disciplined, and the soberest army that had been known in these latter ages.'[10] An Act of Parliament enabling disbanded soldiers to exercise trades certainly helped, but the vast majority returned to civil life as compliant, if not enthusiastic, citizens of the new order. Samuel Pepys reported that 'Of all the old Army, you cannot see a man begging in the streets. You shall have this Captain turned shoemaker, the Lieutenant a baker … tis common soldier a porter; and every man in his apron and frock as if they had never done anything else.'[11]

Orders in Council listed sixteen regiments of horse and dragoons and twenty regiments of foot for disbandment,[12] of which nine regiments of horse, fourteen regiments of foot and eight companies were in England.[13] Some estimates give the number of soldiers released by this measure to be as great as 60,000; Macaulay says 50,000;[14] however the strength of the Army during the last year of the Commonwealth was only 30,000 throughout the whole of the three kingdoms, but not including Dunkirk.[15] In the end, Monck's own regiment was retained, not least because the abortive insurrection of John Venner and his fifty or so miserable Fifth Monarchy Men on 6 February 1661 exposed the fact that in terms of security and public order, the emperor had no clothes. The militia had neither the training, nor the equipment, the leadership nor the willingness, to deal with disorder. However this still left a considerable body of trained military manpower that future insurrections might enlist.

After the Peace of the Pyrenees in 1659, France officially abandoned her Portuguese ally. However there were considerable advantages in keeping Spain tied down. Marshal Frederick Herman, Duke of Schomberg, was sent as military adviser to Lisbon by Cardinal Mazarin and his master Louis XIV in the first year of his personal rule, on the advice of Marshal Henri de la Tour de Turenne, with the secret approval of the still-exiled Charles II of England. This was at a time when no power had yet established an embassy in Lisbon and the Pope still refused acknowledgement of the dynasty. Turenne acted as the agent through whom the Portuguese would recruit soldiers in France in order to distance the French government from such an obvious breach of the treaty – not that the Spanish were in any way galled by this, or by Turenne's protestations of innocence. It was Schomberg above all others that Turenne recommended to the Portuguese and when he agreed to go, further to maintain the official fiction Louis deprived Schomberg of his French staff officers and all outward appearances of support.

Schomberg was the half-English scion of two old families: the von Schönbergs in the Palatinate and the Suttons in England. He was born at Heidelberg, the son of Hans

Meinard von Schönberg and Anne, daughter of Edward Sutton, 5th Baron Dudley. Both his parents died while he was in his infancy and he was therefore brought up and educated by family friends, among whom was Frederick V, the Elector Palatine, in whose service his father had been. After studying at Bouillon's military college at Sedan,[16] he began his military career under Frederick Henry, Prince of Orange, and in 1634 entered the service of Sweden. After only a year, he transferred to the French service where his family, through the allied house of the Saxon Schönbergs, was already well established. For a short interlude he retired to his family estate at Geisenheim on the Rhine, but in 1639 he returned to military service, this time with the Dutch, in whose service, apart from a few intervals at Geisenheim, he remained until about 1650. He then rejoined the French army as a general officer under the patronage of his relative, Charles de Schomberg, Duc d'Halluin. He served under Turenne in the campaigns against the Protestant rebel army under Louis de Bourbon, Prince de Condé and Duc d'Enghien and was promoted to lieutenant-general in 1655.

According to the terms of the bargain with the Portuguese, concluded on 24 August 1660, Schomberg was to receive the title of *Maestro de Campo* General, roughly equivalent to a lieutenant-general – and position of general of the forces in the province of Alentejo, a yearly salary of twelve thousand *cruzadoes*, two thousand *cruzadoes* daily for table-money, as well as appointments for his two sons, Frederick and Meinhard. In order not to compromise the French government, the arrangements were completed in England, where the negotiations on the Marriage Treaty would provide cover.[17]

> The consequence of the nomination of a general of such reputation was that a great number of French officers and experienced soldiers, who were left without employment by the peace, offered themselves for service in Portugal. Schomberg chose the most able to form a regiment of horse of six companies, under his own command, which would serve as an exemplar to the Portuguese troops.[18]

When Schomberg's transports dropped anchor at the Dunes, the regiment was embarked with a strength of twenty-four officers and 353 men. In addition there was a second regiment of horse, the regiment of Montjorge, with only seventy-four men in three companies and an independent company of forty-seven dragoons under Captain Rafael de Aux.[19] To these, several hundred more French officers and reformadoes were added when towards the end of October, Schomberg made rendezvous at Le Havre. These men formed a second regiment of horse under Lieutenant-Colonel Jeremiah Chauvet, which absorbed the regiment of Montjorge and the company of Rafael de Aux and mustered another 400 men; and a regiment of foot 600 strong. Two companies of Catalans joined Schomberg's Regiment after it arrived in Portugal.[20] In addition there was Schomberg's own company of guards – a French brigade therefore of about 1,800 men, mostly mounted.[21]

In England, Schomberg met Charles and advised him to send to Portugal 'the military men that had served under Cromwell, whom he thought the best officers he had ever seen: and he was sorry to see, they were dismissed, and that a company of wild young men were those the King relied on'.[22] Schomberg had of course a vested interest in the quality of troops sent to Portugal, but Charles, who also created Schomberg Baron Thetford, accepted his advice which in any case, coincided with his own interests. Burnet, who is seldom accurate but always opinionated, had this to say:

As the treaty with Portugal went on, France engaged in the concerns of that crown, though contrary to their treaty with Spain; but to cover their proceedings, Count Shomberg, a German by birth and Calvinist in religion, and who would therefore be less suspected, was sent thither to negotiate some matters very privately. He was the Prince of Orange's particular favourite, but had so great a share in the last violent actions of his life that he left the service upon his death, and gained in France, next after the Prince de Condé and the Maréchal de Turenne, the reputation of one of the best generals they had. He had been intimately acquainted with the King at the Hague, and therefore, as he passed through England, he had much free discourse with him, and took an occasion to give his advice as to the business then in agitation – the sale of Dunkirk … But to alleviate this loss it was soon pretended that Tangier, which was offered as a part of the Infanta of Portugal's dowry, was a place of much greater consequence.[23]

While Cromwell's army was being disbanded in England, three of his foot regiments remained in Scotland from the original six regiments of foot and four of horse there.[24] These had been left in Scotland under George Monck's command to garrison the conquered country after the campaigns of 1651 and 1654 had completed the victory of Dunbar and imposed the rule of the Protectorate. Now, the Scots were vigorously urging their removal, having been taxed for the maintenance of their occupiers at the rate of £120,000 a year during the period of occupation. In the last months of the English occupation of Scotland during this period of rapid change, the position of the troops was extremely uncomfortable, for the population showed their dislike freely. There was rioting in garrison towns, the worst being in Stirling. The removal of these regiments would, it seemed, not only quiet the Scots but also provide the bulk of the required foot regiments for Portugal – thus neatly killing two birds with one stone. The men could not be obliged to go overseas as they would be maintained in foreign pay, rather than the pay of the English crown, and so volunteers were called for.

The garrison in Scotland was commanded by Major-General Sir Thomas Morgan, a hard case if ever there was one in an age which did not tolerate a soft touch among military officers. Morgan was a Welshman and a professional soldier with service in many foreign armies, especially in Germany under Bernhard of Saxe-Weimar, and in France.[25] He commanded the troops at the capture of the fort of Mardyck and was wounded at the storming of St Venant in 1657. At the capture of Dunkirk in July 1658, when a Cromwellian brigade had fought for the French against the Spanish – whose ranks had included a brigade of exiled English and Irish royalist troops – he was visited by the two most eminent personages of the French army: Cardinal Mazarin and Marshal Turenne. What they saw was not what they expected of such a considerable military reputation:

whereas they thought to have found an Achillean or gigantesque person, they sawe a little man, not many degrees above a dwarfe, sitting in a hutt of turves, with his fellowe soldiers, smoking a pipe about 3 inches (or neer so) long, with a green hatt-case on. He spake with a very exile tine, and did cry-out to the soldiers, when angry with them, 'Sirrah, I'le cleave your skull!' as if the words had been prolated by an eunuch.[26]

Morgan was knighted by Richard Cromwell on 25 November 1658. In spite of his appearance, Turenne took him into his army after the fall of Dunkirk and he was wounded at the taking of Ypres. Here he described in his memoir how three demi-lune redoubts had to be taken by assault. Two were carried by his red-coats 'who threw the enemy into the moat and turned the cannon upon the town.' The French were repulsed in their attempt on the third redoubt and Morgan ordered his men to assist their allies. The soldiers called out 'shall we fall on in order, or happy-go-lucky?' Morgan replied '"In the name of God, go at it happy-go-lucky." Immediately the red-coats fell on and were on the top of it knocking the enemy down and casting them into the moat.' Ypres surrendered the following morning.[27]

In late January 1660, having accompanied Monck as second-in-command on his march south as far as York with the bulk of the army of Scotland, Morgan returned north with two regiments of foot and was named commander-in-chief of the English forces in Scotland, as well as one of the five commissioners for the civil government of Scotland appointed by Parliament. He took a conspicuous part in the celebrations of Charles II's birthday at Edinburgh on 19 June 1660, firing off Mons Meg with his own hand. Charles created him a baronet on 1 February 1661. Under Morgan's command, the three foot regiments that remained in Scotland were, first, his own regiment of foot,[28] which had been raised by William Daniel in May 1650 for service in Ireland. It marched with Cromwell into Scotland in July 1650 and after the campaign there was over, it was left to garrison Leith. When Monck prepared to march into England he made Morgan its colonel, with Edward Witter as the lieutenant-colonel.[29] When the decision was made to employ the troops from Scotland in Portugal, Morgan put the case to the men:

> Yesterday Major General Morgan drew forth his regiment of foot consisting of 1000 proper men besides officers from the cittadel of Leith, and made a short speech to the officers and souldiers, acquainting them how great a value his Majesty had of them, & what care was taken for their present supply both of money and clothes, with assurance of speedy payment of their arrears; that his Majesty had been graciously pleased to design them for honourable service abroad, and that he himself (who had so long commanded them in that country) resolved to ship with them, and made no doubt of their readiness to so honourable an expedition. Whereupon not one man expressing the least unwillingness, they all with great acc[l]amations of joy both officers and souldiers cried out *All, all, all, to follow him to serve their King and country*, and so marcht back again into the citadel, where he gave the souldiers money to drink his Majesties health.[30]

Secondly, there was the regiment of William Daniel.[31] This regiment had been raised by William Herbert; it was given to Daniel by Monck in January 1660 on the dismissal of the republican Robert Overton. Three companies marched with Monck into England, two – those of George Traherne and Robert Laverock – with Morgan's Regiment and Captain Lowrie's company with Mann's Regiment. All three companies returned to Scotland on 24 January 1660 with Morgan. Daniel's Regiment appears to have formed the bulk of the second English regiment for Portugal.

Figure 2 A contemporary drawing of Sir Thomas Morgan, commander of the Parliamentary regiments in Scotland from which the bulk of the English brigade was drawn. (Author's collection)

Figure 3 An English musketeer of the Restoration period, a detail from
Henry Hexham's *Principles of the Art Military*. (Author's collection)

The third regiment was that of Miles Mann, which had first been raised by Thomas Fitch at the beginning of the Civil Wars.[32] When Monck declared for the Parliament rather than the Protectorate in 1659 he appointed Mann as colonel. The regiment remained in Scotland when Monck went south. In April 1662 it was at Inverness, 1,000 strong, from where it was ordered to muster and march for Leith. It appears they were sorry to go, in spite of the reported bad feeling among the Scottish civilian population, which may have been as much political propaganda as truth and probably in any case varied greatly from garrison to garrison depending on the relations established and the behaviour of the troops: 'never people left a place with such relunctancy. It was even sad to see and heare sighs and teares, pale faces and embraces, at their parting farewell from that town. And no wonder; they had peace and plenty for 10 yeares in it. They made that place happy, and it made them so'.[33] Mann's Regiment was probably broken up to complete Morgan's and Daniel's for service in Portugal;[34] the remaining Commonwealth officers were given new commissions from the king.[35] According to John Nicoll's *Dairy of Public Transactions*, the English troops from Leith were shipped out on 15, 16 and 17 May 1662, at which point no English troops were left in Scotland.[36]

It would be easy to see these men as battle-hardened veterans, thirsting for the fray. The Venetian ambassador, Francisco Giaverina, reported that the king had 'decided to send a succour of 1000 horse and 3000 foot ... they will be veteran, so they are sure to render excellent service.'[37] But the truth is probably somewhat different. Even if there had been no turnover at all in the regiments, it had been at least six years since they last saw action. Although disciplined, well equipped and well drilled, they had grown used to peace. Nor is it conceivable that turnover could be zero, so that there would be a percentage of soldiers who lacked any experience of war at all. And rather than longing for battle, it was probably fear of unemployment, in an age when the only relief from hunger was the Elizabethan Poor Law, which motivated the majority. Then again, soldiers tend to stick together: regimental esprit is strong and for many, the opportunity to stay with their comrades in a trade they knew, away from a government that was the opposite of all they had come to believe in, would have been attractive. Even so, some would have decided to leave for civilian life and assuming that the regiments were not in fact at full strength, it would have taken all three regiments in Scotland to fill up the two regiments for Portugal to their established strength. The two new regiments were placed under the command of former parliamentarian officers, Colonels Henry Pearson and Francis Moore,[38] although some sources give James Apsley in place of Moore. Apsley came from a family in Devonshire and had been a royalist officer during the Civil Wars. He later became a privateer and in 1651 achieved notoriety by his attempt to assassinate St. John, Parliament's envoy at The Hague. His brother was Sir Allen Apsley, a close friend of Clarendon, to whose influence he probably owed his appointment.[39] Pearson had been a lieutenant in the Cromwellian regiment of his brother John Pearson, a reputed Anabaptist;[40] his lieutenant-colonel was initially Henry Belasyse, a cousin of John Belasyse who commanded a troop of the horse and a member of a prominent royalist family.[41] Of the remaining officers only Edward Witham, who had been with Morgan's Regiment in Scotland, Charles Serres, a newly commissioned officer, and John Wetmore can be identified.[42] It is not possible to identify any other officers in either regiment – and of course, the non-commissioned ranks were completely anonymous – as they would remain, unless embarked in ships, until the yearly inspection returns of regiments began to list them by name in 1792.

So much for the foot regiments. Next came the problem of the horse. A beginning was made with what remained of Morgan's own Regiment of Dragoons, raised in 1651, which had marched from Scotland with Monck in January 1660 and was disbanded at York in October 1660,[43] with the exception of Morgan's own troop under the Captain-Lieutenant, Francis Kelly, which had remained at Leith. The men were not all eager to go as the newspaper *Mercurius Publicus* contained an advertisement for two troopers who had deserted. Monck's biographer, Chaplain Grumble, had no good opinion of them, saying that the regiment 'had been sinful dragoons, but now converted into troops [of horse]: yet some had turned apostates.' That is, they abandoned their adherence to the strict principles of Puritan Protestantism and accepted such Romish practices as episcopacy. Research by John Childs indicates that Kelly went to Portugal and returned; in 1667 he was given £264 for having taken his troop there.[44] In 1673–1674 he was a captain and then major in the Duke of Albemarle's Regiment of Foot.[45] The man he replaced, John Wetmore, also went to Portugal having, it seems, accepted a drop in rank.[46]

There were several Cromwellian regiments in the garrison of Dunkirk. These regiments lay in uncomfortable proximity to four Irish regiments which had served Charles II in exile and which had fought for the Spanish against these same Cromwellian regiments at the Battle of the Dunes. They had been drawn into the garrison following the king's restoration.[47] One of these old Cromwellian corps was Sir Robert Harley's Regiment of Horse,[48] originally raised by Sir William Lockhart in 1658 to garrison Dunkirk; Sir Robert Harley had taken command of the regiment on 12 July 1660. It had some good officers: Captain Henry Flower, according to Lockhart, 'had given such large testimonies of his courage, good conduct, affectionate to your Highnesses [i.e. Cromwell's] interest, and love of his country in several occasions in the late siege and battle'.[49] There were others not so good: Captain Robert Broadnax for example was 'a pretty man … he seems to promise no extraordinary matters.'[50]

Three troops of the regiment went to Portugal in April or May 1662 under new officers, as an order dated 21 April makes clear: 'Whereas we have ordered ye several troops of horse within our garrison of Dunkerke under ye command of Cap. Michael Dungan, Cap [William] Littleton, & Sir W[illia]m Salkeld, to be forthwith shipped & transported to Portugall.'[51]

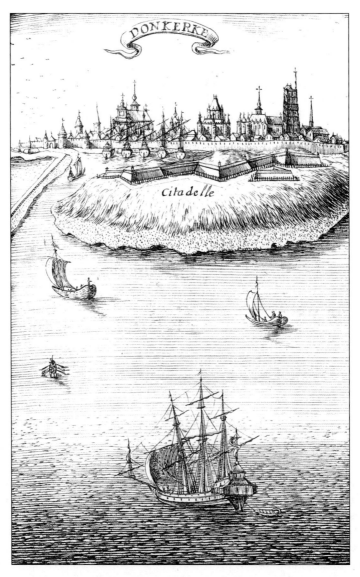

Figure 4 The town and fortress of Dunkirk, from Allain Mallet's *Les travaux de Mars, ou l'art de la Guerre*. (Bavarian State Library)

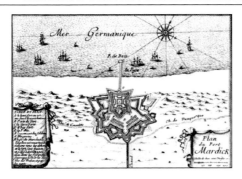

Figure 5 The great fort of Mardyck.

The order continues with instructions for the troops to receive their arrears of pay. Salkeld was a Captain in Sir Robert Harley's Regiment;[52] Littleton had been appointed to a troop of horse in Dunkirk in 1662 and was the son of Sir Thomas Littleton, a prominent royalist during the Civil Wars.[53] The Major, Tobias Bridge,[54] went to Tangier and later raised the Barbadoes Regiment. The ranks seem to have been made up by the offer of places to a few of the royalist Irish, but no names can be identified. These, with Morgan's dragoons, made up the 'four gallant troops'[55] of about 150 men which made up the core of the regiment of horse for Portugal.

Four additional troops were raised from volunteers in England.[56] Some of these volunteers were again old Commonwealth men, as shown by an offer made to some of the officers in Monck's Regiment of Horse,[57] which had been disbanded:

> 18 March, 1662. Letter to Capt. Paddon that there being some horse to be raised by order from Majesty to bee implied in Portugall and the troopers for their encouragement being to have £4 a man for the mounting of them his Grace thought fit to acquaint him with itt, that if he thought fit to raise a troope upon those termes hee should have the naming of his owne officers, and the souldiers to bee taken into pay upon the first muster which is to bee soone as hee has compleated the troope to 70.[58]

As one who joined them wrote, 'This design was cried up to the skies, and extoll'd with such high Encomiums, that he had not the spirit of a gentleman who would not testifie his loyalty by this foreign service.'[59] This was Charles Croke, a member of a royalist family from Buckinghamshire,[60] who later deserted to the enemy and was cashiered in May, 1663. Croke was the author of *Fortune's Uncertainty*, the younger son of Serjeant Unton Croke of Marston and the brother of the colonel of the same name who commanded the regiment of heavy horse in Cromwell's army that had been raised by Sir Arthur Haselrigge in 1650; he was turned out by Monck. Charles served in the same regiment as a cornet. The commanders of these four troops were, however, staunch Royalists, for there were any number of royalist officers, poverty-stricken by the Civil Wars and the interregnum, who sought employment in 1660 and 1661, and the home establishment was far too small to provide places for them all. Captain Guy Molesworth, for example, was an Irish Protestant who had served the king as captain-lieutenant of the Earl of Northumberland's Regiment of Foot during the second Bishop's War against

Scotland in 1640; he had then served under George Monck in Ireland in 1642, establishing what was to be valuable patronage in the years to come. During the Civil Wars he served as lieutenant-colonel of Prince Maurice's Regiment of Horse, in which he had been badly wounded at First Newbury and again at Naseby, where he was captured, imprisoned with Monck in the Tower, but escaped. He recovered from his wounds and with the remnant of the regiment, perhaps 100 men, was still campaigning under Lord Gerard as late as January 1646. In 1647 he fled the new regime for the Barbadoes where in 1649 he was arrested by enemies, his property seized, and he and his family expelled. They had gone to Virginia,[61] returning to England with news of the Restoration. Unable to obtain restitution for the seizure of his property in the Barbadoes and in debt, he opted for the command of a company in Portugal even though he had held the rank of colonel. Captain John Belasyse was a member of a prominent Catholic family, the brother of Viscount Fauconberg – a key supporter of Charles in exile – and a relative of John, Lord Belasyse who was soon afterwards Governor of Tangier.[62] Captain Edward Trelawney belonged to a Cornish family well known to Clarendon. Captain Robert Sutton was probably related to Lord Lexinton, another Catholic who had served Charles I during the Civil Wars and been ennobled by Charles II. It is likely that he was the captain of the Newark troop of volunteers who in later years was killed fighting in Ireland and much mourned, as Thomas Shipman wrote in his volume of poems, *Carolina*:

> He had brave Sidney, and those Sparks outgone,
> Who did at thirty all that could be done.
> But none can limm him right, who have not been
> Where they might him before his Troop have seen.
> How he that day made many Dons to fall,
> When English Swords protected Portugal.[63]

Among the troops of horse were almost certainly reformadoes, or reformed officers, for whom no place could be found as officers; there would also have been gentlemen-at-arms, or gentlemen volunteers. Sometimes these gentlemen were enlisted by captains of companies or troops for higher pay: they might be relatives, or poor gentlemen unable to gain any other living. Many were Catholics, especially after the rigorous imposition of the oaths in 1666.[64] English recusants such as the Catesbys and Treshams, for example, were found as volunteers in the Spanish service. In the armies of Parliament the duties of the reformado had included being 'a sort of storekeeper for the regimental arms and ammunition; he was responsible for the marking, presentation and repair of all arms.'[65] In Tangier in 1664 there was one in every company.[66] But they might also be experienced fighting men and as such, they were greatly valued in any army, since not only did they provide much excellent military experience, but also they were better motivated, more skilled, and less prone to mutiny and desertion than the common men. The establishment, however, did not pay them and they were often paid out of false musters or by the colonels of regiments and captains of companies from their own means.

These four troops numbered about 400 and therefore they brought the horse up to a total strength of about 550.[67] The remainder called for by the treaty were withheld at the Portuguese request,[68] as the nature of the war called more for infantry than cavalry. The regiment was placed under the colonelcy of Michael Dongan, from Harley's Regiment of Dragoons, with Henry Belasyse as lieutenant-colonel; Dongan was an Irish Protestant who had served in Spain in from 1656 until early in 1661.[69] Captain Lawrence Dempsey was another Irishman who had served the King of Spain since 1657;[70] when in 1661 the Catholic clergy of Ireland submitted their *Humble Remonstrance, Acknowledgement, Protestation and Petition* to Charles II, he was one of the laymen who signed it.[71] Captain-Lieutenant Richard Mill, who commanded his troop, was possibly a relative of Sir John Mill who had been killed in the king's service between 1642 and 1646.[72] On arrival in Portugal, the colonelcy passed to the Earl of Inchiquin although Dongan seems to have retained *de facto*, if not *de jure*, command.

In terms of organisation, the Spanish and Portuguese armies in the prospective theatre of operations were based on the *tercio*, as noted in Chapter One. This organisation had been used during the Civil Wars in England, chiefly by the royalist armies, having been introduced by those professional soldiers who had seen service on the continent. By 1660, however, the English infantry organisation was based around the regiment, the building block of all armies and usually the largest permanent unit and synonymous with the battalion. A regiment consisted of between 700 and 1,000 men in eight or ten companies. The two English foot regiments destined for Portugal were each of ten companies initially, each with its own Colour, officers and NCO's. About one-third of the men by this time were armed with the pike, two-thirds with the match-lock musket. The system of Colours followed that developed during the English Civil Wars and can be seen, for example, with details of the uniform then worn, in Dirk Stoop's 1680 painting *The Parade of the Army at Tangier* in the collection of Lord Dartmouth.[73] The Colonel's Colour would usually be a sheet of one colour with the arms or device of the colonel in the centre. The Lieutenant-Colonel's Colour would be a sheet of the same colour with the cross of St George in the first canton. The Major's Colour would be the same, but with the pile wavy added. The Captain's Colours would again follow the pattern of the lieutenant-colonel, but with one, two, three or more small devices or numerals to distinguish their seniority.

Horse regiments were generally smaller than foot regiments, consisting of 300 or 400 troopers in six or eight troops;[74] in the case of the English horse in Portugal, there seem to have been eight troops: four troops with 40–50 men each and four with around 100 men each. Generally there would be no permanent organisation for the artillery other than a few master gunners and their mates – trains of artillery were put together for each campaign; the same applied to the engineers, sappers and miners. Engineering stores, pontoon bridging, digging equipment, fascines and gabions usually travelled with the artillery in its wagons.[75]

Uniform was not standard until the 1630s, but had been adopted by most armies between 1640 and 1660. In England, the New Model Army had provided its men with standard clothing: one suit of clothes consisting of a red coat, grey breeches, a hat known as the Monmouth cap, linen shirt and worsted stockings, snapsack and one pair of shoes per man per year, at a cost of £1/6/3d[76] – but this allowance had to be supplemented by a soldier's own clothes, especially for cold weather.[77] It is known that the English foot regiments in Portugal wore the red coat, which soon became an object of inspiration to their allies and respect to their enemies.[78] The two regiments in Portugal were distinguished by different coloured linings – facings – to their coats although the particular colours are not known.[79] A contemporary writer further remarked that the English wore red and

Figure 6 A regiment of horse in three troops, from Allain Mallet's *Les travaux de Mars, ou l'art de la Guerre*. (© Royal Armouries RAL. 08482)

blue caps made from mantles worn by the country women.[80] The pikemen might still wear armour: a pot helmet based on the Spanish morillon, back and breast plates, and tassets to protect the thighs. Heavy horse, sometimes called harquebusiers, at this time still wore three-quarter armour while dragoons wore the tanned leather buff coat – buff being a corruption of *boeuf*, rather than a description of its colour – with the lobster-tailed cavalry helmet, long boots and gauntlets. In some cases armour, in the shape of the back-and-breast plates, was also still worn. A description of the English horse in Portugal, however, suggests that it was equipped as dragoons, not as heavy horse: 'all in buff coats'.[81] Arms and armour, including ancillaries like powder flasks, bullet moulds and bandoliers were provided by contractors engaged by the government – a musket typically cost more than a month's pay for a soldier; musketeers and arquebusiers drew slightly higher pay than pikemen, but paid for their own powder and shot; cavalry men similarly were paid higher wages to cover the cost of buying, equipping and feeding their mounts. When pay was badly in arrears, the first thing to go would be the cavalry horses – but not the draught animals.

This organisation brought together many former enemies for as well as the mix of former Cromwellians, Parliament men and Royalists within the regiments, there were more Royalists, and Catholics too, alongside Morgan in the hierarchy of the force. Murragh O'Brien, Earl of Inchiquin, was nominated as General-in-Chief of the British contingent. O'Brien had studied war in the Spanish service and fought against the confederate Catholics on the outbreak of the Irish rebellion during Charles I's reign. He was made governor of Munster in 1642 and held command until a truce was brokered with the rebels. He was forced to submit unwillingly to Parliament in 1644, as the Parliamentarians controlled all aid to the Munster Protestants by sea. O'Brien gradually became master of the south of Ireland, and declared for Charles I in 1648, fortified the southern ports against Parliament and signed a truce with the confederate Catholics; he himself was converted to Catholicism in 1656. After Cromwell's landing in 1649, he retired to the west of the Shannon and then left Ireland for France in 1650, where he became a member of Charles II's royal council in exile and in 1654 was created Earl of Inchiquin. He entered the French service and went to Catalonia during the autumn of 1657 to fight against the Spanish.

The Peace of the Pyrenees destroyed his chances of further employment and distinction in Catalonia, but Cardinal Mazarin connived at his going with Schomberg to Portugal; he started for Lisbon in the autumn of 1659. On 20 February 1660 it was reported in Paris that he and his son William had been captured at sea by the Algerine pirates. The English council wrote on his behalf to the Pasha, and by 23 August he was in England, but his son remained in Africa as a hostage until ransomed. Inchiquin went to Paris soon afterwards and returned with Queen Henrietta Maria, of whose household he became high steward. During 1661 he signed the declaration of allegiance to Charles II by the Irish Catholic nobility and gentry and on 23 June 1662 it was noted that 'this famous soldier in Ireland'[82] sailed as General-in-Chief of the expeditionary force. He was seconded by Sir John Talbot, an old royalist soldier, scion of an ancient and famous Catholic family in Cheshire. He had raised and commanded a regiment in 1640 in Prince Maurice's army, and fought at Edge Hill and Second Newbury.

For Charles II, any expansion of the army, especially overseas, was an opportunity to provide employment for Catholic officers and men who had supported his father and himself in exile, away from the scrutiny and hostility of a Protestant Parliament and press In England. These were men to whom he owed a debt of loyalty for their service; and in many cases they were also good soldiers. Between 1660 and 1667, twenty-seven commissions were granted to Catholics in line companies on the home establishment, nine in the guards, ten in garrisons and six abroad. Of seventy Catholics known to have been commissioned by Charles II throughout his reign, twenty-one were Irish. Distance lent enchantment here, for among many in England it was firmly believed that the Stuarts had Popish tendencies and that if this was encouraged, then Charles, like any Catholic ruler of a Protestant territory, would be under constant pressure from his confessor and the pope to extirpate heresy and impose Catholicism, a task so meritorious that breaking oaths and laws would count for nothing. He would try to overturn all laws, fill offices with Papists and atheists and rule by armed force:[83] the massacre of St Bartholomew's day pointed the way. The series of plots and conspiracies – fabricated and real – during Charles II's reign did nothing to alleviate this general feeling of anti-Catholicism; nor did the obvious Catholicism of the king's brother and his second wife, Mary of Modena, nor indeed Queen Catherine.

Catholic officers like O'Brien and Talbot were chiefly career soldiers who lived by their profession, rather than the occasional soldiers from the shires – those gentlemen or peers who would turn out in times of national emergency and who thus have no bearing on this study. Many of these professionals were younger sons of good families, who used their portion of the family estate to purchase a commission. Catholic career soldiers would have even less chance of employment on the home establishment than officers and so would generally seek service abroad; and Catholics were in theory at least disbarred from receiving pensions.[84] In addition, many Catholics employed in English armies were Irish or Scots soldiers of fortune, aliens whose loyalty, as seen by English Protestants, would be initially to their paymaster, but ultimately to the Pope.[85] All the Catholic officers on the Army List lost their places in 1667 as the government sought to encourage fear of Popery and pin on Catholics the blame for the Great Fire and the Medway defeat.[86] However, in spite of hostility at home, there is no evidence that the laws laying down the requirement for taking the Oath of Supremacy or the imposition of the later Test Acts, which specified that soldiers or officers serving abroad had to take the oaths, were actually imposed in stations like Tangier and Portugal; although some may have done so voluntarily.[87]

*   *   *

Although it might be tempting to see the officers and men in Portugal in modern terms, as mere mercenaries, matters stood very differently in the seventeenth century. The political structures of states did not necessarily correspond with the demographic distribution of people, from which troops could be drawn.[88] The Tudors, for example, employed Albanian cavalry and a Spanish infantry regiment in the war against the Scots from 1544 to 1551. Spain, facing the manpower crisis from the 1590s onwards described in Chapter One, routinely employed Italians, Walloons, Burgundians, Germans plus a more widely-cast net. Contrary to urban myth, contingents of English, Scots and Irish troops served the Spanish cause in Flanders from 1580 onwards, often opposing the reinforcements the English government sent to bolster the Dutch rebels, or changing sides as conditions altered.[89] Many of these were Catholic recusants who had fled abroad to escape persecution in England but after the Anglo-Spanish peace in 1604, direct recruiting began. Thomas, Lord Arundel, raised a complete regiment in England and Henry O'Neill another in Ireland. Protestant England was alarmed and Parliament passed a law requiring any citizen entering the service of a foreign power first to swear an oath of allegiance to James I and give a bond against reconciliation with the Roman Church. Even so, with the conclusion of the Twelve Years' Truce in the Netherlands in 1621, intensive recruiting raised the strength of the English contingent in Spanish service to 4,000.[90] This remained steady throughout the 1630s, but the outbreak of the Civil Wars in England greatly reduced the available manpower, until Parliament's victory produced a surge in defeated Royalists and Catholics.[91] These British officers and men were all engaged under contract and being mainly asylum seekers, they were bound to the King of Spain and his cause and should not be seen as mere mercenaries.

Contract was one of three means employed by Governments in this period to raise troops; the others were commission and compulsion. Commissions came from the monarch to a particular captain or lord, specified the area from which troops were to be drawn, the numbers to be raised and their employment, thus retaining full control with a minimum of compulsion. The colonel named his captains and they in turn named the junior officers and non-commissioned officers. The captain could demand assistance from local magistrates in raising volunteers who were paid enlistment bounties and pay thereafter. Compulsion meant either local conscription or else pressure on prisoners of war to change sides – both were widespread during the Civil Wars in England. Contract meant that the government paid the contractor an advance plus a regular sum for wages thereafter in return for a specified number of troops, usually assembled rapidly.

For the Restoration government and army in England, foreign service on contract – often effectively the hire of British forces by foreign states – became an important method of maintaining military forces, available for recall at need, but maintained at the expense of another government. When contingents of troops left the British Isles under these terms they ceased to be part of the English or Irish establishment and became the direct responsibility of the hiring government for their pay, food, clothing and equipment. Foreign service thus provided the English Crown with a corps of trained veterans, hardened by active service, and yet maintained at no cost to the Exchequer. This gave the king a professional reserve army which could be recalled into England at any time. There were two additional advantages in the system: Parliament could not complain of a large standing army in England, while it allowed Charles to fulfil his treaty obligations without committing the country to a war with another power – in this case, Spain.

Within these general principles there were several variations. First, there were officially sanctioned bodies of troops sent to assist a friendly foreign power at its expense, such as the brigade in Portugal and the Anglo-Dutch Brigade which served in the United Provinces, both of which were composed of soldiers raised directly for service in those theatres. Since 1585 when Elizabeth I had sent 5,000 men under Robert Dudley, Earl of Leicester, to the United Provinces, a British brigade had been in the Dutch service. By 1593 a separate regiment of 6,400 Scots was also in Dutch pay;[92] the English and Scots were grouped together and referred to as the Anglo-Dutch Brigade. The King of England had the right to recall these men home at any time and this was twice exercised by the later Stuarts: Charles II recalled the brigade at the beginning of the Second Dutch War in 1665, although many did not obey the recall and even fought against England;

and James II did the same in 1685 when he needed experienced troops to help suppress Monmouth's Rebellion.

Secondly, there were contingents like the brigade that served Louis XIV of France during the Third Anglo-Dutch War which were drawn from the English standing army. Thirdly, there were a number of individual regiments almost permanently in the employment of foreign governments like the Irish and others in the service of Spain; and after 1678 Thomas Dongan and then Justin Macartie commanded a large Irish regiment in French service, forming the foundation of the later Irish Brigade in the service of France.[93] One of the most enduring examples was the Royal Regiment of Foot, later the Royal Scots, which was first raised in 1633 by Sir John Hepburn under a royal warrant from Charles I, on the Scottish establishment, for service in France. It was formed from a nucleus of Hepburn's previous regiment, formerly in Swedish service, which had been in existence since 1625. When in France it absorbed the remnants of a number of other Scottish mercenary units which had fought in Swedish service and by 1635 had swelled to some 8,000 men. Hepburn was killed at the siege of Saverne in 1636; the regiment was taken over by his nephew, Sir John Hepburn, who was killed in action the following year. Lord James Douglas was then appointed colonel. In all the regiment served in France from 1633 to 1661, when it was recalled to England, for it was legally part of the English Crown's armed forces, even though it had been out of the country for three decades. As such, it was recalled to help secure the restoration and coronation of Charles II after the general disbandment of the old armies of the Protectorate. The regiment returned to France from 1662 to 1666 when it was again recalled for the Second Dutch War; and then again from 1667 to 1678, when it was finally placed on the home establishment and given precedence as the senior regiment of the line.

Thus a state's standing army could be made up of both national units, raised in the state itself and non-native troops like the Scots regiment in the Dutch army, or the Irish in the Spanish armies. The state paid and funded both contingents. In addition, there could be non-national troops paid for by the state but not part of the standing army. These could be subsidy troops serving under a treaty between states; or refugee and émigré troops like the Catalans in the Portuguese service or English and Irish Catholics in French and Spanish service; or deserters; or mercenaries in the old sense like Hepburn's Regiment in France in the 1630s. A third element, which David Chandler referred to as 'subsidy troops', were the troops raised and maintained by one state, but for which that state received money from another state, such as the regiments which Portugal was to keep in the field against Spain under the 1666 treaty with France. Many of the distinctions are to do with motivation. For refugee or émigré regiments this could be relatively uniform and easy to establish – often it was religious or ethnic discrimination at home; but for the rest, this could be a more complex matter ranging from ideology to money, or unemployment, or local allegiance or even being fugitive from the law. But once a regiment had been sent abroad either under a treaty or in return for financial return, motivation became irrelevant except in so far as it contributed to fighting power. And once battle had been joined, the composition of any regiment could be fluid in the extreme given the frequency of desertion, capture, amalgamation, heavy casualties and the disbandment of weak units.

Wienand Drenth noted a shift in these various methods of employment of foreign troops by various states through the course of the seventeenth century and the nature of these troops. In the first part of the century they seemed to be of the mercenary or military entrepreneurial type: a leader with influence and martial ambitions would sign a contract with a foreign monarch; then, with or without the consent of his own sovereign he would then recruit a regiment – for example, the Scots regiments in Swedish service. After about 1680, it seemed that foreign troops employed by another state were mostly drawn from that foreign state's standing army, with the government acting as entrepreneur. Thus contracts were signed between states, not between a state and an entrepreneur.[94]

It could be argued, therefore, that a relationship developed between this shift from the use of mercenaries, towards contracts between states and with this, the increase of standing armies, the rise of nation states and government rather than seigniorial control over finances. To address this question one must examine in each individual case the underlying mechanisms which led to a contract. These mechanisms could include dynastic marriage; alliance, treaty or other obligations; the need to enhance national prestige; money; or simply fear of powerful neighbours.

Drenth also suggests that in order to understand the nuances of differentiation between various non-national units employed within an army, a number of criteria need to be considered. First, the source of pay and supply for the unit, which might change over time. Secondly, who raised the unit – military entrepreneur, government or foreign head of state – and what was the origin of the unit and its service before it went into foreign service, if any. Thirdly, the nationality, religion and prior service of the colonel, the officers and men. Fourth, the command arrangements: whether the units were placed under the overall authority of the army commander, or if by contrast they retained an independent command within a coalition.

*   *   *

The various contingents that were to make up the brigade in Portugal now had to be shipped, at Charles's expense, to Portugal. The regiments of foot from Leith were embarked under Sir Thomas Morgan's command on 15, 16 and 17 May 1662, as we have seen.[95] They went first to Plymouth and departed from there on 18 June: 'The same success that attended the forces under Major-General Sir Tho. Morgan's command from Scotland to Plymouth, hath waited on them all along the voyage to the expected harbour. The 18 June we set sail from Plymouth and arrived at Lisbon the 27'.[96] The four troops of horse at Dunkirk sailed from that place on 6 May 1662 and after losing their convoy and being intercepted by Spanish ships, finally made their way to Portugal, landing the men and horses at Lagos and Faro.[97] Finally, the four troops of horse from England were shipped from Plymouth to Portugal on 20 June 1662, along with 1,400 French soldiers.[98] Charles Croke reported that he had

> listed himself in a Western Gentleman's troop [probably Trelawney's] which then lay at Plymouth ready to take Shipping; and by the favour of his new Captain, mustered a man: Being thus provided with a couple of able Geldings, and good Clothes, and Money, he took Shipping with the rest of the Souldiers; and by the favour of a fresh and moderate Gale they soon arrived at Lisbon, where they found a plausible reception at their first landing, with Bonfires and ringing of Bells.[99]

By the end of June, therefore, the whole force was assembled.

4

The English Brigade, 1662–1663

'Over the hills and o'er the main,
To Flanders, Portugal and Spain'[1]

Ann, Lady Fanshawe, described Lisbon – the first place in Portugal that the arriving English soldiers saw – as 'the goodliest situation that ever I saw; the city old and decayed, but they are making new walls of stone which will contain six times their city … The nation is generally very civil and obliging; in religion divided between Papists and Jews; the people generally not handsome.'[2] Those among the English soldiers whose only experience had been life in England or Scotland were in for something of a change in their familiar horizons of landscape, climate and culture. Portugal lies on the western littoral of the Iberian Peninsula; it is bound by Spain to the north and east and the Atlantic Ocean to the south and west. The land border between the two countries runs for around 1,000 kilometres (625 miles). Some of it follows defined features such as the rivers Douro, Tagus, and Guardiana; however much of the land border is unobstructed and ill defined. This was a major factor in defining the nature of the war in the 1650s as essentially raiding at points of choice.[3]

In order to make any sort of sense about what happened during the Restoration War, where it happened and why, one really has to travel to Iberia and walk the ground. Not just for a few hours, but for days, even weeks – and then at different times of the year. Only then will one see what tourists in the Algarve do not: that Portugal is mountainous, arid, poor, thinly populated and difficult to cross. In the north-east of Portugal, the highlands of Beira Alta and Tras-os-Montes which rise above 2000 metres (6000 feet) are a continuation of the Castilian Plateau; while further south, the Beira Baixa and Alentejo regions are part of the same geographical area as the Extremadura region of Spain. The central mountain range that slices Portugal diagonally in two, the Sierra da Estrela, is a westward continuation of the Gata, Gredos and Guadarrama ranges of Spain. Similarly the two principal rivers – the Tagus and the Douro – are also Spain's. Thus the strategic and operational geography of Portugal cannot be separated from its larger neighbour. The political border between the two is one based on language rather than geography but it is dominated by high, rough and dry terrain for most of its length. Roads are few and in the seventeenth century, they were poor even by the standards of the rest of Europe at that time. Rivers and streams, usually deeply incised, ran in torrents that obstructed movement for a few months of the year and then, perversely, they dried up during the heat of summer, leaving deep channels that had to be traversed without the benefit of anything to drink for the parched soldiers and animals who had to struggle over them. It could take a whole day for even a moderate army to cross a river obstacle, even if the river was low. In both

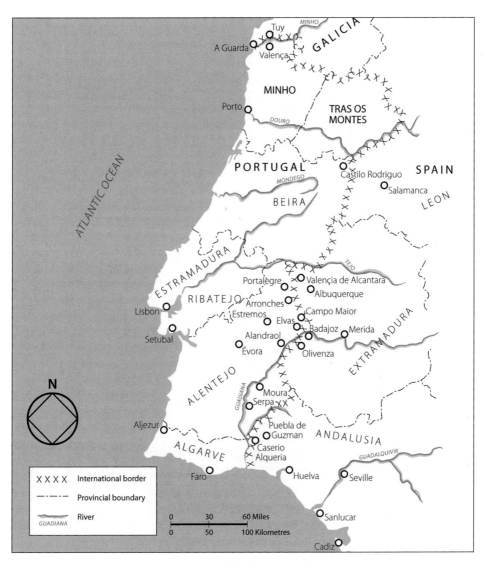

Map 3 Portugal and Western Spain.

Figure 7 This is the view that Ann, Lady Fanshawe, described and that the English troops would have seen as they arrived by sea. *A view of the Royal Palace in Lisbon*, by Dirk Stoop in 1662. (British Museum M36.43)

1662 and 1663 the Army of Extremadura had thrown two wooden pontoon bridges over the Caia River to increase the pass rate, but even so, crossings were choke points that could be attacked.

Portugal has two climatic zones. The northern zone is Atlantic, characterised by an average annual rainfall of 991 mm (39 inches) with temperatures influenced by the ocean air currents and the Spanish Meseta. The smaller, southern zone, which has a Mediterranean climate with hot, dry summers and mild, wet winters, has weather conditions influenced by high pressure systems which develop over the Azores. It was in this latter climatic regime that most of the English brigade's fighting was done. Average temperature ranges in Lisbon are from 8 to 14°C (46 to 57°F) in January, to 17 to 28°C (60 to 82°F) in August. From mid-November, rain, cold and sometimes snow restricted the ability to move on the roads as well as being outside the growing seasons; it was because of this that the rivers and streams became torrents impossible to cross except on the very few bridges at this time of year, so that campaigning stopped. Traversing the country only became possible from mid-April but even in spring, heavy rain could turn roads into bogs. In summer, high temperatures, lack of food and water obliged the armies to cease campaigning again: these conditions of climate combined with geomorphology produced the two short campaigning seasons of spring (mid April–mid June) and autumn (mid September–late November).

As the English troops were arriving in Portugal and settling in, their commander, the Earl of Inchiquin, had the task of opening negotiations with the Portuguese over the implementation of the terms on which they were engaged. It rapidly became apparent that they differed over the interpretation of that part of the treaty which specified the date on which Portugal would take over responsibility for the payment of the troops.[4] Initially Charles II and the Portuguese government had agreed that the men were to be paid by the English Crown for the first three months, but after that responsibility for payment was to pass to Portugal. Thomas Maynard, the English government's consul-general in Lisbon, calculated the cost of paying the English brigade as 13,000 *cruzadoes* each month.[5] But native Portuguese troops received only seven or eight months' pay in a year as opposed to the twelve months of the English soldier. With some justification, the Portuguese authorities argued that to pay the English at this rate would cause jealousy, and possibly even mutiny, amongst the Portuguese and French soldiery. The Portuguese refused an increase in the English pay, stating that the wages given to their own soldiers were quite sufficient as Portugal was a cheap country in which to live.[6] This was a mealy-mouthed response, given that the cost of feeding and paying the army of Alentejo, as already noted, came to just under 214,000 *cruzadoes* each month and the proportion consumed by the English brigade was therefore modest.[7]

If the English soldiers learned that delays in pay were likely, the senior officers feared that they would mutiny and force the seamen of the fleet to take them straight back to England. After swearing the regimental officers to secrecy, Inchiquin ordered the troops to disembark, after which they were then drawn up in review and he addressed them, saying that:

> they were two of the best regiments (for proper persons of men) that ever he had seen, but his only fear was that they would destroy themselves faster than their enemies, by taking too much wine and fruit, and gave the assurance that for

his part he would take all possible care of them; whereupon the soldiers joyfully acknowledged their general with several acclamations.[8]

The bulk of the brigade, it appears, marched directly up-country to their quarters in and around Estremos, arriving there by early August.[9] Inchiquin's assurances were soon seen for what they were, however. From the beginning of the expedition until its end, the pay of the English troops was in arrears; the correspondence of their commanders, of Maynard and of Sir Richard Fanshawe, the English ambassador, was full of complaints on this score. Schomberg remarked that 'Our English troops would be on a very good footing if they were paid with some regularity'.[10] Moreover, relations between soldiers and civilians deteriorated quickly, even by the standards of an age in which the quartering of troops on civilians at the charge of the community and the rowdy behaviour of Thomas Atkins were almost always causes for complaint. On the other side of the coin, the troops complained that their quarters were poor and the civilians gave them no assistance.

Lawrence Dempsey of Pearson's Regiment insisted that the indiscipline and bad behaviour of the English troops had been grossly exaggerated and that the fault lay entirely with the Portuguese,[11] but in truth the blame lay with both sides. Sickness also took its toll. Maynard described the soldiers as 'mouldering away', the horse having only 250 effective men and the foot only 1,400. Without food and other necessities the soldiers turned to robbery and begging, further antagonising the civilians who retaliated by murdering any soldiers who strayed from their quarters. Several killings of soldiers led to reprisals by the English, who were said to have exacted two or three victims for every one of their comrades murdered.[12] Three months after their arrival the troops were reported as being in an uproar, 'all being weary of the service, wishing themselves home again.'[13]

Active service in the field would probably have solved most if not all of the problems, but there was no campaigning in prospect as the winter approached. Inchiquin therefore granted passes to officers who wished to return to England on furlough and many, including Sir Thomas Morgan[*] and several other senior officers, took advantage of this and left, pleading 'want of due pay and regard.'[14] Samuel Pepys noted that 'We fell to business of the Navy. Among other things, how to pay off this fleet that is now come from Portugall; the King of Portugall sending them home, he having no more use for them, which we wonder at, that his condition should be so soon altered. And our landmen also are coming back, being almost starved in that poor country.'[15]

Inducements were also offered to deserters by the Spanish, which fell on fertile ground in the climate of neither pay nor new clothing; and in November 1662 a party of English went over to the enemy, to be followed by others in the following March. Fanshawe wrote to Clarendon at the close of 1662 painting a gloomy picture: the regiments still held together, but 'in such a mouldering, perishing, discontented fashion as gives me no confidence of their continuing so a fortnight longer.'[16] In another letter he wrote that 'Upon the whole, my Lord, there appears to me no cement at all in our troops, being

---

[*]   Morgan died in 1679 having been Governor of Jersey. His son, Sir John Morgan, was colonel of the 23rd Royal Welch Fusiliers from 1692 until his death early the following year.

admirable individuals but the worst body that ever was … In fine, break I see these troops will at a most unlucky hour – without a miracle – in a thousand pieces',[17] Charles II could barely afford to help. About £40,000 had been spent from the Privy Purse in raising the troops, who had then been paid for several months longer than expected. Charles found it impossible to relieve the troops' condition or to send recruits without better assurances from the Portuguese.[18]

Religious divisions did not help the general tone of disquiet. Portugal was, of course, an intensely Catholic country – as was Spain. Not for nothing was the King of Spain styled 'His Most Catholic Majesty'. Efforts had to be made to make the command at least of the brigade acceptable to the Catholic Portuguese: Inchiquin and Talbot were both Catholics, as were a number of the officers as already noted. But the Portuguese seem hardly to have been aware of these efforts, probably believing that since the king of England was a Protestant, so too must be all his subjects: this after all had been one of the principles established at the Peace of Westphalia and the Catholic Church issued a proclamation protecting any Portuguese citizen who might wound or murder an Englishman.[19] For their part, the soldiers of the Protectorate would have had neither love nor respect for Catholicism. The bulk of the foot regiments, being old Protectorate men, were indeed hard-line Protestants and although Monck had purged the officers of extreme elements, the ordinary soldiers still ranged in their views from Presbyterians and Erastians, through Independents to Congregationalists, Separatists, Anabaptists, Levellers and Diggers.[20] It was as well that the treaty of 1642 had contained protection for them, ratified under the new treaty, in a country where the Inquisition had been active since 1536. Should any of such heretical views have been taken up and put to the question, it would have gone very hard indeed with them – very hard.[21] Even within the brigade, the religious mix caused tensions, as it did to an even greater degree in Tangier,[22] where the garrison was described in parliament as 'a seminary for Popish priests and soldiers too.'[23] In 1662, sixty percent of the officers there were Catholics, and in 1667 the figure was still as high as forty-five percent. Many were Irish and there were several documented fights and resulting courts-martial between adherents of the former protectorate and the monarchy.[24] Of course, there was bound to be tension between members of a force composed of men who until a year before had been fighting on opposite sides of a long and bitter civil war. In modern times, we have seen the equivalent in the re-formation of the armies of Zimbabwe, South Africa, Germany and Iraq from former opponents. It is seldom an easy business.

That said, the Spanish had, of course, used Protestant troops – although this had been largely for service in the Low Countries and not close to the heartland of Castille. Lutherans had been recruited in Hamburg in 1646; the army of the deposed Duke of Lorraine was taken into service in 1633; and troops loyal to the Prince of Condé were taken up between 1653 and 1659. In 1649, Don Ambrosio Mexía was given permission to raise a regiment in the United Provinces and although he concentrated on Catholic areas like Limburg and North Brabant he also enlisted many Calvinists. This is not to say that the Spanish were without misgivings: one senior officer wrote of the troops raised in Germany that 'The troops to be raised there will be excellent, except that they will be heretics to a man; but this was realised when the levy was ordered, and the extreme shortage of infantry in all parts will compel us to take them wherever they may be found.'[25] To reduce friction, foreign troops were usually kept as separate administrative units by nationality: only Spaniards could serve in and command Spanish contingents; English officers could not command Scottish or Irish units; Milanese or Roman soldiers could not serve in Neapolitan contingents and so on. This general principle seems to have been adopted for the English and French troops in Portugal.

Shortly after Alfonso VI's coming-of-age in June 1662, the twenty-six-year-old Count of Castelo Melhor,* leader of an impatient young faction among the nobility, saw an opportunity to gain power at court by befriending the young king, who is generally regarded as having been mentally sub-normal. According to Samuel Pepys, 'That the King of Portugal is a very fool almost, and his mother do all, and he is a very poor prince.'[26] Another commentator described him as 'a young prince with a very negligible education, without money, soldiers, allies or a single decent minister; happily however still under the management of his mother, a most prudent princess.'[27] In short, Alfonso VI was a man who had been brought low by debilitating illnesses in childhood and was left with a withered body, a defective mind and a tendency towards cruelty and violence. Castelo Melhor convinced the king that his mother was intent on taking the throne and sending Alfonso into exile. As a result, on 23 June 1662, Alfonso took control of the government. In May of the following year, his mother was sent to the convent of Xabegras, near Lisbon, which she had herself founded, and remained there until her death in 1666.[28] The king appointed Castelo Melhor as his secret notary (*escrivão da puridade*), a position in which he was able to exercise the functions of first minister and, given the weakness of the king, to become the real ruler of Portugal.

Castelo Melhor belonged to the Francophile party at the Portuguese court and over time he remodelled the government on the lines of the autocracy of Louis XIV. To consolidate his position he caused a King's Council to be appointed, headed by himself and packed with his place-men: the Marquis of Nisa, the Marqis of Marialva, Francisco de Mello, now the Marquis de Sande, the Conde de Arcos, the Conde de Santo Lorenço, the Conde da Myranda, the Abbot of Brago, Don Remy de Moira Belbes and Secretary of State Antonio da Souza de Macedo.[29] He accordingly inclined away from an English alliance towards a French pact and therefore also towards Schomberg. Relations between Castelo Melhor and Inchiquin thus deteriorated to the point where he too asked to return home.[30] In November 1662 he left, leaving his brother, Major-General Christopher O'Brien, in command of the brigade.

Christopher was no more successful than Murrough and his fall was precipitated by the court-martial of Guy Molesworth, the old royalist colonel now a captain of horse, who was arraigned by an English court-martial at Moura on 19, 20, 21 and 22 February 1663 under the presidency of another old Royalist, Colonel James Apsley. The proceedings tell us at least something about the relationships between officers and men, and between different political interests in the contingent as well as about the networks of patronage and influence at home.[31] Molesworth had a history of feuding, as already mentioned: he was quarrelsome, arrogant and undisciplined; he was also well-connected at home – with Prince Maurice and George Monck in particular but also with Fanshawe who was an old personal friend. Fanshawe tried to have the hearing held in England and to stand bail for him, but O'Brien refused and the trial went ahead.

---

*   Luis de Vasconelos e Sousa, 3rd Count of Castelo Melhor (1636–1720).

The first of a series of articles against Molesworth set out, with an evident ring of truth, 'that hee shoulde have spoken reproachful words against his Majesty's sacred person'. The witnesses to this article were Lieutenant Charles Croke and Corporal Charles Ward, who had heard Molesworth say that 'hee himself and thy party were to be made slaves of & to be destroy.' Trooper Theobald Nichols heard him say that 'if the king had any honest cavaliers he shoulde send them to be destroyed in a company of Rebels.' Trooper John Paine attested that Molesworth had said that 'the King had sent him into this country to be destroyed, and that he would seek instruction in ye faith' – presumably that the king was preparing to convert to Catholicism and betray the troops to the Spanish as evidence of good faith. George Chapse related how Molesworth said that he wished the king had sent him to Tyburn rather than to Portugal.[32] These witnesses were articulate and may well have been reformed officers, former Royalists who disliked hearing the king abused by an Irishman.

The second article, in which the witnesses again were Croke and Chapse, alleged that Molesworth had insulted the honour of both O'Briens 'by calling them cheats and saying they were neither true to king nor country'. A third article that accused him of inciting mutiny was dropped because of insufficient evidence. Next, it was reported that he 'daily disheartened the foot soldiery by telling them that they were but Cromwell's whelps and rebels, and that they were sent here for murthering the late King and were banished men.'[33] The witnesses here were old Cromwellian soldiers: Sergeant Thomas Bankes, Privates John Paul, Thomas Ely and Ralph Stevenson who were probably disheartened even before Molesworth's ranting began, having been neglected from the start by their own government and the Portuguese regime. Not content with abusing the men, he had moreover defrauded his troops of their pay, 'the witnesses sworn in this article were the officers of his troope because ye Colonel [presumably Dongan] excepted against ye soldiery.' This must have rankled with the old Cromwellian, Dongan, but he clearly had a strong sense of fair play. The three officers, Lieutenant William Grant, Cornet Robert Meakinge and Quarter-Master George Chapse, were only too happy, it seems, to take the part of the men against their captain.

Molesworth, although an Irishman himself, was a Protestant and had no opinion whatever of the O'Briens. Several articles allege that he had disobeyed orders many times, had fomented mutiny, encouraged disobedience and 'contempt to superiors' in the soldiers; he made application to have his trial conducted by a Portuguese court rather than an English court-martial. Finally, 'He swore that if Jesus Christ himself were come from Heaven and were an Irish man, he would not obey him'. As well as the witnesses, Molesworth's own letters provided ample testimony of this. Molesworth went further, accusing both Inchiquin himself and Christopher O'Brien of plotting with the Spanish to march the English brigade into Spain and there hand them over, a charge which seems to have struck a chord with the paranoid Portuguese high command who insti-gated a commission of inquiry. As a result of this, on 7 March 1663, a despatch from James Apsley to Fanshawe reported that Christopher O'Brien had had 'delivered himself prisoner' to Apsley as president of the court-martial, and demanded to be examined by a court of the English officers in Portugal. Molesworth was summoned to produce his witnesses and could only nominate Captain South, 'who upon oath … denied that he ever heard the Major-General say such words, or intend such an unworthy trai-torous action'.[34] This effectively sank Molesworth without trace: he was condemned for misdemeanour as well as being found guilty on the other charges. He was 'disgracefully cashiered' and sentenced to death. Twenty officers, including Henry Pearson, signed a deposition in which they declared that:

> the penalty of the sayd articles beinge by his Matie ordained to bee death, from which wee have noe Liberty to recede, wee doe hereby order that Collonel Guy Molesworth bee shott to death or otherwise punished and siposed of according to the will of Major-Generall O'Bryan, for whose Mercy wee are supplicants.[35]

But Molesworth again repeated his allegations: James Apsley testified on 29 March that Captain South had told Cornet John Crossman that O'Brien meant to march the English into Spain and hand them over if they were not paid. O'Brien defended himself vigorously, but he was returned under arrest to England towards the end of March.[36] These destructive proceedings dragged on well into 1663,[37] as both parties mobilised their networks of patronage. The charges against O'Brien were examined by an inquiry of two commissioners, who unhappily for O'Brien were George Monck and Sir Henry Bennet, both patrons of Molesworth. Fanshawe joined in against O'Brien, providing a dossier of allegations supporting the claim that O'Brien had conspired with the Spanish. Although the evidence was thin, O'Brien was not able to convince the commissioners of his innocence and had to resort to petitioning the king for what had been 'unjustly layd on him in Portugal.'[38] As a result, Charles directed Bennet to acquit him: 'there was not much ground in either the Council's nor Colonel Molesworth's accusation of him, not enough to punish him here or indeed enough to detain him any longer prisoner'.[39] However in spite of that, O'Brien was finished anyway. The final result of O'Brien's examination and discharge did not reach Portugal until June 1663, when Fanshawe noted to Schomberg that in a letter from Sir Henry Bennet, 'which I wish were known to the soldiery there with you for the better clearing of his honour and innocency amongst them, whilst I shall be as industrious in this court to obtain his quietus est from hence, which I expect to be able to do, because I believe they never really thought him guilty.'[40] O'Brien had done what he could to contain the disruptive influence of Molesworth, but Molesworth's disdainful, quarrelsome nature, his close ties with Fanshawe and with those in power at home, the fragility of the governments in both London and Lisbon and the suspicious nature of the Portuguese all combined to undo him.

Molesworth's conviction did him no harm, probably because he enjoyed the patronage of the Duke of York, Prince Maurice, Gervase Holles and George Monck and surprisingly perhaps he was granted an interview by Charles II, at which although no record survives, they appear to have parted on good terms;[41] however over the coming years he repeatedly petitioned the king for employment in return for his years of service. The sentence of execution was quickly and quietly dropped and he was appointed to several civil posts – such as warehouse keeper in the Port of London – that would provide him with an income.[42] He was the major of Lord Alington's Regiment of Foot in 1667, knighted in 1680 and was made colonel of the Duchess of York's Regiment before his death in 1680.[43]

The court-martial of Molesworth raises the question of discipline. The organisation of disciplinary affairs rested with the regimental provost martial, then on to the council of war which made disciplinary decrees and could act as a court. The proceedings would have been governed by a code of military justice similar to those used in both Tangier and Dunkirk at this time; these in turn bore close similarity to the *Laws and Ordinances of War Established for the Better Conduct of the Army* by the Earl of Essex in September 1642, modified to include duties to His Majesty the King. The use of such a code ensured that jurisdiction over the troops remained with the national military authorities rather than the Portuguese, even though they were paying the wages. Similarly, the *Orders and Articles of War* for the English Army published in 1666 took military justice at home away from civil magistrates.[44] Not that discipline had ever been much of an issue for Protectorate troops and the regiments in Scotland, from which the brigade had been formed, had been kept to a high standard of conduct by Monck. In one court-martial, he had dealt with two soldiers caught plundering the citizens of Dundee. They were 'sentenced for robbing two country-men near the Town … to be led with ropes about their necks to the gallows, there to be tyed up and receive 30 stripes a-piece; then to ask forgiveness to the Country-men upon their knees, and to be kept with bread and water in prison, until they should restore four-fold for what they had taken away.'[45]

With the departure of Christopher O'Brien, the command of the demoralised English brigade devolved on Schomberg and this was to prove a turning point.[46] Schomberg, described as a man of 'indefatigable zeal, imperturbability in the face of danger, moderation in victory, open nature, politeness'.[47] As a Protestant with an English mother, he was favoured by the majority of the men. When the colonelcy of the horse regiment, which had been held by Inchiquin, was conferred on Schomberg the announcement of his appointment was received by the troopers with cries of 'à Schumberg, à Schumberg!' and assurances of loyalty by all the officers.[48] The transformation of a rabble of disgruntled soldiers into an effective fighting force must be attributed to Schomberg.

Schomberg had arrived in Portugal at the head of the French contingent described in Chapter Three on 3 November 1660,[49] where 'His troops took the field and passed in review to the great admiration of the Portuguese. Schomberg himself passed the rest of the year at court, in order to become acquainted with the senior figures.'[50] His mandate was to exercise command of the forces in the field in the province of Alentejo, as well as to reorganise and retrain the whole army. As a Frenchman who had taken the trouble to learn Portuguese – remarked on by Richard Fanshawe[51] – he was favoured by the Portuguese people and the king's ministers in the new government. However a faction among the grandees in Portugal wanted to refuse Schomberg's appointment and to be rid of him and all foreigners, as they were perceived as being more likely to do the bidding of France and England rather than Portugal. His experience, seniority and religion however excited envy and resistance among the grandees; this attitude, which endured to an extent throughout Schomberg's time in Portugal, along with shortages of money, munitions and food, meant that he found it very hard indeed to fulfil his task.

In effect, the command arrangements in Portugal were all that is worst in an alliance or coalition force, where national interest is of more importance than the defeat of a common enemy. Only the threat of catastrophic defeat will be enough to persuade nations to subordinate their common interests in a single cause. But at this point, the Portuguese simply did not feel threatened enough to give ground. Schomberg claimed the sole authority to give orders to the foreign contingents; but the Portuguese resented this, nor would their generals cede him any authority over Portuguese forces. For their part, the French and later the English would only take orders from Schomberg.[52] Unity of command is a principle of war, but one that only near defeat would oblige the Portuguese to obey.

Opposing Schomberg, the command of the Spanish armies fighting against Portugal was in 1661 placed in the hands of Philip IV's illegitimate son, Don John of Austria the Younger.* Don John was a nobleman who was, in the words of d'Ablancourt:

> Proud of his Birth, and puff'd up with the Glory of having formerly reduced *Barcelona* and *Naples* under their Obedience to his Catholick Majesty, promised himself nothing less than the entire conquest of Portugal ... he had come on account of his Honour, that he might attempt some great Thing, to retrieve the Reputation he had lost at the Battel of Dunkirk.[53]

Don John was the only natural son of Philip IV of Spain to be acknowledged by the king and trained for military command and political administration. He had advanced the causes of Castile militarily and diplomatically in Naples, Sicily, Catalonia, the Netherlands and Dunkirk. He had 'arrived at Zaffra on 24 May 1661, passed his infantry and cavalry in review at Truxillo and put his artillery and supply arrangements in the best possible state ... In effect, the Spanish army that was to be used against Portugal had never been in better order since the beginning of the war. The well-known bravery of Don John had again excited new ambitions and the ambition of Don John himself was that Portugal could be re-conquered and that he himself would take the title of King, subordinate to the crown of Spain.'[54] He immediately began raiding into Portugal.

All that Schomberg was able to do was to assemble the Portuguese army, numbering around 13,000 men, at Estremos, try to prevent Spanish encroachments and subsequently personally pursue the Spanish back to their bridgeheads as they retired. Once Don John was reported as being in his summer quarters, the Portuguese troops were dispersed among various towns with orders to fortify them. Schomberg saw the Portuguese army into its quarters and was then recalled to Lisbon – he did not know why.

Rather than lapse into idleness Schomberg set about the education of the officer corps in the arts of war; in teaching practical matters like drill, discipline, musketry; and in seeing to necessary improvements to the fortifications in Alentejo. He also reformed the haphazard methods of arranging march, quarters and billeting: the practice had been that every quarter-master, according to seniority, chose a billeting place for his regiment. The next morning, the whole army would have to be re-assembled, given orders and sorted out according to precedence – so that it was seldom before noon that the army began to march.[55] Schomberg made sure that the army would be formed on the march and at rest in battle order; ensured that marches were not made during the worst heat of the day; and insisted on efficient arrangements for the reception of units at the end of their day's march were in hand. All this was 'a mighty Advantage to new levied Troops and to Militia.'[56] Finally he attempted to reorganise the Portuguese cavalry, which was

---

* John of Austria the Younger (1629–1679) remained a significant popular hero even as the fortunes of Imperial Spain declined. In 1677 in a palace coup he took control of the monarchy of his half-brother Charles II of Spain, but he proved not to be the saviour of their fortunes that the Spanish had hoped. He remained in power, but without effective authority over the declining empire, until his death.

the arm which was most markedly inferior to the Spanish. He attempted to group the many independent companies of horse and dragoons into a two or three regiments, or *troços*, on the Spanish model, however he met with so much opposition from the council of war that no progress was made for the next two years.[57]

In April of the following year, 1662, Schomberg had taken the army into the field and attacked a major Spanish convoy of 150 wagons escorted by six squadrons of cavalry and much infantry. He dispersed the escort, plundered the convoy and burned the wagons.[58] However, his authority was superseded by the official Portuguese commander-in-chief. The Marquis of Marialva, who had been sent from Lisbon to replace d'Atouguia, risked a meeting engagement with the Spanish against Schomberg's advice. He marched against Don John with 2,500 horse and 6,400 foot against the Spanish 5,000 horse and 9,000 foot. But by the time contact was made, the Spanish army had been reinforced to nearly 20,000. A council of war was convened where it was agreed to withdraw; the Portuguese army fell back in disorder to Elvas, its equipment in bad order and its morale badly shaken, only saved from pursuit and destruction by 'the nonchalance of the Spanish'.[59]

Marialva and his generals retired to Vila Viçosa; Schomberg's advice was to protect Estremos, where lay many of the stores and supplies of the army and which he regarded as 'the key to Lisbon.'[60] Eventually Schomberg got his way and Estremos was put into a state of defence. Meanwhile, Don John was anxious to attack the Portuguese base at Elvas; however his second-in-command, the Neapolitan general Francisco de Tuttavilla y del Tufo, Duke of de St-Germán,* saw this as too high-risk and instead advised the capture of Juromenha, on which Don John then advanced, 'burning small towns, villages and farms that lay in his path'.[61] The fortress was garrisoned by 2,000 foot and 100 horse, with all that was needed to withstand a long siege. Schomberg thought the place in no immediate danger and, with a field army now 15,000 strong, advised the seizure of Albuquerque from the Spanish. This advice was rejected by the Portuguese who preferred an operation to relieve Juromenha, with the idea that once Don John saw the approach of a relief force, he would lift the siege. Don John was not, however, distracted and after four fruitless days the Portuguese drew back to Vila Viçosa. The Spanish fell on the Portuguese rear-guard and handled it very roughly. The consequence of this mistaken expedition was that the garrison of Juromenha, disheartened, surrendered on 9 June.

The two armies then retired into summer quarters and the Portuguese troops dispersed into various garrisons. But Schomberg, who was in despair at being unable to influence matters, at least to be able to redress the follies of the Portuguese generals, returned to the court and asked leave to resign. This coincided with the palace revolution which brought Alfonso VI and Castelo Melhor to power; d'Atouguia, who at the queen's command and at Schomberg's request had been removed from the governorship of Alentejo, was one of the principal drivers of this revolution and thus became one of the king's chief ministers in the new government. The representations of Schomberg on his ignorance and lack of resolution, as well as the uselessness of Portuguese generals, had made him many

---

*   St Germán (1604–1679), also Duke of San Sasón, was a Neapolitan general in the imperial Spanish service.

enemies who lost no time in speaking against him in the new government.[62] Although he did not know it, he was also being undermined from within by Lieutenant-Colonel Chauvet, a former protégé of Turenne who had been advanced by Schomberg, who 'on all Occasions us'd him with great Respect, whereby the Heart and Spirit of *Chauvet* was visibly puffed up with Ambition, and a good Opinion of himself, which yet he covered with a seeming Modesty, and much civility'.[63] Chauvet threw in his lot secretly with those of the court who opposed Schomberg, in particular, Castelo Melhor, with the aim of supplanting him as commandant of all the foreign forces in Portugal. Schomberg had no inkling of this at first and although his suspicions grew, he had no proof.

Schomberg therefore made up his mind to return to France and his decision was accepted by the king. He sent off his baggage and servants, embarked his horses and was himself on the point of taking ship on 9 October if the wind was favourable. But then several factors changed matters for the good of Portugal. First, the council of Tradesmen in Lisbon – the equivalent of the Guilds of the City of London – sent their president, who had the privilege of waiting on the king, to tell Alfonso that 'he ought not to let the Count of Schomberg depart, that they could be no other but Enemies of the State, who had advis'd his Majesty to grant him his leave, seeing the loss of Portugal would in a short time follow.' The king had replied, somewhat puzzled, 'That a due regard should be had to this Remonstrance.'[64] That same evening, French messages of support were very quickly given shape and form with the arrival by ship of Charles Colbert du Terron, Marquis de Bourbonne,* a Counselor of State. Colbert was also the Superintendant of La Rochelle and he brought a letter for Schomberg from Louis XIV, asking him to be patient and that his services would be recognised and rewarded. More publicly, he had come to negotiate terms for a contingent of 20,000 French troops, but consequent on accepting peace with Spain in contradiction to the obligations in the treaty with England. Schomberg took Colbert to dine with Fanshawe, who reported of Schomberg that he 'was absolutely going, until this person came … and now stays'[65] for Colbert had come at the behest of Schomberg's patron, Turenne.

Fanshawe shrewdly remarked that 20,000 men was too large a force either to be disguised as mercenaries, or for the French to commit directly against Spain, breaching the treaty of the Pyrenees in doing so, unless Louis would as a result be able effectively to annex Portugal. Fanshawe was, not surprisingly, fearful for England's future influence in the face of such a force. Interestingly Schomberg seems to have done all he could to balance loyalty to Turenne and the French court, with a desire to keep Charles II well informed and engaged. Schomberg was thus the servant of three monarchs: Alfonso VI, Charles II and Louis XIV but Fanshawe was greatly relieved that Schomberg was to stay in command, for he preferred the devil he knew, as any new appointment might be a man less amenable to the interests of his master Charles II.[66]

Now that he was in command of the English troops as well as the French, Schomberg took up the cause of the English soldier's want of pay, telling Fanshawe that

> if the [Portuguese] Court does not pay them something the troops will be very feeble a month hence … only the foreign troops can be relied on, and if they are

---

*   Charles Colbert du Terron, Marquis de Bourbonne et de Torcenay (1628–1684).

paid so badly they will not stay. The English are in great need, and the Comte de Castelmelhor must do something for them … So far not a single soldier has given up, which I think is very good.[67]

However, the threat of invasion was of more immediate import to Schomberg and Alentejo was the most vulnerable part of the frontier, the most likely avenue of approach for a Spanish invasion. After his time spent gaining an understanding of the political realties, complexities and intrigues of the court in Lisbon, Schomberg had returned in January 1663 to Alentejo to inspect progress on the improvement of the frontier defences.[68] He established his headquarters at Elvas, close to the border, which had the strongest fortification in the province, dominating the direct route from Badajoz towards Évora and Lisbon. According to Maynard he visited Évora, Campo Maior, Vila Viçosa, Portalegre, Moura, Marvão and Castel de Dive,[69] and found little in any place to encourage him: 'whereof the Garrisons were in very bad condition, since the siege of Badajoz, where the Choice of the Portuguese Infantry were lost'.[70]

Schomberg's position was further strengthened by the arrival, in March 1663, of a new French envoy, Nicolas de Frémont, Sieur d'Ablancourt, a fellow Huguenot, as clandestine envoy of the French government.[71] But at roughly the same time, Schomberg was taken suddenly and mysteriously ill – it was thought that he had been poisoned – and it was not until the end of May that he was able to sit on horseback, 'but two years in Portugal was more than enough to upset the health of any honest man.'[72] Before Schomberg could formulate any real operational plans following his recovery, the Spanish army under the command of Don John crossed the Guardiana and captured the town of Arronches.[73]

5

The Capture of Évora, May 1663

'The English poured in all their shot'

After the inconclusive campaigning of 1662, Spain committed herself to a major effort to end the Portuguese rebellion. During the late winter, an army of 20,000 men was assembled at Badajoz under Don John's command. To generate this number of troops, Don John had stripped the garrisons of Aragon and Old Castile;[1] on 27 April 1663, as soon as campaigning was practicable, he invaded the Portuguese province of Alentejo with close to 14,000 foot and just over 6,000 horse, carrying six weeks of provisions in his baggage train and clearly poised for a determined effort to win the war.[2] His timing was excellent, for Schomberg himself had told Fanshawe that in his view, 'the Portuguese can no more be prepared in point of time for Don John, than they can they can plant timber in the space of a year.'[3] As soon as he had recovered from his illness Schomberg, with a premonition that a Spanish attack was imminent, had urged that the defences and garrisons of Évora and Vila Viçosa should be strengthened; but the Portuguese had neglected to fortify the latter even though 'it could have been done in a fortnight.' He wrote again to Fanshawe that 'These people will not believe that the enemy will dare to advance so far into their country, but they will presently see the truth of what I have often said'.[4] Vila Flor had agreed to a limited reinforcement of men with four guns to Évora 'just to please me'.[5] The town was garrisoned by 5,000 armed men augmented by 3,000 local militia with 600 horses, but without a single officer of rank who had any idea of how to defend it.

Don John of Austria's objective for the campaign of 1663, although it was never set out in writing, must be deduced as having been to conquer Lisbon and re-establish Spanish rule over Portugal. The land campaign was not, however, properly coordinated with maritime power against Lisbon through blockade or with the landing of a force from the sea – although by 1663 it was too late for such operational reach to be effective, as Dutch and English naval forces were on hand to redress the balance. Nor had Don John moved his headquarters rapidly onto Portuguese territory and thus to make maximum use of the short campaigning seasons, along with his enemies' food supplies, so shifting the enormous burden of war from the Spanish population to the enemy.

Don John made a reconnaissance of Campo Maior, razed during his march several forts that the Portuguese had erected on key terrain, took the fort of Ouguela close to Campo Maior and then invested Arronches. The fortress surrendered without a single shot being fired and was taken by Don John as his base of operations. Don John left his infantry to fortify the place, which they did to the extent of not only repairing the breaches made in the walls, but also adding five bastions, four demi-lunes, a forty-foot-wide moat and a covered way on the counter-scarp.[6]

Concurrently with his move against Arronches, Don John sent 4,000 of his horse towards Estremos with the object of drawing out the Portuguese garrison. Having received the news of Don John's advance, the Portuguese generals made a sortie from Elvas and arrived at Estremos on the same day as Don John set down in front of Arronches.[7] Schomberg proposed that the army should be placed between Campo Maior and Arronches, from where he could interdict the Spanish supply convoys and divert Spanish attention away from Arronches. Don John knew the danger of such a move, for he did not move his main supply base from Badajoz to Arronches after its capture and we must ask why not? Probably because he understood better than the Portuguese that the supply route to Arronches could be blocked by Portugal's two main fortifications at Elvas and Campo Maior. However, no-one in the council of war objected to Schomberg's proposal but the governor of the province, the Don Hieronimo de Ataida, Conde d'Atouguia, would not take responsibility for supplying the move or providing regional forces without reference to Lisbon for approval. D'Atouguia 'was a man full of probity, disinterested [i.e. not corrupt] and personally brave, but as ignorant of the military arts as of all the others.'[8] He sent a courier to the queen and in the delay thus caused, the opportunity to destroy Don John was lost: 'This lack of resolution lost the opportunity to occupy an advantageous position … d'Atouguia took the blame for this, the queen herself recalled him before the onset of the campaign. He was forced to look for employment abroad.'[9]

Castelo Melhor, who was now anxious to placate Schomberg, nominated a new governor in Alentejo, the Conde de Vila Flor, who was regarded as 'the most able and successful Officer of Portugal. In his Youth he had served three Years in Flanders … he had defended Elvas against Don Luis de Haro.'[10] However this did little to ease the

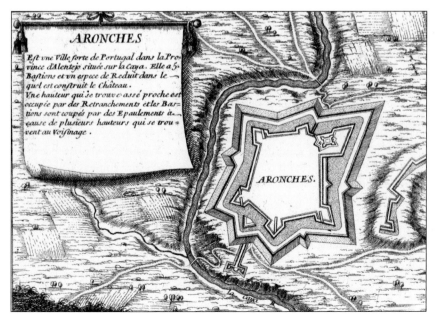

Map 4 The fortifications of Arronches, contemporary map. (Author's collection)

tensions of the divided command between Schomberg and the Portuguese. These tensions could well have forced Schomberg from Portugal had he not, as we have seen, received direct instructions to the contrary from the Kings of France and England. A conciliatory Castelo Melhor hastened to explain that to satisfy national honour, the Portuguese army must be seen to be under the command of a Portuguese general. However, Vila Flor would be told that in all circumstances he must accept the advice of Schomberg – who would in addition have unrestricted command over the foreign contingents.[11]

*   *   *

The character of continental European war in the late sixteenth and seventeenth century, as distinct from the type of warfare based on pitched battles that had been the norm in Britain during the Civil Wars, was dominated by major innovation in the science of fortification. The Italians were the first to experience the new technology of gunpowder weapons and it was in Italy, after about 1530, that the development of fortification began to take account of it, both in mounting and resisting cannon. The defensive works that resulted were built on a thick but low profile of rammed earth and rubble faced with stone and the trace, or ground plan, was designed on mathematical lines, hence the name these works were given: the *trace italienne*. Looked at from above, the ground plan resembled a star which allowed interlocking and mutually supporting fields of fire for guns that were fully casemated and thus protected from counter-battery fire; there was no cover for an attacker and the besieger's artillery could be kept at arm's length until extensive systems of entrenchments were constructed to bring fire within a range sufficient to breach the defences. Towers were remodelled as pentagonal bastions, shaped to eliminate dead ground that could favour the attacker and throughout the latter decades of the sixteenth century, the defence became more and more one of depth. Deep ditches with covered ways were backed by a sloping glacis, low ramparts with bastions, and redans. Further to obstruct the attacker, bastions were supported by outworks: ravelins, hornworks, crownworks and demi-lunes – so called according to their shape – to guard the approaches.

It was the French engineer Vauban,[*] who combined all these developments into a single code of practice, building or remodelling some sixty fortresses during his career.[12] Vauban was Louis XIV's Chief Engineer and as well as developing fortification and siege techniques, he also founded the corps of engineers in the French army. Warfare thus became as much science as art and as it did so, the thinking of men like Vauban became more scientific. In the late seventeenth century, we see an increasing emphasis on observation, reconnaissance, intelligence gathering, analysis and evaluation – on rationality and calculation.[13] Vauban also developed a comprehensive scheme for the defeat of fortresses by siege warfare, for only formal sieges could break such fortifications and they needed heavy artillery, from 32 to 64 pounder, to create a breach, supported by heavy mortars to lob shells inside fortifications to kill defenders, cause fires, blow up ammunition and reduce the will to fight. Meanwhile, the attackers would dig lines of circumvallation, as they were known, for their own defence, and then open a parallel trench line opposite the

---

*   Sébastien le Prestre de Vauban (1633–1707).

area where a breach was to be made. From this first parallel, a zig-zag sap would be dug forwards until a second parallel could be opened More sapping would advance a third parallel until the attackers were within storming distance. Usually the outworks would be taken first, and then the garrison summoned to surrender on relatively easy terms. If they refused, the main defences would be breached and the defenders summoned once more. If a garrison refused terms and the attackers then got into the town with their blood up, there would be no quarter for the enemy's soldiers and little for the civilian population. There had been sieges during the English Civil Wars, but these were mainly of towns like Bristol which were protected by garrisons behind entrenchments, or of castles and fortified manor houses like Old Basing. These were small beer in comparison.

Wherever war seemed likely, defences would be built – from Lombardy to the Low Countries – and the huge increase in fortification stultified warfare. In mobile operations, the ascendancy of the pike ensured an advantage to the defence and this advantage became the norm in siege warfare as well, as even a relatively small fortified town would be strong enough to resist siege, even with heavy artillery, for weeks or months provided it was well stocked with food and munitions. The heavy armoured cavalry, once the unrivalled king of the battlefield, was eclipsed by the infantry, the gunners and the sappers who were needed to form garrisons or invest forts. In 1639, for example, no less than 208 fortified areas required garrisons in the Spanish Netherlands involving over 33,000 men, from Dunkirk with its 1,000 man garrison, to a mere ten men at La Grande Misère near Ghent.[14] As an example of the national investment required, each of Amsterdam's twenty-two bastions cost half a million florins, while Vauban took six years and 5 million livres to fortify Ath. On the other hand, the siege of La Rochelle cost 40 million livres.[15] This was the nub of the concept: although the initial investment was huge, fortification was cheaper than paying a large standing army. A defended, fortified town with a garrison of 1,000 men needed at least ten times that number to reduce it. Thus a well-designed system of fortifications could delay and obstruct an attacker at little cost. They might not be able to win wars, but they could prolong them and increase the attrition on powerful opponents. Thus for a field commander, it became very difficult to reach a decision by battle. Moreover for a government, attrition caused war weariness and increased the willingness to reach a compromise peace. That said, the growth of fortification did not end pitched battles entirely, for aggressive commanders like Gustavus Adolphus and indeed Schomberg would seek battle on favourable terms in order to reach a decision. In so doing they not only offered battle, but accepted the risks it brought along with the costs and benefits.

In Iberia, the fortifications of Badajoz and Salamanca anchored the frontier fortifications with Portugal. But Badajoz, the major Spanish headquarters on the border, was not a strong base of operations: the Guardiana River was not much of an obstacle except in mid-winter; its stone bridge actually made it an attractive target as well as a choke-point. Moreover its fortifications were still incomplete in the 1660s and it would not therefore stand a determined formal siege. Its saving grace was the large circumference needed for any besieging force on both sides of the Guardiana, which would divide any enemy force and greatly increased the need for large numbers of troops and guns.[16] Ironically it was the improvements carried out to defend Badajoz against two British expeditions in the middle seventeenth and early eighteenth centuries, which made it so difficult a nut to crack for the Duke of Wellington and his army in the early years of the nineteenth century.

On the Portuguese side of the frontier, the major fortifications were at Valença, Elvas, Almeida, Estremos and Lisbon. The long delay between the outbreak of war in 1641 and the campaigns of the 1660s had given the Portuguese the chance to transform their medieval frontier castles into modern fortifications on the lines of *trace italienne*. Olivares had warned Philip IV of Spain of this danger as early as June 1641,[17] but by 1661, Spanish commanders like Don John were confronted by state-of-the art fortresses equipped with modern guns. To seize a fortress like Elvas should have required weeks of formal siege-work with all the problems of feeding and supplying a static army that that inferred, in either the heat of summer or the misery of winter. Meanwhile desertion and sickness would take their toll. As it was, even a couple of minor sieges could eat up all the time available in the short campaigning seasons. Elvas, which was opposite Badajoz and about 9.7 kilometres (6 miles) away, was the designated Portuguese headquarters early in the war. From 1643 onwards its fortifications were extensively remodelled on the style of the *trace italienne*, making it capable at least of delaying any invasion long enough for the Portuguese field army to assemble. Don John's capture of Arronches in 1661 however compromised the usefulness of Elvas. Arronches was a salient into Portugal so that Don John could now assemble an army on Portuguese territory, under the cover of the guns of Arronches, on the western side of the Caia River. The Portuguese therefore moved their headquarters to Alentejo to Estremos, where it remained for the rest of the war.[18]

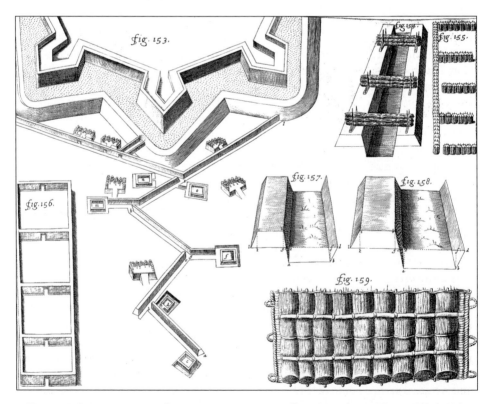

Figure 8 Instructions on the proper preparation of siege-works in Henry Hexham's *Principles of the Art Military*. (© Royal Armouries RAL. 08487)

* * *

A decisive Spanish campaign aimed at Lisbon would need to be launched from a point which meant finding the shortest and easiest approach for marching troops, animals, wagons, and for resupply. Because of the strategic geography and the distribution of fortresses outlined above, there were only two main avenues of approach for this.[19] The first was in the north, from Ciudad Rodrigo to Coimbra along the northern edge of the Sierra da Estrela, then south along the old Roman road to approach Lisbon on the north side of the Tagus. The second was from Badajoz through Alentejo following one of two Roman roads: either crossing the Tagus by the bridge short of Abrantes, or passing through Évora and crossing the Tagus by ferry. By 1662, the southern corridor had become the Spanish preferred route, for the northern corridor was more mountainous and the roads were poor. The south also offered the best going for cavalry, in which the Spanish possessed a clear advantage over their enemies because of the superior agricultural base in Spain and the consequent ability to raise large numbers of livestock. Moreover, reinforcements were readily available from the militias of Andalusia and Toledo, or from contingents sent from abroad and disembarked at Seville.

The southern corridor had an additional significant advantage for both sides: food. Supply, now known as logistics, had already become a significant factor in warfare. In Iberia, along with the environment, time and space it was one of the factors that bore equally on both sides in war and with which every commander had to reconcile his operational objectives. Seventeenth century armies were in effect itinerant cities, moving at a few miles a day, with all the problems of food and fodder supply, cooking, sanitation, health care, fresh water, law and order, and traffic control that cities had then. For besides the soldiers in any field force, there would normally have been a considerable train of supporters and followers, who allowed the moving city to function: grooms, carters and drivers; servants and the staffs of the senior commanders; smiths and farriers; sappers and miners; armourers and cutlers; surgeons and priests; wives, sweethearts, washerwomen and whores. These could easily add up to 50 percent of the number of fighting men, and it is the total figure, not only the total of fighting men, that mattered, for it was this figure that determined the demand placed on the supply system. As well as the people there were horses, mules and oxen – the latter both as mobile food and as draught animals – all of whom drew on supplies of food and water. To give an idea of the scale, the Spanish Army of Extremadura in 1662 was accompanied by 900 ox carts, 500 mules to draw the artillery, 110 four-wheeled wagons each with four mules, 5,500 pack horses and mules and fifty donkeys, as well as a hospital train with fifty carts, one long covered wagon, six other wagons; and then a supply train with 5,696 pack animals and 1,989 ox carts.[20] In addition, the general and his principal subordinates might easily require 100 carts for their retinues – Prince Maurice of Nassau in 1610 required 129 for this purpose.[21]

Given the numbers of people and animals in a field army, the most bulky logistic problem of the period was food and fodder. Most professional soldiers agreed that a satisfactory ration for a soldier consisted of about 2lbs of bread, one pound of meat and a gallon of water per day of which the most important ration item supplied to troops was bread: wheat, barley or rye, in loaves of 1, 1½ or 2lb. The minimum daily ration was usually 1½ lbs per man per day, paid for by stoppages of pay. This had to be

Map 5 The fortifications of Elvas, contemporary map. (Author's collection)

supplemented by meat or other protein, and beer or wine since water was seldom safe to drink unless sterilised by alcohol. Based on 16th, 17th and 18th century figures for requisition, an army of around 20,000 people and 9,000 animals could consume 17,500 lbs of bread, 6,000 lbs of meat, 50,000 bushels of oats, 70,000 lbs of hay and 100 barrels of wine or small beer *per day.*[22]

When advancing through friendly territory, the army could buy or requisition from the local area, or draw on the stocks held in depots and fortresses. In enemy territory, organised plunder was the general rule. Soldiers' songs tell us much about daily life in an army and one in particular, *One and All,* alludes to this subject:

As soon as you come to your enemies' land,
Where fat goose and capon you have at command,
Sing take them or eat them or let them alone.
Sing go out and fetch them or else you'll get none.[23]

However, the larger the army, the less effective this was: small armies were easy to feed and needed little in the way of a regular supply system. The time of year also mattered greatly: was the grain harvest in or not? What was the nature of the grain – wheat, barley, rye? Were there animals in the fields, or had they been slaughtered? Requisition was therefore the main method of securing food for men and horses in either friendly or enemy territory. This was surprisingly an orderly process in which subordinate commanders were allocated particular areas. Random plundering caused not only indiscipline but also problems with the population.

It is the problem of feeding the army that has probably undergone the biggest change in the intervening years between the medieval period and today. With the technology to can, dry, condense and freeze food, the field ration requirements for the combat elements of a modern brigade of around 3,000 men – the same as the brigade in Portugal – can be carried on a single supply vehicle. Seventeenth century armies, by contrast, had to be voracious foragers. One might expect the inhabitants of the country over which campaigns were fought to be stripped bare, but the truth is rather more complex. Even with a system of supply, living off the land was an absolute necessity, for an army of more than 10,000 men could not possibly carry all its food for men and animals, without ceasing to do everything else. Secondly, for an army in the field, a standing crop, other than grass, was not the same thing as food: the army had to spend time gathering raw materials, grinding corn, baking bread, slaughtering animals, salting meat and so on.

Martin Van Crefeld has calculated that given the population density and agricultural practice in Europe at the time, an army of 30,000 people could be comfortably supplied with food by a strip of country measuring sixty-five miles by seven miles and would consume only fifteen percent of the available food as it passed through this corridor.[24] It is however important to understand that this would not be a uniformly distributed slice of fifteen percent, which would make the peasant farmer's life more difficult but still tolerable: in reality, some farms would be stripped bare while others would escape untouched: the effects of war were therefore patchy, tended to cluster around the more accessible areas, and produced extreme hardship in some localities.

Because of the quantities needed, local supplies of animal fodder were the most important resource for a pre-modern army. A horse required a daily ration of about 20 kg

(50lbs) of green forage, or 4 kg (10lbs) of hay, plus (2.5 kg) 6lbs of oats and 1.75kg (4lbs) of wheat or barley in its stead in winter – and three bundles of straw every week. Horses could graze on the march but in camp, foraging was required every third or fourth day. Armies foraged to the front and flanks, leaving the rear intact to support a retreat. Foraging grounds were thus often disputed and escorts were needed; a fight for food. A grand forage could involve most of the army as mowers and gatherers or as covering troops.[25] Sixteenth century figures suggest that 400 acres of fodder each day were be needed to feed 20,000 animals. Therefore the same strip of sixty-five miles by seven miles would provide fodder for the military force as it passed through, provided that the agriculture of the area was functioning properly and had not been heavily despoiled. But it was every army's insatiable appetite for green forage that restricted the campaigning season to the growing season – and in Iberia, this was confined to the months between the cold of winter and the hot drought of high summer – the two short campaigning seasons in the spring and the autumn.

These severe logistic limitations meant that there were distinct differences in the types of operations that could be conducted in Portugal in spring as compared with autumn: spring offensives meant that an army had to keep moving – and raiding – in order to find food; and sieges had to be undertaken close to home and near water. Until the rain brought growth in the pastures, an autumn campaign would be limited to defensive operations. A large army could carry no more than thirty day's bread and twenty day's

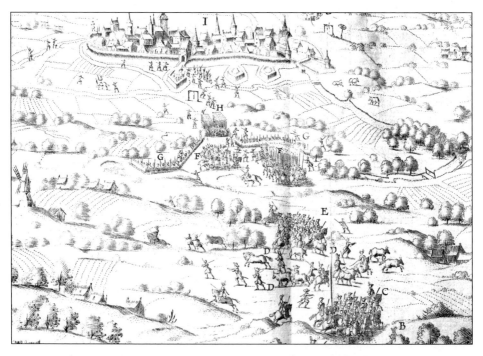

Figure 9 A grand forage, from Ludovico Melzo's *Regole della cavalleri*.
(© Royal Armouries RAL. 08686)

barley for horses, so its maximum range without resupply or requisition was half that distance, given the need to march out and back. These two short campaigning seasons made it very difficult for a field commander to develop any real operational tempo, nor to achieve other than local penetrations into the enemy's territory – let alone develop a strategy and a set of operational objectives to deliver that strategy. This must be seen as one of the reasons why the war had lasted so long – this and the inability of either side to generate decisive force ratios: the Portuguese because of their limited resources, the Spanish because of their strategic overstretch.

For Don John and the Spanish armies, the terrain of the southern approach into Portugal was favourable for cavalry raids against small populations, concentrated into unfortified settlements amongst rich agricultural areas. As well as forage and grain, the armies could requisition vegetables, fruit, wine and huge numbers of sheep, goats, cattle and pigs – but chiefly sheep. This was especially so in Extremadura where the migration of enormous flocks meant that the province was at risk from Portuguese raids for months.[26] On their own side of the border, there was easy access for the Spanish armies to the large supplies of grain available in Extremadura. Lorraine White cites figures for 1641 of 2,119 tons of barley produced in the province in what was accounted a poor year.[27] This could be supplemented within a month by additional supplies from Sicily, Andalusia and La Mancha. Ann Lady Fanshawe certainly had a rosier view of the delights of Spanish food than of Portuguese:

> We do take it for granted in England there is nothing good to eat in Spain, but I will assure you the want is money only ... here is not in the Christian world better wines than their midland wines are especially, besides Sherry and canary. Their water tastes like milk; their corn white to a miracle; and their wheat makes the sweetest and best bread in the world. Bacon beyond belief good; the Segovia veal much larger, whiter, and fatter than ours. Mutton most excellent; capons much better than ours ... They have the best partridges I ever ate, and the best sausages, and salmon, pikes, and sea-breams ... and dolphins, which are excellent meat; besides carps, and many other sorts of fish. The cream called *nata* is much sweeter and thicker than ever I saw in England. Their eggs much exceed ours; and so all sorts of salads and roots and fruits.[28]

In Portugal, Alentejo was also a major producer of grain, especially in the districts centred on Évora; however the Portuguese were always short of horses, not having the large areas of grazing available in Spain.[29] Both Extremadura and Alentejo provided plenty of forage in spring, although a hot summer dried up the pasture before it was possible to make hay. But water disappeared in summer – a major factor for an army with thousands of animals, not to mention the production of flour from water-powered mills, which was also curtailed, making it necessary that stock-piles had to be built up in advance to provide the soldiers' bread ration.[30] Thus when Schomberg had first arrived in Portugal in 1661 he had made a tour of inspection of the frontier fortifications and deduced that the route from Badajoz must be the most likely avenue of approach for a Spanish army bent on capturing Lisbon.

Turning to the supply of small-arms, armour, powder and shot, soldiers would come to a campaign fully armed and equipped by means of contract. Replacement equipment would be provided in the same way or else by plundering defeated enemies: one great advantage of warfare at this period was the huge commonality of weaponry throughout Europe. One pound of powder would provide about eight charges for a gun, or fill up to forty rounds for a musket, harquebus or cavalry pistol; for the small arms, this would be about half a day's expected expenditure in battle. One pound of lead would make about twelve rounds for a musket, up to sixteen for a pistol or arquebus. One day's battle would therefore deplete the stocks of powder and shot by 2lbs of powder and 5lbs of lead per man, without taking into account the needs of the artillery. For a force of 18,000 men – the size of each army in the

Figure 10 A rare contemporary image showing the manufacture of gunpowder, from Allain Mallet's *Les traveaux de Mars, ou l'art de la Guerre*. (© Royal Armouries RAL. 08482)

campaign of Ameixial, for example – this meant 16,000 kg (36,000 lbs) of powder and 41,000 kg (90,000 lbs) of lead per day – all of which would have to be carried on the man, or in the baggage train of the army. In addition, the artillery – where sieges were expected, would require another 320,000 kg (700,000lbs) of powder for a campaign along with forty rounds of shot per day. This amount of supply, if carried with the army, would have required nearly 800 wagons and 32,000 horses, mules or oxen. In addition, the heavy siege guns required for the *trace italienne* might be split between several vehicles. For an average artillery train one can add up to forty more carts and 200 horses for the guns.

Then came the problems of roads and their capacity. The first requirement was to assemble the armies from their winter or summer quarters, for which, being dispersed, several days or even weeks were needed. The Portuguese normally reckoned on five days to assemble at Elvas, the Spanish about the same at Badajoz. By the 1660s, up to fifteen days could be needed to summon cavalry from further dispersed quarters, plus any time required for moving contingents between fronts. The Spanish usually relied on troops from Andalusia and Toledo, and occasionally *tercios* from the Armada. These could require several weeks for orders to reach them, troops to be assembled, equipped and victualled and then marched to the assembly area. If these troops arrived late in the theatre of operations, then the campaign would begin late: the already short campaigning season would be further curtailed and objectives drawn ever less ambitiously.

*   *   *

By this time, the Spanish armies had been greatly reduced in numbers and capability by the effects of war in Europe and throughout the whole of the empire they probably numbered no more than 77,000 men: 19,000 in Flanders, 16,000 in Italy, 4,000 in Catalonia, 18,000 in Extremadura and 22,000 in the rest of the Iberian peninsula. It was this dispersion of resources that prevented the assembly of a force large enough to achieve a decisive victory in Portugal. According to various sources, the 12,000 foot in Don John's Army for the campaign of 1663 were formed into fifteen Spanish *tercios* with 202 companies – an average of around thirteen companies per *tercio* – five Italian *tercios* with fifty-eight companies – those of Lombardia, Milan, Modena and two from Naples – and three German regiments with twenty-six companies. The Spanish *tercios* were, first, one old, regular *tercio viejo* – the *Armada*; secondly, another regular *tercio*, that of Aragon with ten companies; then nine provincial or temporary *tercios*, five of which had only just been formed – those of Toledo, Madrid, Burgos, Valladolid and Cordoba[31] – along with the older *tercio* of Lisboa and three of the Extramaduran militia – those of Castilla, Viejo de Estremadura and Nuevo de Estremadura. These provincial units had been formed since 1635 as they were needed, usually by noblemen or by provinces and city administrations. As well as a varying number of soldiers – just short of 1,000 if the figures are correct, *tercios* would have been commanded by a *Maestro de Campo* with a small regimental staff plus about twenty officers for each of the 286 companies in the army, and as many reformadoes to stiffen the poorer quality of the troops. In addition to the foot, the horse numbered 6,144 horsemen divided into ten *trozos* of cuirassiers, each of 500–600 men: the *trozos* of Rossellon, Ordenes, two *trozos* from Milan, Osuna, Borgoña, Alemanes (or Germans), Wallonia, Extremadura and Valones; and nine independent companies all drawn from the Horse Cuirassiers and Horse Arquebusiers of the Guard of Castile.[32] The army carried twenty guns in its artillery train. Adding their crews, and the various support troops and staff, the army numbered around 20,500 men.

The Spanish advance continued towards Évora, passing within 'half a league' of Estremos, where Schomberg had established his headquarters and such reserves of troops as remained after he had garrisoned the frontier fortresses, according to James Apsley.[33] Apsley's estimate of the available troops is largely borne out by the official records, which give a figure of 5,469 men at Estremos: the English regiments, seven *terzos* of foot, two *terzos* of auxiliaries and two companies of Catalans. The remaining 7,500 men of the Army of Alentejo, in eleven *terzos* of foot and four of auxiliaries, with the French brigade and the English horse, were dispersed either in billets or in the fortresses of Portalegre, Castelo de Vide, Campo Maior, Elvas, Vila Viçosa, Mourao and Moura.[34] This was a meagre force with which to oppose Don John but even so, Schomberg began launching raids to harry the Spanish army on its line of march and interdict its communications. These attacks forced Don John to adopt a tactical march column, the troops ready to fight, which slowed him down.

The progress of the Spanish army was again slowed dramatically by a day and a night of rain that turned the road to mud: the artillery train fell three miles behind the infantry with the supply train a further three miles behind that, obliging the army to halt until these long lines of wagons could catch up.[35] Another opportunity to intercept the invaders was thus lost as the Portuguese and allied army was still dispersed. On 1 May, the Spanish crossed the Tera River; on 3 May they were at Évora-Monte, 'a small Town that stands on a high Hill, two Leagues from Estremoz and four from Ebora, enclos'd with a single Wall wherein is a Castle.' The high hill is almost 550 metres – more than 500 metres (1,500 feet) – high and steep to the point of inaccessibility. It would be very hard to take by assault and no guns could be brought to bear from the plain because of the height and gradient. Don John summoned the garrison, which was commanded by Colonel La Cote, a French officer, to surrender; La Cote however, 'answer'd him so resolutely, that Don John marched away without attacking it.'[36] Given the strength of his position, it is no surprise that La Cote was defiant and one presumes that Don John did not wish to incur either delay in trying to starve the garrison out, or the severe losses that would be incurred among his best troops should he storm the place – for only his best troops would take on an objective like that.

The next day he marched on to Évora and established his headquarters in the convent of the order of St Jerónimo at Espinheiros.[37] This convent had been built between 1412 and 1458 on the site of an apparition of the Blessed Virgin Mary and had been richly endowed by the Portuguese royal house. It had subsequently been used by Philip II of Spain. Comfortably ensconced in the best guest bedroom, therefore, Don John immediately invested the city. Fanshawe reported that 'Now is come to pass which Count Schomberg forespake many months ago, though neither their ministers nor their commanders could believe it till they saw it: namely Don Juan de Austria besieging Évora, leaving near fifteen leagues of many strong towns therein.'[38]

Given all that has been said so far about the time and resource constraints of conducting lengthy siege operations there is no surprise that Don John, an experienced and able commander, seemed intent on the seizure of a relatively weak target – Évora – while avoiding the main fortresses of Elvas, Campo Maior and Estremos. Equally, as

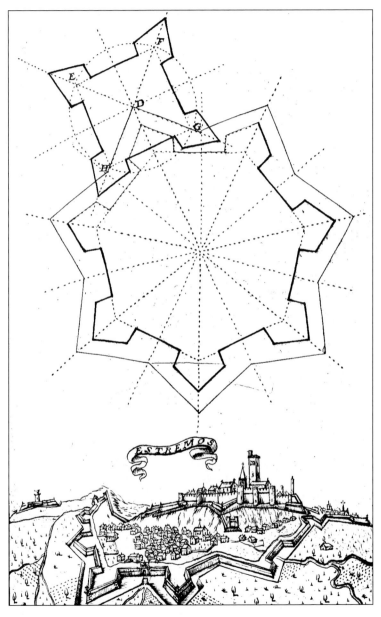

Map 6 Estremos, the base of operations of the Portuguese and allied armies in Alentejo, contemporary map from Allain Mallet's *Les traveaux de Mars, ou l'art de la Guerre*. (Bavarian State Library)

Figure 11 Évora Monte, from Allain Mallet's *Les traveaux de Mars, ou l'art de la Guerre.* (© Royal Armouries RAL. 08480)

Figure 12 A modern photograph of the same site. (A.M. Goulden)

the campaign unfolded he seemed unwilling to force a big battle. We can only deduce, therefore, that he believed that the capture of an iconic Portuguese city would trigger a popular uprising that would bring down the government, prompt the collapse or betrayal of other fortresses and result in a negotiated end to the revolt.[39] Évora, although significant, was not fortified to the same extent as the frontier towns. Its medieval wall ran for approximately 3.5 kilometres (2 miles), was of varying thickness and rose to about 6 metres (20 feet) in height. Some bastions had been added to mount guns but there was little real strength or depth in the fortifications; nor was there an inner castle or citadel to which the garrison could withdraw once the outer walls were breached. D'Ablancourt confirms this, describing Évora as a large city standing on the plain, surrounded by a fair wall in good condition but without any other defences: no moat, some incomplete bastions and the beginnings of a citadel near the convent of St Anthony. It was held by around 3,500 soldiers and about the same number of armed citizens, under the command of the governor, Don Antonio Henriques de Miranda.[40]

D'Ablancourt may never have visited the place, for his reference to the convent of St Anthony makes no sense. The convent sits in the middle of the strongest and most modern of Évora's fortifications, the outlying fort of the same name about 300 metres (325 yards) north of Évora's walls and astride what was probably the key to the city – the huge 16th century Aqueduct da Prata. Almost none of the contemporary accounts mention this feature, which is strange: perhaps it was taken for granted. This aqueduct was however probably the most important hydraulic structure of the country, built between 1533 and 1537 to service the needs of the royal court during the dry summer period. The aqueduct runs for 19 kilometres (12 miles) from the springs of Divor, all but a kilometre or so of which runs on arches. Sever the aqueduct and the city would rapidly succumb to thirst.

On 5 May, Don John placed a siege battery in what d'Ablancourt described as the 'Carmelite Convent, just fifty yards outside the town walls'. This again makes no sense as the Carmelite house was – and is – inside the city walls. We must conclude that the battery was placed in the Carthusian monastery, close to the north wall of the fort of St Anthony, and was used to seize the fort as an enabling step towards breaching the walls of the city itself. Don John was also, concurrently, dealing with spies and potential traitors who might betray the place. The Portuguese high command believed that the town could hold out for at least a month but even so, letters from Vila Flor underlined the need to relieve the town even if this precipitated a battle; Schomberg was quietly asked not to obstruct this course of action. In answer, Schomberg wrote to Castelo Melhor, setting out:

> what twenty-five years' experience of war has taught me, that we have only raw troops and raw officers, that we can hardly put as much infantry together as the enemy, and have only three thousand horse to their six ... and that if they wish to hazard the kingdom on one battle it would only be right to send from Lisbon all the nobility, all the infantry, and all the horse.[41]

But once again, Schomberg complained that there was an ingrained dislike among the Portuguese against accepting advice. On 9 May, Schomberg had a despatch from Don Antonio de Sousa de Macedo in Lisbon, who told him that letters from both Estremos

EVORA en Portugal de la Province d'Alentejo est vne grande Ville dans vne espece de Plaine fermée d'vne assé bonne Muraille, et d'vne fausseBraye revetue qui regne au tour de la Place, il y a quelques Bastions çà et là le Fort de S.ᵗAntoine, du côté du convent de ce nom, avec vn autre Fort au dessous. Il peut y avoir dans cette Place 3.ou 4000 Bourgeois ou Habitans capables de se deffendre sans la Garnison.

Map 7 The fortifications of Évora, contemporary map. (Author's collection)

Figure 13 A modern photograph of the fortifications of Évora. (A.M. Goulden)

and Évora were very cheering, that Don John's army had suffered losses from harassment by the Portuguese cavalry and that their logistic situation, especially in food, was poor. The Portuguese, on the other hand, were well supplied and itching to attack: 'If Don John escapes it will be as much as he can count on.'[42] Only three days later, however, Évora surrendered to Don John, on the assurance that the lives and property of the people would be protected. James Apsley wrote that the size of the garrison of Évora 'did not terrify Don John in his intended enterprise ... Partly through the ignorance of those who should have defended it and partly through their treachery, Don John had persuaded those gentlemen and citizens to surrender it ... when they had not been besieged above five days.'[43] The answer could be much simpler of course: thirst. If Don John had cut off the water supply through the aqueduct, the town would not long hold out – but conspiracy could be offered as an excuse to disguise a failure to rectify this reliance on a single source of water.

Don John made a ceremonial entry through the Portas de Aviz, where he was met by two emissaries of the city governor, the Rector of the University and other Jesuit professors. Don John, it seems, went out of his way to be agreeable – even going so far as to destroy taxation records – and to curbing the tendency of his troops to plunder.[44] Don John garrisoned Évora with 3,700 of his own troops – 700 horse and 3,000 foot; the latter probably from his least experienced Spanish units but as was seen later, stiffened by at least one German unit – the equivalent of thirty-five companies, or the best part of four *tercios*. Moreover he had so little regard for the capabilities of the Portuguese officers that he did not even place them under the normal restrictions of prisoners of war, but let them go where they pleased.[45]

The news of the fall of Évora caused an eruption of popular emotion in Lisbon and consternation throughout Portugal. There was rioting and the sack of houses belonging to government ministers, for there was now no major terrain feature or river obstacle to

Figure 14 Siege-works from a contemporary illustration in Allain Mallet's *Les traveaux de Mars, ou l'art de la Guerre*. (Bavarian State Library)

delay a Spanish advance on Lisbon, only 135 kilometres (85 miles) away. The shock was even greater because Évora had huge symbolic importance. It was a royal city: here, in 1481, John II had publicly executed his rival, the then Duke of Braganza. The city had also been the home of the Jesuit University since 1558; the Jesuits represented a progressive contrast to the Inquisition and in the choice of Évora, the Spanish were making a religious point as well as a statement about sovereignty, for the Inquisition on both sides of the border was a firm supporter of Iberian unification. Ann, Lady Fanshawe, reported on 15 May that:

> there happened in Lisbon an insurrection of the people in the town, about a suspicion, as they pretended, of some persons disaffected to the public; [in] which they plundered the Archbishop's house and the Marquis of Marialva's house, and broke into the treasure. But after about ten thousand of these ordinary people had run for six or seven hours about the town, crying, 'Kill all that is for Castile!' they were appeased by their priests.[46]

Charles Croke commented that 'whether the success of that bold achievement [i.e. the capture of Évora] was by the Spanish valour or Portuguese treachery, I will not now question; but certain I am, that the loss of this City did not only surprise, but likewise startle and discourage the whole army at the news of it'.[47] The king announced himself ready to march to the city at once and large numbers of citizens declared themselves ready to follow. The king was restrained by his council, but immediate orders were sent to Vila Flor to engage Don John – in spite of Schomberg's continuing reservations about the poor quality of the Portuguese army and in particular its want of cavalry.

The Portuguese forces had by now been reinforced by troops from the northern province of Beira and by other second-line units.[48] Schomberg had 17,000 men: 12,000 foot of which 2,000 were in the English regiments and 1,600 in the French brigade. There were 4,000 horse, of which 400 were in the English regiment and about the same in Schomberg's Regiment of French Horse; and between fifteen and twenty artillery pieces had concentrated in and around Estremos. From there, a reconnaissance force of 200 horse under Chauvet was sent forward. Schomberg also sent sixty English and French horse to Montemor-o-Novo to dissuade the Portuguese peasants from supplying food to the Spaniards. For many days there had been no reports of Spanish artillery firing on the city, which was taken as a good sign, and the army was actually marching to relieve Évora when news came of its surrender: Schomberg himself met Don Pedro Pissingo, a Sicilian colonel who had commanded a regiment of foot in the Portuguese service since the revolt of Naples against the Habsburgs and who had been in the garrison of Évora. Schomberg was surprised to see him and asked news of the siege: Pissingo told him shortly, in evident disgust, that the place had surrendered – but not why.

Given the changed situation, the army halted for a council of war. There was an unanimous view in favour of Schomberg's proposal that the army should use the advantage of the mountains and observe the enemy rather than give battle in a head-on clash with a Spanish army in possession of a fortified base. An indirect approach was considered the least risky course of action, particularly as Don John had 6,000 excellent horse, Schomberg only half that number, and a meeting engagement in open country would be very disadvantageous. Both armies were approximately equal in terms of infantry.

Schomberg realised that without overwhelming numbers and without enough ammunition, food and money for a long campaign, Don John would not be able to maintain Évora and then extend his line of communication without capturing either Rodondo or Terena, thus avoiding interception around Estremos or a long detour to Arronches, and then bringing up considerable resupply; he urged Vila Flor to fortify both places, 'but they do not listen to what one says to them. They would not put their troops in order during the winter before the enemy came'.[49] However, such a course was against the direct orders from Lisbon, a letter should be sent to the court, signed by all the general officers. Putting this together took until 10 o'clock that night. As this was being done, Schomberg was told privately by Simon de Sousa, commander of the Portuguese *Terzo* of the Armada (the nearest equivalent to a regiment of guards in the Portuguese army), about the disorders in Lisbon and the threat of a pro-Spanish coup. Schomberg called d'Ablancourt, who immediately left to assess the situation.

In order to understand how the campaign unfolded from here on, one must study the map of this part of Portugal. Once one does, Schomberg's view of the matter becomes clear. Estremos lies *between* Évora and Badajoz, thus severing Don John's direct line of communication and increasing the pressure of lack of resources on the Spanish. Schomberg was also able to persuade Vila Flor's endless councils of war to march the army to Alandraol, severing Don John's secondary line of communication back to Jerumanha.[50] Don John's problem now was simple but compelling: the Spanish army had marched from Badajoz to Évora, besieged it for nine days, by which time the cavalry had eaten up 'all of the sown fields for up to three leagues (14.5 kilometres or 9 miles) around.'[51] Having by-passed both Estremos, he had given Schomberg the opportunity to sever his eastward line of communication back to Badajoz. Don John had taken a big risk and ignored the need to establish secure lines of communication, guarded by well-garrisoned fortresses so as to avoid either envelopment or starvation – or both. By late May, the rising temperatures had begun to burn off the pasture so that without supply, he had to disperse. Don John was forced to send his horse four leagues (19 kilometres or 12 miles) away for subsistence in unfortified farms, villages and towns. Nor could supplies be taken from the Portuguese, as the harvest was still some weeks away. Don John continued to improve the fortifications of Évora with his infantry, but by 20 May, his supplies of fodder and food were so reduced that he was forced to send out a large force of 2,000 horse and some mounted infantry on mules deep into Portugal, to Alcaçovas and then on to Alcacer de Sal, to bring up as much corn and meal as they could gather and burn both towns – which they did but without gathering enough in the way of provisions to satisfy the needs of their army.

When the move of this foraging expedition was reported by his scouts, Schomberg proposed that the army should march as rapidly as possible to interpose itself between the two bodies of Don John's troops – and thus be in a position to deal with each part in turn, on favourable terms. The lengthy deliberations in council that this required, along with the slow pace of the supply train, meant that the Portuguese arrived three hours too late to achieve Schomberg's design.[52] James Apsley reported: 'Upon the first advice of the marching of this party we removed from Landraol with all speed and diligence to use our endeavour to have cut off those troops, but they having understood what we were endeavouring they took a great compass about to shun us, insomuch as it was impossible for us to hinder their joining'. This is hardly surprising, since Alandraol is more 40

Edward Hyde, Earl of Clarendon, engraved by Michael Loggan after Sir Peter Lely's portrait. (Author's collection)

Frederick Hermann, 1st Duke of Schomberg, engraved by Simon Gribelin after Michael Dahl's portrait It was Schomberg's abilities that brought vistory in the field in the Portuguese Restoration War. He commanded the English brigade from 1663 to 1667. (Author's collection)

Sir Robert Southwell engraved by John Smith after the portrait by Sir Godfrey Kneller. It was Southwell's mediation that brought the war between Spain and Portugal to a conclusion – although the credit was given to the Earl of Sandwich – and who secured the arrears of pay for the English brigade after a long struggle. (Author's collection)

Murrough O'Brien, 1st Earl of Inchiquin, by an unknown artist. O'Brien commanded the English brigade for the early period of its deployment to Portugal. (Author's collection)

Antonio Luis de Meneses,
1st Marquis of Marialva,
by an unknown artist.

Francisco de Tuttavilla y del Tufo, Duke of San
Germán, Don John of Austria's deputy
during the campaign of 1663.

A contemporary sketch of Don
Francisco de Mello.
(Author's collection)

Luiz Vasconcellos e Souza,
Conde de Castelo Melhor.

Charles II, King of England. (Soham Roots)

L'entrée du prince de Ligne à Londres, 1660 by François Duchatel. This painting shows the arrival of Jean-Charles de Watteville in early September 1660 and the environs of the Tower before the Great Fire; it was also here that on 30 September, French and Spanish soldiers fought a major street battle.

Luis de Benavides Carrillo de Toledo 3rd Marques de Caracena, by Philipp Fruytiers.

Marie-Françoise de Savoie-Nemours, Queen of Portugal by an unknown artist.

Alfonso VI, King of Portugal by an unknown artist. The King is wearing full armour in recognition that his country was at war, even though he himself never took the field.

Queen Catherine of Braganza, wife of Charles II of England, by Jacob Huysmans. (Trustees of The Queen's Royal Surrey Regiment)

Sir Richard Fanshawe, 1st Baronet, (1608–1666), by an unknown artist. Fanshawe was the English Ambassador to the court of Portugal and Spain until supplanted by Sir Robert Southwell. (Government Art Collection, 1175)

Philip IV of Spain in Hunting Attire, by Diego Velázquez.

Don John of Austria the Younger by an unknown artist.

A contemporary illustration on tiles of the battle of Montes Claros. (Author's collection)

The Parade of the Army at Tangier by Dirk Stoop (1680). This near-contemporary illustration shows the dress, equipment, Colours and organisation of a mid-seventeenth century English army as well as giving an accurate view of the situation of Tangier. (Lord Dartmouth collection, BHC 1942)

A Prospect of the Magazine and Platforme of Portsmouth ... This illustration, which shows the entrance to the harbour as it would have been seen by the returning officers and men from Portugal in 1668, comes from a survey of the fortifications of Portsmouth and the Channel Islands undertaken at the orders of George Legge, Lieuenant-General of the Ordnance, in 1680. This same George Legge was, in 1668, Governor of Portsmouth. (National Maritime Museum L4386)

kilometres (25 miles) from Évora, giving the Spaniards at the very least a full day's start, and probably two days.

The march of the Portuguese army had brought it close to Évora from the north-east, from Redondo, and this approach had been observed by the Spanish. When Schomberg rode forward to observe the Spanish dispositions, he could see that they were being drawn up in battle formation on the western side of the River Degebe, about three miles east of Évora: the two armies were thus arrayed astride and with their backs to each other's direct line of communications. The river, according to d'Ablancourt (who was not present, as he had returned to Lisbon), was passable everywhere except close to two

Figure 15 A modern photograph of the incised course of the River Degebe at the point where the Portuguese army crossed. (A.M. Goulden)

mills and was 'dry'd up early, there being no Water to be seen, but in the deep ditches.'[53] The two mills appear to have been the Molino de Caiado and the Molino Encarnado. According to Schomberg, the Portuguese were camped in the Val des Palms, or Vale de Palma,[54] (the valley of palm trees) between 5 and 8 kilometres (3 and 5 miles) east of the city. This was an unconscious – or possibly conscious, irony, for another Valle or Vale de Palma lay 12 kilometres (7 miles) north-west of Évora: it was the home of the painter and poet Jeronimo Corte-Real (1533–1588) who had written a poem in praise of the victory over the Turks at Lepanto by Don John the Elder.

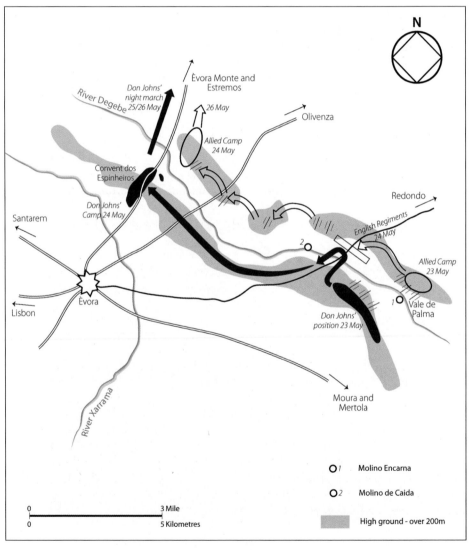

Map 8 The situation around Évora, 23–26 May 1663.

Don John really had no option but to dump as much of his heavy baggage and the heaviest guns (i.e. those most useful for siege rather than field operations) as he could so as to move fast, leave 3,000 foot and 500 horse to garrison the captured fortress, and try for the shortest route to supplies and security: due east, back towards Spain, to Jerumanha where there was a good crossing point over the Guardiana River. But to reach safety, he had first to defeat the Portuguese army which lay in his direct path. The Degebe is not a large obstacle in itself – no more than ten metres wide – but it is deeply incised, thickly lined with trees and thorn bushes, and muddy: passable therefore by infantry and cavalry but not by wheeled vehicles and guns without a bridge or ford.

Don John's cannon bombarded the Portuguese camp all that night; 1,500 Portuguese deserted. Vila Flor spent most of the night in another interminable council of war; Schomberg however spent the night moving the army to a position closer to the river, where it was less exposed to the enemy's artillery and better able to block any attempt at a crossing the next morning. The next day, 24 May, Don John did indeed attempt to force a passage of the river at the ford on the Redondo road, in order to clear his escape route: 'In the morning early Don John had ordered his army in *batalia* over against the river, as if they had intended to have fallen upon us, for he sent some commanded foot with five or six battalions to second them'.[55] D'Ablancourt said this force was three battalions and three cavalry squadrons. The attempt was repulsed by the two English regiments, who composed part of the Portuguese advanced guard force, led by a screen of 200 picked musketeers:

> who suffered the enemy to come within musket shot, lightly skirmishing with them, but reserving the most part of their fire for a better opportunity. At last the enemy adventuring to approach nigher, the English poured in all their shot upon them at once, and with a small party of horse passed the river and routed those commanded foot, together with the battalions which were second to them, and caused them to retreat in disorder. In the meantime our cannon were placed very dexterously and advantageously to endamage the enemy, for they killed very many officers of quality and missed but little the person of Don John.[56]

This fight lasted no more than an hour, but Schomberg generously acknowledged the valour of the English on this occasion, asserting – probably in the aftermath of the night's desertions – that in the whole army only the foreign troops were reliable.[57]

Don John made another attempt to cross with his main army but the effects of the superior artillery fire of the Portuguese under the command of a French officer, Colonel Desfontaines, and the appearance of the main Portuguese force to second the English regiments made Don John change his plan. Having failed with the direct approach, he tried the indirect. He decided to cut the army's rations by half and strike north-east for Arronches on the east bank of the Caia river, for word had reached him that waiting for him at Arronches were 4,000 fresh troops and a large supply train.[58] For the rest of that day, Don John 'made his army march by the left, coasting always the Eugebe [Degebe], on level ground which began to rise as it approached Évora where there was cover available from trees and vineyards.[59] The Spanish passed in front of Évora, the Portuguese shadowing them on the other side of the Degebe, 'removing our cannon from one hill to another with great effect, till at last they insensibly parted from us, so that we lost the sight of their march for above three or four hours.'[60] This makes sense, as the ground rises towards the north and the Spanish army probably crossed the crest. According to Schomberg's account, the artillery 'disturbed the enemy at a bridge where they quitted the high road [N.B., probably where the road towards Estremos crosses the Degebe, about 3 kilometres (2 miles) north-east of Évora]. In the evening we saw them passing the stream, protected by the vines and wood near the convent *dos Pinheros*, where they camped that night, while we made our camp'.[61]

According to D'Ablancourt, the Spanish crossed the river on the main road towards Estremos. As Schomberg said in the reported passage above, they made camp around the Convent dos Espinheiros, no more than two miles from Évora, where Don John had earlier established his headquarters. The Portuguese and their allies camped about two miles to the east of them on a ridge overlooking the road, 'The enemy finding it a long way to come to us, especially on our right hand, our left being defended by the river.'[62] In other words, they were orientated towards the north, parallel with the road and on the south side of it, rather than blocking it. This is odd given that Schomberg had blocked Don John's earlier attempt to force the Redondo road and one can only conclude that whatever he said publicly, he did not wish to bring on an engagement here. This may be because the terrain was highly favourable to cavalry – which indeed it was – and the Spanish were much superior in this arm. Alternatively Schomberg may have felt that the enemy would be weakened by a few more days on low rations and hard marching and therefore easier to beat later than now.

Don John planned only three days to cover the remaining 70 kilometres (45 miles) from Évora to Arronches. His first day's march was to cover 35 kilometres (20 miles) and a crossing of the Tera River, a long march but on a good road with an easy gradient. He therefore took only eight light guns with enough ammunition for a single day's fighting;[63] but he also had 3,600 prisoners from Évora to consider, who would not have made speedy marching easy for their captors. Schomberg gave out publicly that the next morning Don John would take his opportunity to give battle on the open plain, taking advantage of the fact that he had 6,000 horse against the Portuguese 3,500, as well as being able to bring up the troops and guns in Évora. That would have held good had he blocked the road, but by adopting the position he had, as discussed earlier, Don John had been offered an escape route. That night, therefore, the Portuguese and their allies prepared what entrenchments they could. However instead of attacking them, Don John spent the whole of the next day, 25 May, in bringing up his baggage train from under the walls of Évora, putting the garrison he had left in the fortress in a state of defence, and marshalling the convoy of Portuguese prisoners. These were to prove fatal errors in terms of loss of time and speed: according to Don Luis de Meneses, because of this, the Portuguese were able to move faster 'because the great number of wheeled vehicles that it [Don John's army] was convoying obliged the entire army to march slowly, and our forces had no hindrance at all'.[64]

That night the baggage train was sent off 'by the same way which he came to Évora, and by this his diligences he came to encamp on this side of the river Bera.'[65] This is the current N18 towards Estremos and from there, he intended to strike northwards to Sousel and then Arronches. It is surprising that the Portuguese and their allies did not hear the thunder of the Spanish army passing – but perhaps as already discussed, Schomberg was willing to let them go. Early next morning, Schomberg's scouts reported the move and Schomberg issued orders on the assumption that Don John was heading for Estremos – the only plausible explanation. He too decided to march on the main road, the present N18, through Évora-Monte, and catch up with Don John near Estremos. He therefore 'sent his own baggage train back to Estremos and by a forced march, which killed many Portuguese soldiers through heat and thirst',[66] came up with Don John on the River Tera – for Don John had not made the distance he had planned. On the night of 26 May in the old Julian calendar, the two armies made contact, camping two miles apart on either side of the river.[67] The next day, 27 May, both armies resumed their march and skirted around Estremos on the southern side before turning north. Both armies halted that night after a march of about 15 kilometres (8 miles) near the village of Ameixial.

The battle that followed was known variously by the names of the settlements of Ameixial, Estremos, and del Canal by the four nations engaged. Schomberg seems to have believed that the broken country around Estremos, where he caught up with Don John, was the last piece of favourable terrain for battle before the Spanish irrupted into more open country, where their superiority in cavalry would give them a significant advantage. If the Spanish made it through to Arronches they would be reinforced and resupplied, presenting the Portuguese with two problems: fighting a large army in the field and recapturing Évora. But if the Portuguese fought and lost, there would be nothing to prevent Don John from marching directly on Lisbon. It was make or break: the Portuguese had to win.

6

Ameixial, May 1663

'There come the English Redcoats'

The initial phase of the Battle of Ameixial took place on the following day, 28 May 1663. Don John appears to have reached the conclusion that he could not outrun the pursuit any longer and must therefore stand and fight. He therefore placed his guns on three small hills forming a strong advanced position on the Sierra Ruivina, north-west of Estremos, with a screening force of musketeers commanding the main road – probably to buy time for the Spanish army to establish its main defensive line. This position was to be about 1 kilometre (half a mile) further back, on the ridge formed by the two hills of the Monte Granja and the Monte Mourada, and the saddle between them.[1]

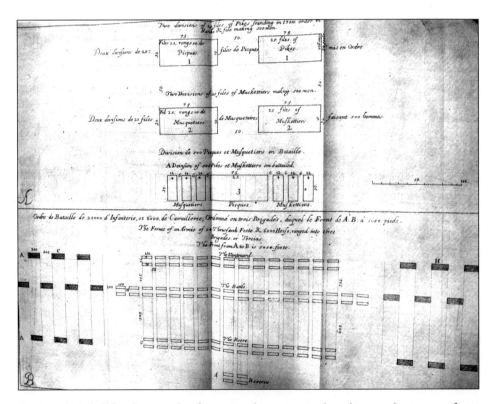

Figure 16 A drill-book example of an army drawn up in three lines and a reserve, from Henry Hexham's *Principles of the Art Military*. (© Royal Armouries RAL. 08487)

The English horse under Dongan, supported by two Portuguese *terzos* of infantry, was ordered to attack the Spanish infantry on this advanced position to clear them away. Cavalry charges in the mid-seventeenth century were not the wild affairs they had been in earlier days – nor the shock events that they would once again become under Napoleon Bonaparte. They were more controlled advances, since a charge could not break the tight blocks of the *tercios*, bristling with pikes as they were. Instead the method used was the caracole, in which several ranks of horsemen trotted close to the enemy, fired their pistols or carbines, and then retired to reload while the next ranks moved forward. Only when fire had broken up the tight formation of the foot would the horse close with the sword; the exception to the rule was the controlled shock attack with the sword practised by the horse of the New Model Army – to which many of Dongan's men had either belonged or had faced. Dongan's men succeeded in driving the Spanish foot from their position below Ruivina and then pursued them across the low ground between Ruivina and the main ridge, where they became entangled in an unequal battle against far larger numbers of Spanish horsemen who had hastened up to reinforce the musketeers.[2] Had this attack been properly supported, it might have been able to push on and roll up the main Spanish position that day; however Vila Flor insisted on breaking contact and Don John was able to move his guns from the advanced position to the main ridge – no mean feat given the rough ground, for they would have had to have been manhandled or broken down and carried by pack animals rather than being towed. The Portuguese therefore contented themselves by occupying the ground that the horse had won and moving up their guns to the positions vacated by the Spanish.

Meanwhile, Don John had organised his main army. The baggage and prisoners were to continue their march through Sousel, to Arronches, which was still 35 kilometres (20 miles) away. The baggage train was composed of about four thousand *Mancha* wagons, each about 3 metres (33 feet) long, drawn by mules or oxen. This huge procession moved at a stately pace in a column of march stretching for more than 3 kilometres (1.5 miles). Its movement was to be covered by the main army, which took position to the east of what is now the village of Santa Vitoria do Ameixial – Our Lady of the Victory of Ameixial – but at that time was just Our Lady of Ameixial. Here, the long ridge of higher ground ran from the south-east to the north-west, cut towards its western extremity by a saddle sometimes referred to as Perdicus: that is, partridge, since the birds are common in this part of the world. This feature divided the position into the two *sierras* of Granja and Mourada. Below the ridge, to the south-west, lay the plain of Estremos and northwards the ground continued very broken until it again fell away after about 2 kilometres. Don John's escape route, the narrow road towards Sousel and Arronches – the present route N245 – ran between the two hills: the modern road by-passes Granja to the west but Don John's deployment would make no sense at all if the road had taken this course in 1663. Some sources suggest that as it ran northwards, the old road was almost in a canyon for a short distance but there is no sign of this being so; however it is dominated by higher broken ground for 2 kilometres which would mean that wheeled vehicles were confined to it and these would have formed a considerable blockage to men and horses. Contemporary accounts also suggest that the plain was heavily farmed but the high ground was at least partly wooded on the lower slopes, probably with olive groves, as still grow there, although now the whole area is thickly covered with vines and olives.

Figure 17 Contemporary illustrations of heavy cavalry and arquebusiers from Henry Hexham's *Principles of the Art Military*. (© Royal Armouries RAL. 08487)

The Spanish were drawn up with half their foot, in two lines, on each of the two hills. The most reliable and experienced regular *tercios* were on Don John's right – i.e. on the westernmost of the two hills – the Sierra Granja. These were probably the five regular Spanish *tercios* and the five Italian *tercios*. This was because the position could be most easily turned by an outflanking movement from this direction, which would sever the route along the main road northwards. On the easternmost hill, the Sierra Mourada, which was the larger and more severe of the two and therefore offered the best protection to the least able troops, were what remained of the Spanish territorial *tercios* after the garrison of Évora had been extracted, with the two remaining German regiments which were named by Schomberg as those of Chemy and Kaisterstein.[3] Four guns were also deployed on each hill. The Spanish horse – the strongest and most manoeuvrable element of the army – was placed in two divisions below the hills, the right division covering the exposed flank and the left division covering the road and the gap between the hills, for if a penetration was made here then the Spanish line would be severed, the two bodies of foot would be surrounded and defeated in detail. It was a formidable position: James Apsley thought that 'by his order of *batalia* their baggage lay under a good covert.'[4] Don John is said to have told the King of Spain that his troops were as safe on these hills as if they had been in the citadel of Milan.

The allies were drawn up with the bulk of the Portuguese *terzos* on the right and the English and French foot on the extreme left, again in two lines, with their guns placed between the squares so as to be able to deliver direct fire. The first line was commanded by Alfonso Turtoda de Mendoza and the second line by the Conde de la Torre; the artillery was under the nominal command of Don Luis de Meneses. The horse was likewise in two lines: the first line, a mere advanced guard of about 800, consisting of the English and French regiments. Behind them were the 2,000 Portuguese horse, commanded by Dionysius (or Denis) de Mello, reinforced by bodies of musketeers drawn from the *terzos*.[5] Thus the most reliable troops – the foreigners – faced the most dangerous of the Spanish units. All this can be seen in the contemporary picture of the battle entitled *Emtrada do Exercito del Rey de Castella, Governado por D. Joam de Austria*. This picture is more about propaganda than strict interpretation and as with many such images of the period it captures not one snapshot in time of the battle, but the whole sequence of the action through its various phases within the same canvas – and so must be carefully interpreted.

The infantry of both armies was formed in the conventional formation of the day, sometimes known as the Dutch method: regiments in six ranks, with their pikemen in the centre to give protection against cavalry and to form the offensive arm in the advance to the 'push of pike'; musketeers on the flanks, able – at least in theory – to maintain a continuous fire as each rank discharged its weapons and was relieved in place by the next rank passing through and thus break up an enemy formation so that the pikes could push in. This alternating arrangement of blocks of pike and musket gave the battlefield of the seventeenth century a characteristic chequerboard appearance, which can be seen in the picture. The English had adopted a variation of the Swedish methods during the Civil Wars: at very close ranges (about fifty yards), the six ranks of muskets could be rapidly formed into three, thus increasing the weight of volley fire for the decisive moment. Once a heavy weight of fire had been delivered – and the weight of shot from a matchlock musket was around 2 ozs, as against 0.9 ozs from an arquebus[6] – the foot

Figure 18 A modern photograph of the Spanish position on the Monte Mourada, taken from the south. (A.M. Goulden)

Figure 19 A modern photograph of the Portuguese position on the Monte Ruivino, taken from the south-west. (A.M. Goulden)

would then attack rapidly and violently with the pike, sword and clubbed muskets: the forerunner of the volley and bayonet charge which later characterised British infantry tactics on the battlefields of the 18th and 19th centuries. This tactic of fire followed by charge was also widely used in the Spanish armies of the day: the Duke of Alba had recommended opening fire at a range of a little more than two pikes' length (about 10 metres or 36 feet), especially if the opposition force was wearing armour.[7]

Much of the following day, 29 May, passed in an inconclusive artillery duel. However late in the afternoon it was noticed that the Spanish fire seemed to slacken – they had after all only eight pieces of artillery and limited ammunition. Schomberg also received word from his scouts that the Spanish baggage train was preparing to move off

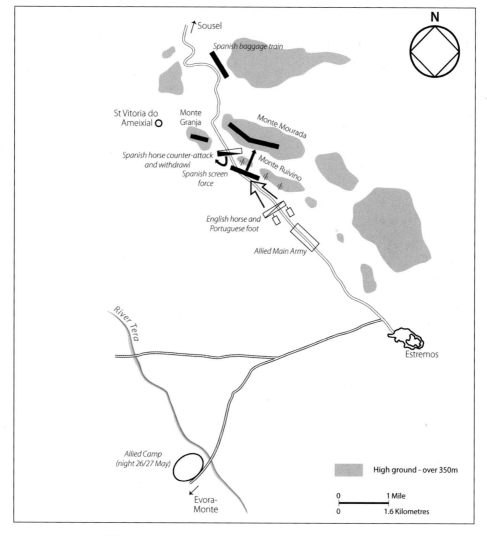

Map 9 Ameixial: the opening moves, 28 May 1663.

northwards, escorted by two squadrons of horse. The Portuguese generals again took council, irresolute but conscious of the orders of the king to give battle and anxious not to allow Don John to slip away – however the Spanish position was a strong one and they held a considerable advantage in cavalry. Schomberg decided to take a risk and 'he resolv'd, to tell the General Officers who were with him, how he would have things order'd for the Battel, representing to 'em, that to wait any longer for the Resolution of the Count of Vallaflor, would be to let slip this Occasion.'[8] His sense of urgency carried the day. He at once ordered De Mello to move the horse to the left flank, using the cover of the ground to conceal the move, and then, reinforced as he was by infantry to reduce the disparity of numbers, engage the Spanish horse there while the infantry assaulted the high ground. This move could have been made with a degree of concealment, for the lower slopes of Monte Granja, to the west of the position are, although not steep, convex. De Mello, however, made no haste and took little care, so that the move was observed by the Spaniards. They in turn redeployed their horse on the same flank. One hour before dusk, Schomberg ordered the English and French horse forward in the centre.

Colonel Michael Dongan, at the head of the English horse and three troops of French cavalry, attacked the flower of the Spanish horse – the guard of Don John. Without discharging their pistols, Dongan led the allied horse straight at the enemy, in the face of heavy fire and smashed the Spanish first line, the remnants of which recoiled on their own second line. During the mêlée, the French horse under Colonel de Saussay captured the great prize of Don John's royal standard; Don John's guard was all but wiped out.[9] Without hesitation, Dongan fell on the second line but the expected support of that part of the Portuguese horse which had been allocated to the centre failed to materialise. With his three French troops, Dongan and the English horse took cover behind a series of low walls and rocky outcrops to rally.[10]

While the English re-formed, the Spanish horse also rallied. On their right, the allied left, their general noticed how Schomberg had placed bodies of musketeers between his un-engaged Portuguese cavalry squadrons, in order to spread the line out to the same length as the longer Spanish one. He immediately attacked these bodies of foot, which were not protected as was usual by pikemen to keep cavalry at a distance, dispersed them and put the Portuguese horse to flight.[11] It was again time for the English horse to re-enter the fight. Taking no account of the disparity of numbers, Dongan led his troops for a third time, passing behind the rear of the allied infantry on their left, to attack the right division of the Spanish cavalry, and engaged them so fiercely that they were not able to break off the action and take part in the decisive phase of the battle between the infantry of both armies, which was developing along the main position. Had he not done so, this body of Spanish horse would have been able to turn in and take the advancing allied infantry in the flank. Apsley, however, thought that 'the English horse were too forward in charging … and at their last repulse they were able to charge no more.'[12] Dongan was killed here at the head of his regiment along with Captain Paulinge and Cornet John Wharton, while none of the surviving officers was unwounded; seventy-five troopers were dead and another 100 wounded, many of whom were not expected to live.

Meanwhile, the allied foot advanced against the two hills. The two English regiments were on the left wing of the army, in two echelons, opposite the toughest of the Spanish units – one of which, probably the *Armada* – was held to be invincible. On their immediate right advanced two Portuguese *terzos,* led by the *Maestro de Campo* Juan Furtado de Mendoza and Francisco da Silva. As they moved forward, the Spanish artillery gave them its full attention but without much effect: only three or four men were lost. When Schomberg rode to the left flank, he was delighted to see the spirit with which the English troops advanced and how ineffective the Spanish artillery was. He therefore ordered his own regiment, led by Francis Moore, to press on as far as some peasant hovels ('masures') which gave cover from musketry. This order was obeyed with great precision and without loss in spite of heavy Spanish fire.[13] As we have already noted, the early part of the approach was a steady, not steep, but convex slope that gave a good degree of cover from fire and from view; the peasants' farm buildings, which are still there although in ruins, lie at the point no more than 250 metres (220 yards) from the Spanish main position, where the slope changes, becomes much steeper and is broken by many rocky outcrops. Once in position around the buildings, there was insufficient cover for the

Figure 20 Cavalry formed for an attack. A rare contemporary illustration from Flaminio della Croce's *L'essercito della cavalleria*. (© Royal Armouries RAL. 08686)

whole regiment, so that three companies had to be dropped back to join the second regiment under Henry Pearson.

The soldiers were impatient, so close now to the enemy but not able to close with him. Moore told them on pain of death not to fire a single shot until they came clear of the smoke from the discharge of the enemy artillery. They moved forward, the six ranks of muskets closing to three, and fired a volley so densely and so accurately as to stun the Spanish and cause shock, wounds, flight and death. Another volley threw the Spanish second line into confusion. The English gave a loud hurrah and charged with their muskets clubbed – putting the Spanish to flight, for this combination of lethal firepower at close range followed by shock action was completely outside their experience – surprisingly, given what the Duke of Alba had been recommending to the army. Pressing their pursuit, Moore's men captured the four guns and Don John's personal baggage.[14] Dumouriez claims that at this point the English fell to plundering and that Schomberg himself redirected them – however there is no other mention of this and allowance must be given as Dumouriez was writing a biography whose aim was to enhance the reputation of Schomberg, rather than an objective history.

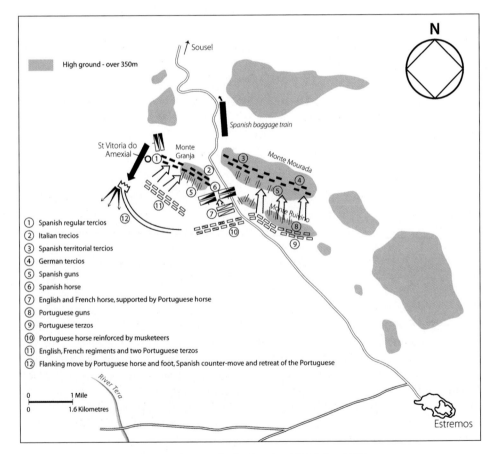

Map 10 Ameixial: the battle of 29 May 1663.

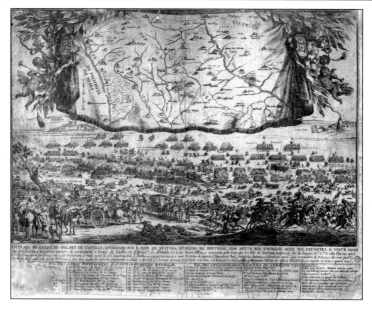

Figure 21 A contemporary illustration of the Battle of
Ameixial. (Author's collection)

While the assault was being made, Vila Flor had established himself on a vantage point on the Monte Ruivina. As the English foot had advanced without firing from long range, as was the Portuguese custom, he believed they meant to turn their coats and surrender to the Spanish – just as Molesworth had claimed. In despair at this supposed treason, 'he vomited a thousand abuses, calling on Heaven to witness that he had played no part in placing these troops in such a position in the order of battle so as to ease their treason.'[15] A party to this outburst was the chaplain of one of the English regiments, Mr Cargill. While he perfectly understood the tenor of the abuse being made towards his countrymen, he did not have enough Portuguese to enable him to respond to Vila Flor. However he found a man in the general's suite to whom he could explain matters in Latin. He said that the English were incapable of such behaviour. While this discussion was in progress, the two English volleys were heard. As the men had closed up into three ranks rather than six, these volleys sounded very loud for a comparatively small body of men. Refusing to accept his error, Vila Flor pronounced that these were certainly salutes fired by the Spanish to receive their English allies. Hearing this, Cargill lost patience and made off at a gallop to rejoin his regiment. On the way he encountered Schomberg himself, who sent him back with news of Spanish redeployments. On his arrival, Vila Flor in his surprise, cried out 'In truth, these heretics give battle better than our saints!'[16]

Back on the hilltop of Granja, Moore's Regiment turned to support of the second English regiment under Henry Pearson, which was in a perilous position. This regiment, having become separated from Moore's, had attacked a large body of Spanish infantry posted behind walls at the eastern edge of the hill. The final approach was steep and stony, but short: the ascent was made and the Spanish put to flight at the first volley. However as the English began to pursue, Spanish cavalry advanced against them – given that there were bodies of Spanish horse on both flanks of the Monte Granja, the enemy could have appeared from either direction very rapidly. Pearson halted his regiment, and formed 'triangle'[17] – what would later become known as the square. In this formation the English repulsed the cavalry attack by four squadrons of cuirassiers; but so repeated and so furious were the Spanish assaults that the English would have been overwhelmed but for the arrival of Moore's Regiment:

> Notwithstanding the rich baggages and coaches and wealthy plunder which were on top of the hill – the English seeing the field not cleared – there was not one man of them stirred out of his rank, but kept close serried together to prevent any second onset, which immediately followed, for they were assailed front, flank and rear by divers of the enemy's troops of horse, but having their fire ready at all hands they quickly quitted themselves of these troops. This was performed rather with an absolute resolution than any conduct or order, for after soldiers had serried themselves close no officer's voice could be heard, but each soldier would give the word of command either as they saw or feared their enemy, but all this while a man could not but joy to see so vivid a courage and so firm a resolution as was in every common soldier to die by one another.[18]

Across on the hill of Mourada, the Spanish left, seven Portuguese *terzos*, supported by five squadrons of horse and led forward personally by Schomberg, had attacked and put to flight the remaining Spanish infantry, where the position was far stronger but the quality of the opposition less. Here they captured the second battery of four guns, which were turned on those squadrons of Spanish cavalry that still held their ground. Schomberg rode back again to the left flank and there he saw that although the English foot had secured the high ground, what remained of the English, French and Portuguese horse was still hard pressed in the low ground. He therefore sent word to the English foot to march down to their left and engage the Spanish horse; he also sent word to Vila Flor, to send up a reserve *terzo* under his personal command – that of Diego Gomes de Figuiredo – which he refused to do; however Figuiredo brought the *terzo* up on his own initiative. The three formations 'immediately advancing to the Front of the Cavalry, made such seasonable Discharges on the Enemy, that the Horse were no longer able to keep their ranks'. In contrast to received wisdom, it was not uncommon for infantry in line to take on cavalry provided they could deliver fire. Having failed to break Pearson's triangle and now seeing the approach of more troops, the cry is said to have gone up from the Spanish: 'There come the English redcoats, who give no quarter!' They fled, leaving the allies in possession of the field,[19] leaving the ground covered with the bodies of a great number of men and horses, 'such that it provided the English with a rampart.'[20]

This retreat forced the rest of the Spanish horse to join the foot and quit the field. In the broken ground either side of the narrow road behind the main defensive position, the cavalry and the remains of the Spanish infantry now found themselves under heavy fire from allied cavalry and infantry, and their own captured artillery from the higher ground above the road. Struggling animals and men were caught up with the baggage and the generals' carriages, all effectively bottled up on the road. What had been the mounted vanguard was now a rearguard intent on escape, trampling their way through and over the infantry. They were not helped by the 3,500 Portuguese prisoners from Évora who,

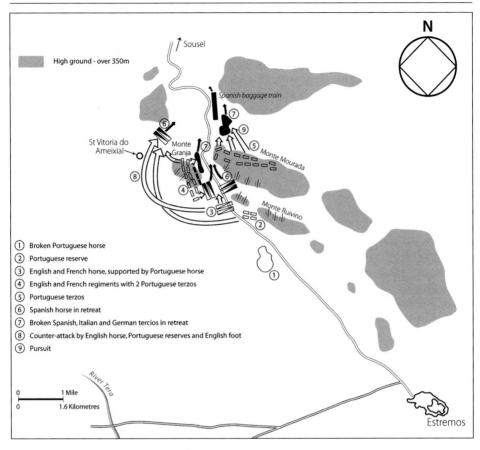

N

High ground - over 350m

↑ Sousel

Spanish baggage train

St Vitoria do
Ameixial

Monte
Granja

Monte Mourada

Monte Ruivino

(1) Broken Portuguese horse
(2) Portuguese reserve
(3) English and French horse, supported by Portuguese horse
(4) English and French regiments with 2 Portuguese terzos
(5) Portuguese terzos
(6) Spanish horse in retreat
(7) Broken Spanish, Italian and German tercios in retreat
(8) Counter-attack by English horse, Portuguese reserves and English foot
(9) Pursuit

0   1 Mile
0   1.6 Kilometres

River Tera

Estremos

Map 11 Ameixial: the battle of 29 May 1663.

seeing how matters were developing, turned on their desperate Spaniard guards, taking their weapons and turning these against their captors. This chaotic episode does much to explain why the tally of killed, wounded and prisoners was so high.

The victory was complete and it remained only to order the pursuit. Schomberg considered the army's weariness, the heavy losses among his cavalry, the approach of night, the enemy's total disarray and sent the order to hold firm. Don John, abandoning the rout of his infantry, his guns and his baggage, made off with his remaining cavalry for Arronches with all the speed they could manage. Apsley recalled of the aftermath:

> That night we kept guard within the wood [i.e., the olive plantations], but the next morning we perceived the field was clear and that it was an absolute victory on our party. The enemy had an inestimable damage, having lost his cannon and train of artillery and generally all the baggage of his army; there were fourteen coaches taken of several Princes, Dukes and Earls. It is such a loss that the Castilians cannot repair in a short time.[21]

Figure 22 A modern photograph of the route of the Spanish retreat. (A.M. Goulden)

To recognise the service of Moore's Regiment, of which he was colonel, Schomberg placed himself at its head as it marched back into camp.

There are various reports on the losses in this battle. D'Ablancourt – who was not present – gives less than 2,000 on both sides. The Portuguese and their allies by most estimates lost about 1,000 men killed and 500 wounded, among the latter was Schomberg's eldest son, who received a sabre cut to the face. The losses of the English foot were surprisingly light: Captains Atkinson and Goudinge are known to have been killed, and about forty men in each regiment killed or wounded. Lawrence Dempsey and Edward Trelawney were both remarked on by Schomberg and both were promoted to major. At some point during the campaign, however, some English soldiers were taken prisoner by the Spanish: in June 1664, a number of them managed to petition Sir Richard Fanshawe from the captivity in Seville, pointing out that they:

> had hoped long ago to hear the joyful news of their enlargement from the miserable captivity which has now lasted twelve months, and praying his Excellency to pardon their importunity, they fearing that the weightiness of his affairs may cause him to be oblivious of them, although they have little reason to suspect it, having so lately received a signal token of his tender affection and care towards his countrymen in distress.[22]

The losses of the horse were much higher. As well as Dongan and Paulinge, Cornet Meakinge and Cornet John Wharton are said to have died of wounds later – however Wharton evidently survived as he is listed as being still in the army in 1676;[23] up to 100 other ranks were killed or wounded out of the total of 400 including, as was noted, all the officers being wounded to some extent. Around 20 percent losses are usually enough to render a military unit ineffective, a figure that does not seem to vary much throughout history.[24] Schomberg wrote that 'the foreign cavalry lost more men than all the other horse put together. My own regiment opposed Don John himself. Most of his squadron were killed on the spot and his standard taken by M de Baubignis [it was later sent to the king] … We have got Don John's carriage at your service.'[25] Ann Lady Fanshawe noted that

> our house was full of distressed, honest, brave English soldiers, who by their and their fellows' valour had got one of the greatest victories that ever was. These poor but brave men were most lost between the Portugueses' poverty and Lord Chancellor Hyde's neglect, not to give it a worse name.[26]

In view of the losses among the horse, most of the surviving officers seem to have been given commands in the two foot regiments; the remainder of the English horse was amalgamated with the French regiment and placed under the command of Schomberg's eldest son, Meinhard, with James Apsley as lieutenant-colonel until Thomas Hunt succeeded him early in the following year.[27] No attempt was made to bring the English horse up to its original strength, presumably because the need was primarily for infantry. Given the constant threat from the superiority of the Spanish horse, this seems odd – but the issue was probably the inability to mount the horsemen properly, rather than the inability to recruit and equip the men.

Some English sources give 4,000 Spanish casualties, including those who fell into the hands of the Portuguese peasants and who received no quarter; the real figure is probably between 5,000 and 7,000 killed, wounded and missing. So ruined was Don John's infantry that he had to abandon the campaign. Among the Spanish prisoners were eight general officers including the Marques of Liche – who was subsequently instrumental in the successful peace negotiations – the Conde Luis de Fiesque, the Conde de But, the Conde de Escalante, the Conde de Lodestein and Daniel de Guzman, son of the Duke of Medina de las Torres; fifty other officers; thirty NCOs; 1,000 wounded and 2,000 unwounded soldiers.[28] The Portuguese also recovered the captured garrison of Évora – including the detachment of horse under Chauvet, who was under suspicion of dealing with the enemy although nothing could be proven; and they took the Spanish guns and baggage train: more than 5,000 wagons and carts and twenty-five carriages; 8,000 valuable mules and 6,000 oxen; 6,000 rounds of artillery ammunition; the military chest containing the funds of the army and all Don John's correspondence. Among Don John's papers was found a detailed account of the army intended for the conquest of Portugal including its artillery and its supply arrangements.[29] In the aftermath, Don John wrote to King Philip, ignominiously attempting to shift the blame for the defeat from himself to the troops, saying that he:

> would prefer to have died a thousand times before obliged to say that your majes-ty's arms have been infamously broken by your enemies, with more unexampled

ignorance that has ever been ... To put it bluntly, no man in the army performed as he should, and I am the first to confess, as I was not smashed in body on that field, to admit the fault and give your majesty this news ... To say further, the vileness of our people is remarkable, for they plundered the baggage and all that could not be withdrawn ... These, Sir, are the facts. The circumstances of my pain can only be written with a broken heart, not that I regret the loss of one battle, for God who is Lord of them, gives victories to those that earn them, and Meneses deserves his triumph. What scars my soul is to the astounding experience of the vileness of our nation and the infamy with which our men behaved generally.[30]

Although the Portuguese soldiery and the regimental officers had done well in the battle and earned his admiration, Schomberg had no such admiration for the high command which had consistently let down their own men. Of his fellow generals, he wrote that 'They understand nothing about war. The soldiers are brave enough, but the chiefs carefully avoid all risks, and as to him who should have led us, no one saw him during the battle at all ... the cowardice with which the commanders have acted is beyond anything I ever saw in any war ... they ought to be hanged.'[31]

The role of the English and French soldiers in providing example, along with the experience and skill of Schomberg, must be seen as crucial. Schomberg wrote that 'Everyone here is pleased with the behaviour of the English troops. We lost about fifty of our Horse, but few of the Foot, although more than eighty were wounded.'[32] As a result of Ameixial, the redcoats gained the reputation of being the best soldiers in either the Spanish or Portuguese armies: in spite of their objections on grounds of religion or behaviour, the Portuguese developed a high regard for them as soldiers and employed them as the backbone of their field army, and as such they were always in the heat of battle. It was reported that the Portuguese 'do say themselves that the English did more than men'[33] and a request was made to Charles II for a further one or two regiments of 800 men. Fanshawe wrote to Sir Henry Bennet that:

I am not ashamed of my former fear or indeed despair of the fortune of Portugal, seeing that it was shared by the Comte de Schomberg himself, nor do I see the error of my conjecture that without a powerful help from England Portugal was lost, but I did not discern that powerful succour to be already here whilst I was soliciting for it, or believe it possible that a beheaded remnant, with so many discouragements to boot, could have proved such instruments of good, for which infidelity of mine I humbly crave his Majesty's pardon and theirs.[34]

Charles Croke wrote that the English troops:

in a great and bloudy fight overthrew the Spanish Army with such a general rout, that the whole plunder of the field, with all their bag and baggage, and thousands of their lives paid for their late bold attempt: the resolutions and valour of the English Brigade, was not a little instrumental in this great Victory, although the ingrate *Portugal* would not acknowledge it. I shall however wave their continued and treacherous baseness which they always shewed to the English Army, which deservedly merited their best esteem; and only let you know, that in the fight there were lost no less than four hundred of the English Cavalry, the whole number being but six hundred; which miserable rack caused the poor Englishmen to return with hoarse Trumpets & dead-beating Drums, notwithstanding a certain and absolute Victory: [I was] at that time a Cornet of Horse, but after the fight there were left more officers than private Soldiers, the number of that gallant Regiment being reduced to a small Troop: this caused a general endeavour by those that survived, to bestow themselves in other capacities, and list among the English Infantry; some got commands by vacancies which the engagement caused; among which by the favour of Colonel *James Apsley,* [I] got a Commission for Captain of Foot.[35]

Croke's version of the casualties among the horse is not borne out by the facts; he deserted to the enemy not long afterwards and was disgracefully cashiered – but as Schomberg remarked, he 'had greatly neglected Trelawney's Company, and he is gone over to the enemy ... but the loss is not great.'[36] Croke for his part claimed that he had been captured, given his parole, and was thus obliged to leave the war.[37]

Pepys noted in his diary that:

Sir G[eorge]. Carteret did tell us that upon Tuesday last, being with my Lord Treasurer, he showed him a letter from Portugall speaking of the advance of the Spaniards into that country, and yet that the Portuguese were never more courageous than now: for by an old prophecy sent thither some years though not many since from the French King, it is foretold that the Spaniards should come into their country, and in such a valley they should all be killed, and then their country should be wholly delivered from the Spaniards. This was on Tuesday last, and yesterday come the very first news that in this valley they had thus routed and killed the Spaniards.[38]

A week later he was shown a report of the battle in the *Lisbon Gazette* and remarked: 'Here I learned that the English Foot are highly esteemed all over the world, but the horse not so much, which yet we count among ourselves the best; but they abroad have had no great knowledge of our horse it seems.'[39]

7

The Recapture of Évora, June 1663

'With such resolution, as so daunted their enemies'

After the Battle of Ameixial, the army was given six days' rest in order, as Apsley wrote to Fanshawe, 'to furnish ourselves with battering-pieces, powder, sale [i.e. shot], scaling ladders and whatever else was necessary'.[1] Meanwhile, there was much rejoicing when the news reached Lisbon. This mood of holiday and of leisure was not to Schomberg's taste at all for having gained the initiative he understood the need to maintain it: 'Although we have won this battle', he wrote to Fanshawe, 'there will be enough for them to do, as the enemy still have four thousand horse. I want to attack Evora, but our commanders here, having done so well, think of nothing but of resting themselves, instead of making use of their victory.'[2]

With the threat to Lisbon removed, the Marquis of Marialva arrived with reinforcements of 5,000 foot and 500 horse from the garrisons there and the two armies made rendezvous on 4 June, intending to re-take Évora. The town, it will be remembered, had been left with a garrison of 3,000 foot and 700 horse by Don John; of these, between 400 and 800 – or a complete *tercio* – held the fort of St Antonio. The English troops, however, refused to march, complaining that they had not been paid with any regularity. This mutiny was suppressed by the arrest of several officers and the hanging of a corporal who had incited the unrest. The officers are not named but there are two who were serving at the time who have no subsequent mention in any record and who were therefore most likely dismissed: Captain Richard Mill and Ensign John Crossman – the latter an old Protectorate man. Schomberg was not unsympathetic, but the standards of the day would not permit of anything that smacked of defiance of authority. He wrote to d'Ablancourt that 'I send to M. de Baubigny, in the first place, to get some money for the English soldiers, whose good services the day before yesterday merit better treatment than they receive.'[3]

Since February,[4] Fanshawe had been reduced to pleading with Charles II to keep the brigade in Portugal, but his case for doing so was weakened when a number of officers in Portugal petitioned Charles II in May 'that they cannot get their pay from the Portuguese ministers and praying for relief, as they are almost starved to death'. The king's answer was to order Fanshawe to give them three month's arrears, amounting to £6,000, from the unpaid portion of the marriage dowry; to promise that if better conditions could not be procured they would be ordered home; but in the meantime insist that they should serve Schomberg 'with such fidelity, courage and patience as may be for the honour of His Majesty and the nation.'[5] Even so, the Portuguese still pressed for a reinforcement of English troops as Fanshawe reported:

> On Thursday, the 14th [of June], I was invited to a conference with the ministers here, who told me that Francisco Pereira was being sent to England, Holland and France to announce the late victory and stir up the allies to send further help of men and money to enable this crown to follow their blow smartly. I told them plainly that the report in England of the treatment of our men would make it impossible to persuade any more to follow them.[6]

As the Spanish garrison in Évora under the command of the Conde de Santirena was completely isolated by Don John's defeat, Schomberg decided to force an entry as soon as possible. On 7 June, Schomberg completed his reconnaissance of Évora and the planning of the attack: he decided on two approaches, the first from the direction of the convent of dos Espinheiros, to the north-east; the second along the aqueduct da Prata of to the Fort of St Anthony, from due north.[7] These were, unsurprisingly, the same approaches as Don John had taken in his assault on the town. On the 8th, the trenches were begun, Apsley remarking that: 'The first two days we did nothing but cut down faggots; when we had enough we began our approaches.'[8] Schomberg meanwhile had found yet another subject to try his patience. The Portuguese had not the slightest idea of how to conduct a siege and an Italian had been engaged by the Crown as Chief Engineer for many years. It was clear from the first opening of the trenches that he was an imposter – to the extent that he directed the spoil (which should have formed a parapet between the besiegers and their objective) to be thrown on the wrong side of the entrenchments, i.e. to the rear. It fell to Schomberg to make good the want of expertise.

On 10 June, the garrison made a sortie from the Gate of Aviz, but this was furiously repulsed by the Portuguese. On 11 June, two batteries were brought into action against Fort St Anthony. That night, the English were assigned the task of making an assault on this fort. Two hundred volunteers from Pearson's Regiment and 200 Portuguese, four companies each commanded by a captain and the whole led by Major Henry Belasyse, with a Portuguese regiment held ready to exploit any penetration, were assigned to the task. The English attacked at midnight, 'with such resolution, as so daunted their enemies, that with the loss of a very few men they presently made themselves masters of it, putting all them to the sword from whom they found the least resistance, though indeed there was a far greater number for the defence of that place than the assailants that took it.'[9] Schomberg wrote that the English lost only three men killed and a captain wounded, although Lieutenant Pollen is later noted as having been killed. Fanshawe wrote at length of this attack to Sir Henry Bennet:

> a party of four hundred of the Portuguese army, whereof two hundred which made the vanguard were English commanded by Major Bellasis, a most gallant young man, brother to my Lord of Faulconbridge, did carry the fort of St. Antonio, suburban to Evora, with the loss of only three soldiers of ours, but of a matter of three hundred Spaniards of six hundred which were the defenders, being the medium of eight hundred which some report were therein and others four hundred. This prodigious action I relate with very great modesty in reference to our English

and their commander, for there are that do affirm that of the other two hundred of the party, which should have seconded them, not a man was come up until ours had finished the work, and that then ours would not suffer them to enter for a share of the honour, the booty not being worth the wrangling for; all I have heard named was a Capuchin's robe [N.B. presumably Carthusian, since the monastery in the fort was of that order], which one of our common soldiers plundered from the owner's back; and to the great merriment of himself and the beholders – of which the friar himself had his part in that he had scaped so well with the loss of his upper skin only – put it upon his own, cowl and all upon his head, saying he would be clad in summer, though he had gone naked all the winter.[10]

A third battery was erected the next day and a mine opened under the main wall of the town.[11] Schomberg wrote that Spanish deserters were saying that the horse meant to make a further sortie, in order to escape: 'I have sent twenty squadrons to stop their way. Don John is said to be gathering troops to relieve this place. I hope he is, and then we will march against him … my belief is that in four or five days the enemy must capitulate, and I think we ought to treat them as they treated our side.' Schomberg's reasons for believing the siege would only hold out for a few days were probably founded on the same reasons that had led to its early collapse against Don John: with St Anthony gone, the medieval fortifications were weak and the water supply was tenuous. However, he was still in despair at the conduct of the Portuguese generals: 'there is not a commander who does anything unless he is obliged. Messieurs de Villa Flor and Marialva set them the example … neither one has been nearer to the town than the quarter where they are lodged and they do not even know on which side we have opened the trenches.'[12]

The development of the siege works went on rapidly. Two days later the Portuguese lieutenant-general who commanded the works approached Apsley and 'did command two hundred musketeers also, Which I sent him under the command of Captain Roach and Captain More … he gave a command that these men should storm a half moon battery of the enemy's and that they should kill all they found in the ditch between that and the wall. His command was obeyed, though we were very sensible of the unreasonableness of it … we lost three men and had four wounded: next morning the treaty was finished'.[13] On 13 June, a major mine was blown under the walls: the commander of the garrison, recognising the inevitable, offered to surrender to Vila Flor, who himself had never entered the trenches. Under the laws and customs of war as then practiced, this was probably his last chance of surrender on reasonable terms. Had he delayed and obliged the allies to assault the fortress then no quarter would have been given to the garrison while the townspeople would have been subjected to all the terrors of pillage, sack and murder.

Vila Flor offered to allow the garrison to march out with its arms and baggage and four guns, with an escort to take it to Arronches where Don John and the Duke of St Germán had retired. Schomberg vetoed these terms of surrender, since Don John had not extended these terms when he had taken the place: he believed it necessary to force the Spaniards' hand and continue the siege. Accordingly the next day, after a second mine was blown, the Spanish governor was obliged to accept harsher terms. The garrison of 3,000 foot and 700 horse became prisoners for three months, until 15 October; the senior officers were allowed to depart under escort. The ten guns and 700 valuable horses fell into Portuguese hands.[14] Vila Flor, in his rage at having his offer countermanded, had remained in his tent. He now came out to take the honour of the surrender and to ensure his share of plunder from the enemy's baggage. But this was the last act of his command. On the day of the capture of Évora, he was recalled to Court, to give account of his conduct during the campaign.

As the Spanish garrison marched out and stacked their arms, Schomberg recognised many Germans among them, old soldiers of the Empire. He decided to recruit them to the Portuguese service and form a regiment from them. The next day, as many as 700 engaged for a bounty of four *cruzadoes* a man; the adjutant-general of the French brigade, Louis de Clairin, was named as colonel of this new regiment. It was added to the French brigade along with a reinforcement of French horse who had arrived via Plymouth in the aftermath of the Battle of Ameixial, divided into two regiments of 300 each, known as Le Comte de Maret and Briquemaut after their colonels.[15] Briquemaut was probably a Huguenot connection of Schomberg and a relative of that Briquemault (or Briquemaut), Seigneur de Franois de Beauvais (c. 1502–1572), leader of the Huguenots during the first religious wars in France. The French horse now consisted of four regiments: those of Maret and Briquemaut in addition to those of Schomberg himself – commanded by his son Frederic – and that of Chavet. This amounted to 22 weak troops, a considerable eclipse of the declining English contingent.

* * *

The surrender of Évora brought the campaign of 1663 to an end and with it, all the Spanish gains of the early part of the year were made void. He also felt that with Évora secure, it would be desirable to advance into Spain, 'if it were not that our men are fatigued and that it is beginning to be very hot, so that it is to be feared that the rest of the auxiliaries would desert and that the troops, especially the foreigners, would perish.' The constraints of climate and supply therefore once again prevented the development of a decisive campaign. For Ameixial is sometimes referred to as a decisive battle, which it was not. There are only two sets of circumstances in which a battle may be described as decisive and both lie within the context of a campaign, that is, a set of military operations planned and conducted to achieve a strategic objective, within a given time and geographical area. This subject will be discussed in more detail in a later chapter, in the context of the battle of Montes Claros. Although destructive to the Spanish cause and the reputation of Don John, and of huge material and, perhaps more significantly moral encouragement to Portugal, Ameixial falls into neither of these classes: the Spanish had lost a battle but they were not ready to acknowledge that they had lost the war – and defeat lies chiefly in the perception of the losers.[16]

* * *

At the end of campaigning in 1663, the army dispersed to quarters. Where and when to go into summer or winter quarters was a major decision by commanders and usually revolved around withdrawing to ports or large towns which could be supplied; or else choosing areas with well-developed agriculture and therefore significant food surpluses. It may be further argued therefore that the ability to supply by river or sea could in fact determine which towns or fortresses were besieged and which left alone, since dispersion was not possible during siege warfare and it was this that led to most logistic difficulties. If our strip of land cited earlier in the calculations for an army on the march, of seven miles by sixty-five, is converted into a circle, it will be apparent that, using the consumption rates quoted earlier, an army that remained static would eat up 15 percent of the available food every six days and therefore consume all available food in about a month – less if the area has already been stripped by a besieged garrison. Devastating the surrounding area was probably the most effective method that defenders could employ therefore, to ensure that they could see out a long siege. Settling down in large numbers also presented almost immediately problems of sanitation and hygiene – and with them to rapid onset of debilitating illnesses in an age where medicine simply could not cope with the problems of the day. As with injuries that were anything other than minor, putting oneself in the care of a seventeenth century surgeon when hurt would simply mean that death might be fended off for a day or two, rather than prevented.[17]

Taking stock while in its winter quarters, the officers of the English contingent concluded that their effective fighting strength had been reduced by casualties, desertion and sickness to about 1,500, of whom just over 300 were in the horse and the remainder in the two regiments of foot. Steps were taken to recruit the foot, but not, as already noted, the horse. In January 1664, the Portuguese government asked leave to raise in Ireland 'one thousand good effective men, all English, with their arms [i.e. armour], muskets, pikes and swords, powder and ball.' In answer to this request, James Butler, Marquis of Ormonde and Lord-Lieutenant of Ireland, was ordered to provide 1,000 soldiers from 'factious and dangerous' elements in the army on the Irish Establishment, whose potential for making trouble would be reduced in direct proportion to their distance from home.[18] So many objections were raised by the Portuguese, however, that this project was abandoned.[19] There were good grounds for such objections, given the large numbers of Irish troops who had served with the Spanish armies in Flanders; and until 1661 there had been an Irish *tercio* in the Spanish army fighting Portugal itself: the *Tercio Irlanda*. Thus the Portuguese preferred English Protestants to their Irish co-religionists, in spite of their heresies. However, some Irish officers and men did appear from Tangier and elsewhere – including perhaps captured Irish soldiers formerly in the Spanish service who turned their coats – for after the eventual return of the brigade to England in 1668, many petitioned the king for employment or relief and their names are recorded.[20] We can thus be certain that the brigade contained a reasonable number of Irish officers and men from this time onwards.

The Privy Council decided that a safer course of action would be to recruit volunteers for the brigade in Portugal from the English counties, primarily in the south-west which was closest to the ports of embarkation. The unpopularity of the Portuguese service soon became evident: in Somerset, for example, a riot occurred and many of the recruits ran away after having been terrified by rumours that they were to be sold as indentured labourers in the sugar plantations of the Barbadoes.[21] Clarendon wrote to Fanshawe that 'you will easily believe the news of the treatment of our English troops have had there is very small encouragement to make new levies here, and to imagine that the king can send troops from hence and take care for the payment of them there is indeed ridiculous, so that they must either resolve to have no need of foreign troops or to provide to have means to pay them punctually'. In the end 730 recruits were shipped out from England, arriving in Portugal in May and June 1664.[22]

Surprisingly, perhaps, no additional troops arrived from the sale of Dunkirk to France, a place which Schomberg had advised the king to hold, for he 'had considered the place well, and he was sure it could never be taken ... the holding of it would keep both France and Spain in a dependence on the king.'[23] Such a dependence might have been valuable leverage in the war in Iberia but the cost of the place, at £73,868 for the period December 1660 to July 1661, was just too high.[24] This equates to £8,700,000 at today's prices,[25] and this was close to 10 percent of the funds available to Charles to meet all his expenses, including Tangier.[26] The sale was therefore finalised in November 1662, probably because those troops available from the garrison were needed in Tangier, which was after all a possession of the English Crown and demanded first call on the available resources of the Privy Purse rather than the exchequer.[27] The troops in Dunkirk went either to England or, in July 1663, to Tangier with the new governor, Andrew Rutherford, Earl of Teviot.

A fair number of new officers did however arrive in Portugal in time for the campaign of 1664: for the horse, Captain Theodore Russell and Cornet Francis Trelawney – probably a relative of Captain Edward Trelawney. In Moore's Regiment of Foot, John Wetmore appears on promotion from the horse, along with Captain William Moore, a Catholic, who had been captain-lieutenant in the Governor's Regiment in Tangier before shipping to Portugal,[28] and Charles Farrell, an Irish Catholic. There are also a number of officers who cannot be identified by regiment or company, or even in some cases by their full names: Captains John Birch, Bourke, Fitzpatrick, Gregory Noland, Henry Travers, Nathaniel Hill and Turner; Lieutenants Morgan, Mulberry, Terry, Fitzherbert; and Ensigns John Bourke, John Harbord, Pettybons and Thomson. Of these, Fitzpatrick, Noland, Cusacke, Terry and Fitzherbert were probably, given their names, Irish, from families that had supported the king in exile.[29] Cusacke was almost certainly a nephew of the Earl of Tyrconnel and owed his place to patronage, therefore.[30] Russell could be a relative of John Russell, who commanded Prince Rupert's Bluecoats at Naseby; Morgan was a nephew of Sir Thomas Morgan.[31] Fitzpatrick, Bourke, Roche and John Harbord had all served in Fitzgerald's Regiment in Tangier since 1662 before exchanging into Portugal;[32] Charles Farrell and John Bourke had served in Farrell's Regiment in Tangier; and finally, Lieutenant Emerson could be the same old Protectorate officer as served in Robert Harley's Regiment in Dunkirk and then Peterborough's Regiment in Tangier in 1662.[33] Some officers also left: Henry Bellasyse returned to England and went from thence to Tangier in 1667;[34] Robert Sutton was given leave to retire by Schomberg.[35]

It was with good reason that the service was unpopular: pay was seven months in arrears: for a captain, this could be as much as £24 and for a private man, 23/- without allowances: the equivalent today of £36,700 and £1,760 respectively, using a calculation of equivalent purchasing power.[36] Given everything that has been said about the difficulty of obtaining rations, it is obvious that for any soldier in Portugal, the matter of pay was of paramount importance – as it was anywhere. Basic pay was miniscule, ten pence each day for a private man in the English regiments of foot, one *real* a day in the Spanish service for auxiliary units – from which deductions were made for all food other than the bread ration, powder and shot – and it was often in arrears; but extra payments were often made for labouring, acting as soldier-servant, recruiting, sapping and mining. Soldiers moonlighted at harvest time or on road-building and could thus support themselves and supplement the basic food ration, as well as gamble, drink, and buy clothes.[37] In units recruited territorially or from auxiliary troops, desertion rates were often extremely high – routinely a third of the fighting strength.[38] This could be far higher during the seasons of harvest or sowing when agricultural wages could be as high as 3 *reals* plus 3 quarts of wine per day in Extremadura.[39] Captains of companies kept a chest from which distributed subsistence wages on account when no money arrived from the Treasury and recouped the sums laid out with interest when cash arrived. Captains of companies of course chose their sergeants and corporals and paid them extra, thus ensuring their loyalty. Enlistment bounties were also paid that could tide a man over for a while if regular pay was not forthcoming: in the Spanish service this could be as much as 18 *escudos* for an infantry man in 1647, 60 for a fully equipped cavalry trooper.[40]

The situation was made worse because the old Cromwellian soldiers were used to a regime under which there was a degree of democracy and meritocracy in the appointment of officers; they accordingly appointed commissioners from each regiment to remonstrate with the Portuguese as they had done over grievances during the Civil Wars and the Protectorate.[41] Even worse, 'several officers and soldiers have been murdered in their quarters'; in February, Lieutenant Ashton and a common soldier were openly killed in the streets – this in spite of the high fighting reputation of the brigade gained at Ameixial and Évora. To add insult to injury, the offenders were freed without charge by the Portuguese courts.[42]

Outside Lisbon, the English troops had a better image. When the English complained of their arrears, the Portuguese authorities had retorted that the French were paid less and did not complain; Captain Andrew Maynard, the consul's brother, replied that this was because the French plundered the people, 'whereas all the kingdom of Portugal … cannot accuse the whole English brigade of the taking of the worth of an egg without paying for it. And thus the officers prefer to engage to make satisfaction to the worth of a farthing for anything that shall be taken from the natives, and severely punish the offenders.'[43] From June 1663 onwards, it was generally acknowledged among the country folk of Alentejo that the English were better disciplined and better behaved than any other nation. The spirit of the New Model was still alive it seemed – at least in the regiments of foot that had been drawn from it – for of them it had been remarked that 'whereas soldiers usually spend and make forfeiture even of the civility they bring into other armies; here men grow religious, and more spiritual-thriving than in any place of the kingdom.'[44]

* * *

In the aftermath of the campaign of 1663, Schomberg was rewarded by the King of Portugal with the rank of Grandee, the title of count of Mértola and a pension of 5,000 *cruzadoes* a year, or 314 German florins – a huge commitment for the Portuguese treasury. This overcame the earlier objection that Portuguese troops must be commanded by Portuguese officers – for Schomberg was now at least an honorary Portuguese nobleman. Vila Flor was removed from the command of the army and this office, with some restrictions, was conferred on Schomberg; the Marquis de Mello was named as general of the horse and John da Silva da Souza as general of the ordnance. Only Schomberg's religion stood against him: according to Frémont, 'tis certain that had he not been of a contrary religion, they would have granted him great commanderies for himself and for his children, and that for ever.'[45]

Towards the end of November Schomberg himself visited Lisbon to persuade the government to make thorough provision and preparations for the next campaigning season – during which he felt a decision could be reached. However after Ameixial, complacency had set in. In 1664, it would all be to do again.

8

Valencia de Alcantara and the Campaign of 1664

'our Red Coats are very terrible to the Spaniards'

Map 12 Valencia de Alcantara and Albuquerque.

In the shadow of the Spanish defeat at the hands of the Portuguese and their allies, diplomatic niceties continued to be performed in defiance of the reality on the ground. The English Ambassador to the courts of both Spain and Portugal, Sir Richard Fanshawe, landed at Cadiz and was received with salutes and formal greetings by the Spanish before going on first to Toledo and then on to Madrid for audience with the King of Spain.[1] But even as Fanshawe travelled in state, campaigning along the frontier began in April 1664, with border raids in which the English horse participated.[2] The successes of Ameixal and Évora had given the Portuguese new confidence in themselves, but they rapidly turned to complacency and even arrogance. Marialva assumed the title of Captain-General of the armies, in spite of the assurances previously given to Schomberg and his title of Generalissimo, and it was Marialva who thus, at least in public, commanded the armies. Schomberg boiled with rage.[3] He was, however, determined to take the fight to the enemy, realise a long-standing Portuguese objective and seize an important Spanish fortress or town as a bargaining chip. He fixed on the capture of Valencia de Alcantara, across the northern frontier of Alentejo from Portalegre and 65 kilometres (40 miles) north of Badajoz. This role as a bargaining chip was the town's only importance except for its bridge, which would allow easier communications between the Portuguese forces in Beira and Alentejo. Most of the Portuguese members of the council of war were opposed to the move, but Schomberg insisted.

The operation was, however, to be carried out on a logistic shoestring: because of the inadequacies of the Portuguese commissariat, Schomberg was able to assemble a mere ten days of supplies, which meant that the fortress would have to be reduced in five days – just enough, just in time – so as to allow enough food for the army to return home after the operation, unless supplies could be augmented by forage. As things turned out, this was indeed necessary. Although the Portuguese had some 20,000 foot and 6,000 horse

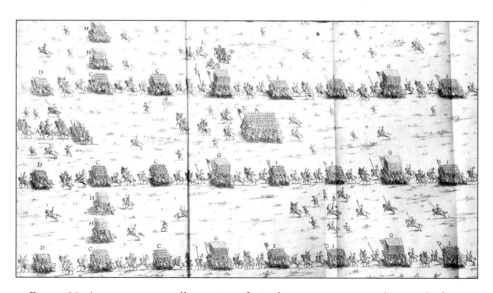

Figure 23 A contemporary illustration of a 17th century army on the march, from Ludovico Melzo's *Regole della cavalleri*. (© Royal Armouries RAL. 08686)

under arms in Alentejo according to Maynard,[4] only a small number of these could be supported by the available supplies once away from their garrisons: numbers are hard to ascertain but given the names of regiments and *terzos* named, it appears that the force included all the foreign troops, at least two Portuguese *terzos* of foot, and a small siege train: perhaps 7,000 men altogether, not nearly enough to overwhelm rapidly the reinforced Spanish garrison, let alone deal with a sortie or a relief. It was 30 May before the troops were assembled and encamped on the Caia River, probably around Portalegre – late, therefore, in the short campaigning season. Here a council of war was held and the selection of Valencia agreed: on 1 June, the army advanced.[5]

* * *

Valencia was a small fortress sited on a rocky outcrop and was a mountain castle whose fortifications had been partly modernised. It was 'surrounded with a Wall, but ill flank'd, having only 4 or 5 little Bastions, and an old Castle within, with some Outworks',[6] the outer walls were triangular in shape, as the map shows, and no more than 300 metres (280 yards) in any direction. The slopes from the river up to the fortress, and indeed from the low ground on the western side, were steep and rocky. Inside the walls, the medieval streets were narrow, cramped and dark. Below the town the river, although shown on maps as a major watercourse, was at this time of the year a dull, small stream and no obstacle to any army.[7] Spanish intelligence rapidly determined that the town was Schomberg's objective and both the town and the fortress of Valencia were heavily garrisoned, under the command of Don Juan de Avila. The castle itself (A on Map 13) was held by Captain Jose Ferran's company; *Maestro de Campo* Pedro Fonseca held the San Francisco outworks, built around the convent of that name (G on Map 13),

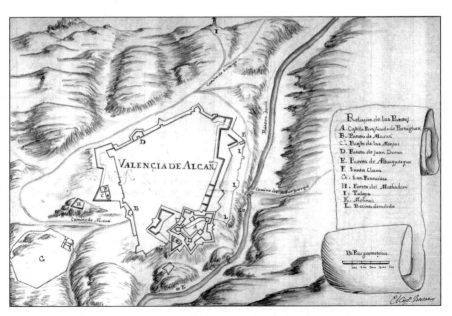

Map 13 Valencia de Alcantara (detail) contemporary map. (Author's collection)

with fifty men of his regiment; another company of his *tercio* held the demi-lune of the convent of nuns of Santa Clara (F on Map 13). Fonseca could count on about ninety effective men of one of the three battalions of his *tercio*, with about 160 civilians to work on the defences. *Maestro de Campo* Juan de la Carrera held the Juan Duran gate (D on Map 13) with 600 Italians of his *tercio*. In the Baluarte de la Magdalena, troops were distributed between the Puerto de las Monjas (C on Map 13), between the curtain wall and the main defences, which was garrisoned by a captain with fifty horsemen of the *trozo* of Don Pedro de Gamboa; another fifteen men and one officer in the tower of San Pedro; and a reserve of 150 men. Securing the Santiago or Marua gate (B on Map 13) were fifty militia men under Don Fabricio Rosi, supported by a company from the *tercios* of Don Baltasar de Medinaceli. Don Bartolomé de Cuellar, Don Martin and Don Alfonso Vargas each provided 150 men to work on the defences and stand guard. A militia battalion under Captain Juan de la Carrera was posted at the barbican (between A and B on Map 13). The townspeople – men, women and children, led by their mayor – the priests and monks even, all turned up to work on the fortifications or take a part in the defence of their town.[8] Given the size of the place, this was an enormous garrison and the place must have been packed with humanity – and with all the problems of feeding, watering, health and sanitation that such overcrowding would have produced.

The allied army arrived at Valencia on the road leading from San Vicente de Alcantara – that is, from the south – on 2 June, at about 11 o'clock in the morning. The troops had marched for 30 kilometres (18 miles), of which the first half had lain through their own territory. The fortress was only 9 kilometres (5 miles) as the crow flies from the border, but a longer route had been taken to bring the army from the south, rather than from the west, since this was a better road and an easier approach. The defenders had thrown out a screen of mounted skirmishers, supported by artillery fire from the fortifications, but these were quickly driven in to the fortress. That night, Schomberg directed the encirclement of the town and the troops worked their way up the river, occupying the mills and tanneries and cutting the road bridge towards Albuquerque. The construction of batteries began at once. Already food was short: Schomberg and Marialva had each to advance money personally to buy food for the army for ten more days.[9] A prudent commander of this date would generally field an attacking force of five to ten times the size of the defending force: about one-quarter of these men would hold the siege works at any time, while the remainder were employed on digging, carrying supplies, serving the guns, or held in readiness to stop any attempts either to relieve the besieged garrison from outside, or by the garrison to sortie out. Schomberg however, did not have the luxury of these force ratios.

When conducting a siege, the first decision for the commander and his engineers was the place and direction of the main attack. It was rare for a general not to have a reasonable knowledge of a fortress before he arrived on the scene. Spies would bring reports of course, but in most cases, plans of varying accuracy could be bought from print shops or stalls in the streets of any large town. In the case of Valencia there was more detailed knowledge, for it had been besieged once before and captured by the Portuguese, in 1644, although not occupied for long, and since then the Spanish had made some improvements to the fortifications, as noted.

On the morning of 3 June, Schomberg completed his reconnaissance and made the decision on where to attack. The river, although only 10–12 metres wide and shallow, flowed through a deeply entrenched valley, making the approach too difficult from that side. He therefore directed an assault on the outlying works around the convent of San Francisco by 1,000 of the English foot, drawn from both regiments, supported by some horse. This assault carried the position rapidly, for it was not a fort on the scale of, for example, St Anthony at Évora, but it lay only just over 100 metres from the town walls. It was at once occupied by the attackers and its few guns turned on their former owners.[10] This was the signal for the formal investment of the town to begin on 5 June; and the work of constructing batteries, trenches and saps by the besiegers went on apace, for given the fragility of the supply situation, the only course of action to seize the fortress was a rapid assault.

On the following nights, various probing attacks were mounted from San Francisco and the trenches advanced across the short stretch of level ground before the walls. The defenders responded with sorties. It was clear, however, that the main objective of the allied attack was the gate of Santiago, or Marua, close to San Francisco and more batteries were erected on the high ground just to the north of the outwork, to dominate the approach. On 7 June, Schomberg opened a parley and offered surrender terms, which were rejected out of hand. Meanwhile, a body of Spanish horse under the John Gaspar de Marsin, Comte de Granville, arrived within cannon-shot of the besiegers' lines and observed matters for two days. Lacking infantry, Marsin made no attempt to break the siege and withdrew. Marsin had been transferred from the Spanish Netherlands, before which he was, in 1647, lieutenant-general in command of the army in Catalonia. During the Fronde he sided

Figure 24 A modern photograph of the convent of San Francisco at Valencia.
(A.M. Goulden)

with Condé against Louis XIV and was imprisoned in Perpignan for thirteen months. When the peace was signed on 30 July 1653, Marsin, like Condé, refused the amnesty and went to Spain where Philip IV appointed him to a command in his army, in which capacity he had accompanied Don John into Portugal. He was an experienced and capable commander, therefore, one whom Schomberg had to take seriously.

By 9 June, a breach had been opened in the wall and Schomberg again offered terms. The defenders were clearly disheartened by Marsin's retreat but even so, negotiations were inconclusive; however by the next day, the breach had been widened to the extent that Avila gave permission for the defenders either to withdraw in contact to the tiny citadel, or surrender in extremis, should an assault succeed in entering the town.[11] If the attackers did get inside in strength, the citadel with its low walls and few guns would not hold out for long. By 11 June the siege-works were close enough to the defences to risk an attempt.[12] The townspeople, knowing what would happen if an assault penetrated a fortified town that had been summoned and had refused terms, implored Avila to accept the enemy's offer. These terms, as offered by Marialva, were lenient, as they had been at Évora: a four days' truce for the army to leave, with Colours flying and drums beating, with its arms and one gun, but all other property to be forfeit.[13] The defenders played for time; but Schomberg had lost patience and ordered an assault on the breach.

Once again, the two English foot regiments led the attack with the supposed support of the French regiment of Schomberg on their left and the Portuguese *terzo* of the Armada on their right. From the Portuguese point of view, it was after all preferable to use foreign allies and mercenaries than to risk one's own troops. Maynard described the attack thus:

> the two English regiments of foot had order to storm at a breach which was made in the wall, and the *terzo da Armada* were to fall on upon the right hand of the English and a French regiment upon the left hand, and in another part of the town the regiment of Casquais was to storm. So about nine o'clock at night, the 9–19 June,* the sign was given, and the English, according to their orders, ran directly to the breach, but not a man besides them stirred out of their quarters but one Portuguese captain, who was so gallant to say, it is a shame to see the English fight and we stand looking on, but before he could get to the breach he was slain with a musket shot.[14]

The defenders had prepared large numbers of grenadoes and these caused many casualties in the breach – this is not surprising, for the troops must have been tightly packed on the very narrow frontage of the attack. The impetus of English assault however carried them through the breach and into the town, where the spearhead of more than 500 men found themselves isolated in the narrow, twisting and barricaded streets. Maynard again:

> The English fought it out above half an hour, to the admiration of all those that stood and looked on, in which short time were slain Lieutenant-Colonel Hunt, Major Wetmore, Captain Travers, Captain William More, Captain Noland, Captain Fitzpatrick, two lieutenants, three ensigns, nine sergeants and one hundred

---

*   Given the chronology already set out, Maynard's date for the assault cannot be right. The attack probably took place on the night of 12 June.

and fifty-eight common soldiers; and wounded Captain Stansby, Captain Hill, Captain (John) Turner, Captain Roch (Roach), Captain (John) Sandys, Captain Baxter, Captain Maynard, my brother, and many others; very few came off without wounds, besides two hundred common soldiers. Colonel Pearson, who got abundance of honour by his gallantry that day, received two shots in his body, but having good arms they did him little harm.[15]

The English pulled back, having lost 200 men; another 250 were badly wounded and many died of their injuries or were crippled.[16] One ensign and five soldiers were taken prisoner in the streets: the ensign may well have been Pettybons, who disappears from the record at this point. The French also suffered losses, including du Fay, lieutenant-colonel of Schomberg's Regiment of Horse.[17] The next day, the allies asked leave to collect the dead under a flag of truce and in spite of the repulse of the assault, Avila knew he could not hold out much longer. But the allies did not know this – as far as they were concerned, the defenders were still in control so that the failed assault delayed the reduction of Valencia by four days. Since only two days' bread remained, the Portuguese were obliged to offer the Spanish garrison the same generous terms of surrender on 14 June that they had previously rejected.[18] These were duly accepted.[19]

*　　*　　*

The taking of Valencia de Alcantara should have been an important victory. It gave the Portuguese a foothold in Castile for bargaining purposes, sure, but it brought material benefit too for from Valencia, a garrison could disrupt and feed off the great Spanish sheep-raising industry by interrupting the movement of the huge flocks to their winter pastures, diverting large quantities of live meat over the border into Portugal. It was proposed that Hertara on the Tagus River, north of Valencia, should also be captured since its 'garrison was very troublesome to the Neighbourhood';[20] In the end, the capture of Valencia and the sacrifices of the soldiers were wasted for the success was not further exploited by, for example, an attack on Badajoz, for want of supplies, the shortage of which obliged Schomberg to disperse the troops to quarters.

In the aftermath, Castelo Melhor acknowledged the contribution of the English brigade, writing that 'the English had done more than could be expected of men, and he believed there were no soldiers in the world like them.'[21] Maynard wrote of the English contribution that 'Our countrymen have added to the reputation they got last year in the field, which cost them dear at Valensa, where they had foul play'.[22] He went on to report that the English commissions of the officers were to be replaced by Portuguese, and henceforth the officers and men would have to take orders from Portuguese generals whom they regarded on the evidence of the previous year's campaigning as incompetent.[23] The separate identity of the English brigade was not only, as already noted, a generally established principle, but also a matter of vital importance to morale and cohesion. Any attempt to break up the brigade or to replace English officers with Portuguese was therefore bitterly opposed:[24]

> notwithstanding all this good service and expense of their blood the Court endeavour to bring them to new conditions: first, by delaying to pay their arrears according

to promise, being indebted to the soldiers almost eight months' pay; secondly, to abate above a fifth part of their pay for the time to come; thirdly, that henceforward they shall not receive their commissions from my Lord Schomberg – which doth a little entrench upon his authority and give him no small disgust – but from the King of Portugal; and fourthly, that they shall at all times receive orders from the General of the horse, Campmaster-General, General of the Artillery, &c, which doth hugely disgust the whole party, who have by their commissioners – Colonel Pearson and Major Rumsey for Colonel Pearson's regiment, Major Trelawny and Captain Russell for the regiment of horse, Captain Hill and Captain Maynard for the general's regiment of foot – given the King their answer that rather than they will abate anything of their pay or alter the conditions made with the Conde de Castelmelhor the 10th of January last, they will all lay down their commissions.[25]

A number of the English officers sent their grievances to Clarendon in London: Clarendon was apprehensive that any attempt to place the English brigade under direct Portuguese authority could make the troops feel absolved of their English allegiance, liable as they were to recall home at need, and to regard themselves as mercenaries. These circumstances, coupled with the seriousness of the arrears of pay, led Clarendon to lobby the Portuguese government. He succeeded in gaining assurances that there was no thought of separating the English.[26] Clarendon replied early in 1665 to the officers' petition that when that year's campaign was over the king would recall the contingent if it was not better treated.[27]

*   *   *

Not long afterwards a Portuguese army under Pedro de Magalhães[*] added to the laurels of the year by defeating a Spanish army under the Duke of Osuna[†] at the Battle of Castelo Rodrigo in the north of Portugal, fought on 26 June 1664. Osuna was a General and Grandee of Spain, a title bestowed by Philip II in 1562. He was later Viceroy of Catalonia, 1667–1669 and Governor of the Duchy of Milan, 1670–1674. After a number of skirmishes, the Duke had attacked the fortress of Castelo Rodrigo with 5,000 men and a huge train of artillery, numbering ninety-five guns of various calibres. The castle was only defended by 150 Portuguese soldiers. Magalhães, who was military commander of the province of Centro, rapidly collected 3,000 men and moved to the rescue of Castelo Rodrigo; a battle took place near the village of Salgadela. After an initial Spanish attack was repelled, the Portuguese counter-attack proved decisive. According to Maynard's account, Magalhães had dressed his men in red coats – although some accounts say red and blue caps made from the mantles worn by the country women:[28]

which the Spanish seeing cried out 'this is the English party', and so threw down

---

[*]   Pedro Jacques de Magalhães, 1st Viscount de Fonte Arcada (1620–1688). His family was that of the famous navigator Magellan.

[†]   Gaspar Téllez-Girón, 5th Duke of Osuna (1625–1694), was a general and Grandee of Spain, a title instituted by Philip II in 1562. He was later Viceroy of Catalonia 1667–1669 and Governor of the Duchy of Milan 1670–1674.

their arms and ran away. I should not dare to give your honour this relation but that I have it from the Spanish prisoners who were taken on that occasion, and from several Portuguese who affirm this to be true. And Count Schomberg hath likewise made some enquiries into the report and is fully satisfied of the truth of this relation; and 'tis not to be doubted but our Red Coats are very terrible to the Spaniards.[29]

1,700 prisoners were taken and artillery pieces captured, for the loss of only twenty Portuguese killed and six wounded. It is said that Osuna escaped disguised as a monk.[30]

*   *   *

The losses of the English brigade during 1664, and especially at Valencia, were heavy: eleven officers, nine sergeants and 158 soldiers were killed; three officers and 250 men wounded, one officer and an indeterminate number of soldiers had been taken captive.[31] Those killed included Thomas Hunt, lieutenant-colonel of the horse, who may be the Royalist Thomas Hunt, who petitioned in 1660 for money to transport home thirty of his soldiers, sent to the Barbadoes by the Commonwealth.[32] Also killed was Lieutenant John Wetmore, one of Morgan's officers in 1659. Three of Pearson's captains were killed – including Edward Witham – and Pearson himself was wounded. It was an insult, therefore, when the Portuguese official account failed to mention the English casualties. Clarendon wrote complaining of this slight and some of the officers remonstrated with the Portuguese Secretary of State, whereupon a more generous account was published.[33] It was a poor consolation for such official disdain, but this engagement again improved the reputation of the brigade with the army and the people, the Portuguese being now of the view that they need not fear the Spanish army, so long as the English were with them.[34]

Perhaps it was a sign of the English government's reservations that little was done to replace the casualties of 1664. A Commission was granted by Charles II to William Sheldon, formerly captain of the Life Guard of Foot, and previously a captain in Prince Maurice's Regiment at Naseby where he had served under the then Lieutenant-Colonel Guy Molesworth. He had later been taken prisoner at the battle of Worcester in the Second Civil War. In England, since the Restoration, he had held both foot and horse captaincies and was now sent to Portugal as lieutenant-colonel to Pearson's Regiment, along with Cornet John Turner who had also served in Prince Maurice's: both men probably owed their places to Molesworth's influence.[35]

Meanwhile, Don John of Austria had left Extremadura, although he remained a significant popular hero even as the fortunes of Imperial Spain began to decline. The command of the Spanish armies fighting Portugal had temporarily devolved onto the Comte de Marsin, who was known to be an aggressive commander. Marsin decided to attack the small fortress of Castelo de Vide, which was lightly held. Schomberg had already told Castelo Melhor that the place should be reinforced, and been told in return that the Spanish would never dare to venture so far. Marsin soon proved Castelo Melhor wrong and in doing so, came up against the two French regiments of Briquemaut and Chauvet. Only 120 men escaped from both regiments combined; Marsin carried off 200 prisoners and killed or dispersed the rest.[36] At the end of September, Marsin then demolished the fortifications of Arronches, on which Don John had spent a great deal of effort. Don John was furious when he learnt of this and took his revenge by securing the dismissal of Marsin from his command. After Marsin's withdrawal, Schomberg ordered the place re-occupied and the damage to the fortifications was soon repaired.[37] Marsin also demolished the fortifications of La Codosera on the Spanish side of the border, which was felt to be vulnerable to Portuguese occupation. Schomberg and d'Ablancourt then tried to plan an expedition into Andalusia to capture the port of Ayamonte, close to Huelva – but this was forbidden by the king on the advice of his ministers.[38]

Schomberg blamed the inability effectively to counter Marsin's incursions on the shortcomings of the commissariat department; and his inability to execute anything resembling offensive operations due to opposition based on jealousy among the king's ministers. He therefore sent the army into quarters and returned to Lisbon in a foul temper, to remonstrate in person with Castelo Melhor. The final straw for Schomberg was the charge of rape against his son Meinhard, who was recalled to Lisbon to face trial by court-martial. No actual evidence was produced, indicating that the episode was just one more attempt by the jealous Portuguese nobility to discredit the man who was trying to engineer their deliverance. The angry exchanges between the Schomberg, Marialva and Castelo Melhor all but led to Schomberg laying down his command. He complained to Turenne and asked Charles II for a command in England.[39] Charles responded rather tartly, telling him to take his orders from the Portuguese, but Schomberg threatened to resign if this were to be enforced: around 6 December, he wrote to Clarendon requesting shipping to embark and evacuate the English brigade.[40] Schomberg was clearly close to breaking point, but the common people had more sense than their nobles and knew his worth. One of the ancient institutions of Portugal, the *Jues do Povo*, (literally, judges of the people) had the right of direct access to the king:

> A fortnight since, when the King began his progress to Santarém, the *Juiz do Povo* told the King that the common people understood that Monsieur Schomberg was put by his command, and was to depart the kingdom, which (said he) is a very great discouragement to the people, and we humbly beseech Your majesty not to rely so much upon your nobility which experience shows us are not fit to command your armies as the Count Schomberg is; to which the King made answer that he knew nothing of Monsieur Schomberg's going out of the kingdom, but did believe he would continue to do this Crown more service.[41]

A reconciliation was effected by d'Ablancourt, which again put Portuguese officers in nominal command but obliged to accept Schomberg's direction. Promises were also made of greater efforts in the following year's campaigning. Even so, Schomberg was unable to convince the Portuguese ministers of the need to consolidate and strengthen the fortifications of Vila Viçosa against a Spanish counter-move, which he felt certain would not long be delayed.

9

Montes Claros, 1665

'This victory is much greater'[1]

Schomberg's view of Spanish intentions was, unsurprisingly, correct. To take Don John's place in command of the Army of Extremadura, Philip IV appointed the experienced and famous Don Luis de Benavides Carillo y Toledo, Marquis of Caracena, who had already begun a programme of reforms in the Spanish armies. Caracena had been distinguished in the wars in Italy and the Low Countries, where he had once before succeeded Don John of Austria after the defeat of the Dunes in 1658 and had been Governor until 1664. He arrived at Madrid in October 1664 and on 1 April 1665 the marquis had, according to Ann, Lady Fanshawe, declared 'that if preparations did not prove as royal and real in all respects as he had been promised, he would not budge a foot, whereby without any fault of his own he might dishonour his master and forfeit to the world such reputation as he had purchased in the wars. Two weeks later he went up to the army amid great expectations.'[1]

To end the war with Portugal, the best available troops that Spain had available were assembled: fighting units of all the nations of the empire, experienced in the wars, from Flanders, Spain itself, the Italian States, Germany, Swiss mercenaries and troops who had fought the French. This army, 'the elite and the fine flower of the experienced and renowned Spanish tercios', as one Spanish source put it, numbered 23,000 men: 15,000 foot and 7,660 horse, but with only a small train of fourteen pieces of artillery and two heavy mortars.[2] Among the *tercios* and regiments were many that had been reconstituted since Ameixial: in the horse, the *trozos* of Rossellon, Ordenes, Milan, Osuna, Borgoña, Alemanes (or Germans), Wallonia, Extremadura and Valones; and the independent companies drawn from the Horse Cuirassiers and Horse Arquebusiers of the Guards. Among the foot, *tercios* from Lombardia, Milan, Modena, Naples, Germany, Switzerland; as well as the Spanish *tercios* of the Armada, Aragon, Toledo, Madrid, Burgos, Valladolid, Cordoba, Lisboa, Castilla, Viejo de Estremadura and Nuevo de Estremadura.[3]

Caracena was determined to finish Portuguese independence once and for all and made a plan to march rapidly on and occupy Lisbon. He would once again use the direct route from Badajoz but would avoid loss of time and troops in investing and then garrisoning either Valencia de Alcantara or Évora; these would fall to Spanish arms anyway as a result of victory; instead he intended first to capture Vila Viçosa and use that as a supply base. He stipulated that the Spanish fleet under the Duke of Aveiro should demonstrate against Lisbon at the same time as he advanced on land and he would then move on to Setubal, which lies immediately south of Lisbon and from which place the entrance to Lisbon harbour can be controlled. He would then surround Lisbon on all sides; controlling the access from the sea would prevent the Portuguese and their English allies from reinforcing or supplying the city.

The Portuguese had failed once again to heed Schomberg's advice and had made few preparations, so that when the Spanish army's move across the Guardiana from Badajoz into Portugal began on 18 May 1665,[4] it met no organised resistance from the field force in Alentejo, which was heavily outnumbered. The Spanish army camped between Campo Maior and Elvas on 27 May and marched on another two leagues (11 kilometres, or 6 miles). The first place they entered was the small town of Borba, on the main road from Évora to Estremos. Its medieval fortifications were not capable of withstanding a determined assault and it had not therefore been garrisoned. The Spanish occupied it without resistance. Vila Viçosa lies just a few miles due south of Borba and by contrast, its fortress was well defended and offered stiff resistance to the attackers when the Spanish stormed it on 28 May; for although the lower town itself was not fortified – and was therefore also rapidly occupied, the fortress had very thick walls and had been much improved and modernised on Schomberg's advice, with five new demi-lune batteries mounting ten heavy bronze guns, several bastions and a covered way having been added.[5] The governor, Cristóvão de Brito Pereira, commanded 1,310 men formed into the *terzo* of *Maestro da Campo* Emanuel Lobato and the auxiliary *terzo* of Maestro da Campo Tomas de Estradas Zuniga, reinforced with a *terzo* from Tras-os-Montes under Francisco de Morais Henriques. With many inhabitants of the town, the garrison retreated to the fortress and there defied the attackers.[6]

The resistance of this small but tough fortress gave the Portuguese time to save themselves;[7] the Comte de St Jean, who had begun to organise the Portuguese troops in the north after the French manner, arrived at the head of 2,300 foot formed in four *terzos* and 670 horse in fourteen companies from the Tras-os-Montes to Alentejo. 2,400 foot in three *terzos* and 800 horse in ten companies came from Beira under Pedro Jaques de Magalhães. A further 2,500 foot, in the *terzos* of Casquais, Lisboa and the Armada, and 300 horse, came from the garrison of Lisbon, under command of Sebastião de Vasconcelos de Sousa António. With them came Don Luís de Meneses, one of the original conspirators of 1640 and the general who had beaten the Spanish in the Battle of the Lines of Elvas, six years earlier. Meneses was placed in nominal command of the army with Schomberg in actual command of a force which numbered altogether 13,500 foot and 5,500 horse, with ten guns. The English and French contingents, which provided more than 4,200 men or nearly 15 percent of the army – and 20 percent of the horse[8] – were called in from their dispersal areas up to 8 leagues (38 kilometres or 24 miles) away, when the whole force assembled at Estremos on 1 June.[9]

The Portuguese court issued order after order to relieve the fortress of Vila Viçosa and to risk a battle if that was the only way to preserve the place. Schomberg, who after personal reconnaissance during the previous years of campaigning, understood all the options and the ground around Vila Viçosa, decided that he would advance from the west as if to relieve the besieged garrison and in doing so, provoke Caracena into attacking him. The prominent, high rocky ridge near Montes Claros, dominating the landscape between Rio de Moinhos and Vila Viçosa,[10] offered the most favourable place to stand on the defensive and bring on a Spanish attack. Schomberg therefore ordered the general of the horse, Denis de Mello, to send the six Portuguese cavalry companies of the vanguard, with the English horse, ahead of the army in order to seize the ridge and

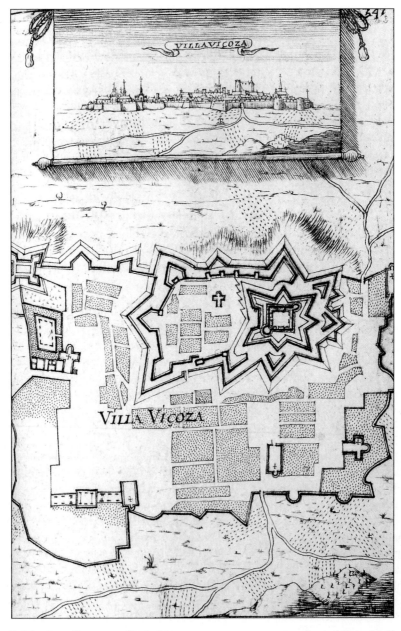

Map 14 The Fortifications of Vila Viçosa, contemporary map from Allain Mallet's *Les traveaux de Mars, ou l'art de la Guerre.* (Bavarian State Library)

from there, observe and report on the movements of the enemy. Six or eight prisoners were brought in, who reported the strength of the Spanish army as 6,000 horse and 12,000 foot.[11] Caracena, warned of the approach of the Portuguese army by his scouts, left a force of 1,800 men with most of his heavy guns to screen the besieged fortress and prevent a sortie by the garrison, and gave immediate orders for the rest of the army to move westwards with the aim of catching his enemy on the line of march.

The Spanish cavalry units sent out on reconnaissance made contact with the allied advanced guard on 6 June and so Caracena knew that Schomberg's objective must be the relief of Vila Viçosa. The battle was therefore a meeting engagement, the outcome of a race in which two forces with incomplete knowledge of each other collide. Victory goes to the side that best and fastest exploits the mistakes of the other in relation to the ground. Making sense of the engagement now, however, is becoming almost impossible. The reason why the ridge is so sharply prominent is its geology: it is made of marble: a metamorphic rock composed of limestone and dolomite that has been changed chemically as a result of movements in the earth's crust. This ridge was originally limestone, laid down on an ancient lake or sea bed, which had then been thrown and twisted through ninety degrees by violent epeirogenetic activity. The softer sedimentaries around it had been weathered away over the millennia that followed, exposing the hard, residual marble as a ridge. But marble is, of course, commercially valuable and large parts of the ridge of Montes Claros are now giant quarries, a scene of utter devastation that within a few years will wipe from the face of the earth, the site of the battle that secured Portugal's independence as a nation. No-one, it seems, cares.[12]

Figure 25 A modern photograph of the ridge of Montes Claros, as seen from the direction of Schomberg's advance. (A.M. Goulden)

The Portuguese and allied main army began to move very early on 7 June 1664, while it was still dark, so probably at about 3 o'clock in the morning. After a march of about 17 kilometres (12 miles), the army halted near several springs to water and to close up the rear-guard: it was now about 7 o'clock in the morning, and full day. Schomberg rode on with his staff to the advanced position on the ridge of Montes Claros. As he did so, ten Spanish cavalry squadrons debouched from a valley south and east of the ridge line; another ten followed and a short time later the enemy's whole body of horse could be seen advancing towards the intended Portuguese right flank in two lines, each of twenty-two squadrons, with accompanying light guns.[13] The first line was composed chiefly of Italian and German units under Alessandro Farnese, Prince of Parma,* the second line was Spanish commanded by Don Diego Correia.[14] Alessandro Farnese was an Italian general in the imperial Spanish service, who was later Governor of the Spanish Netherlands from 1678 until 1682. He is not to be confused with his better known great-grandfather Alexander Farnese, Duke of Parma.

Caracena knew the value of the position as well as Schomberg and was also, probably, intent on seizing it; why he had not done so already is hard to fathom. But on the Portuguese side, De Mello had not, as ordered, sent six companies to secure the position but only thirty men – thinking this sufficient. 'Yes,' said Schomberg, 'sufficient to have your head cut off, for you had your orders in writing.'[15] Schomberg therefore had barely time for a glance over the terrain and to secure his right flank, which was fixed on a deeply entrenched dry watercourse, by throwing into the walled court of a ruined mansion – now disappeared – several companies of Portuguese infantry with two guns; and to form the army in three lines – probably according to a pre-arranged plan.[16] Schomberg's left flank was covered and protected by vineyards and broken ground dissected by stone walls, to the east of a monastery known as the Convent of the Light – it is still there. The allied foot was in two divisions, each formed in three lines. In the left division, the two English and two of the French regiments were, as usual, stationed on the flank,[17] with two regular Portuguese *terzos* of Alentejo and four territorial *terzos*. In the right division were the remaining three territorial *terzos* and the Portuguese regular infantry of Lisboa, Tras-os-Montes and Beira.

Schomberg's first line of horse consisted of six companies of horse from Alentejo, six companies from Tras-os-Montes, His own guards, and all the English and French horse. The Portuguese were, as usual, greatly outnumbered and outclassed in cavalry and Schomberg was obliged to mix four infantry *terzos* with the second and third lines of Portuguese horse, a total of thirty-four companies, in order, as at Ameixial, to present a line of equal length and strength to the Spaniards so as to avoid being enveloped. He kept a reserve of six cavalry companies and four companies of infantry from the auxiliary *terzo* of Mourao, under António de Sequeira Pestano, and sent two cavalry companies to support the infantry on his left flank among the vineyards. To counter-balance the disparity in cavalry, the Portuguese were superior in numbers and quality of artillery – for it will be remembered that Caracena had left his heavy guns

---

*   Alessandro Farnese (1635–1689) was an Italian general in the imperial Spanish service who was Governor of the Spanish Netherlands from 1678 to 1682. He is not to be confused with his better-known great-grandfather Alexander Farnese, Duke of Parma. This Alessandro was often called Alessandro di Odoardo (son of Edward).

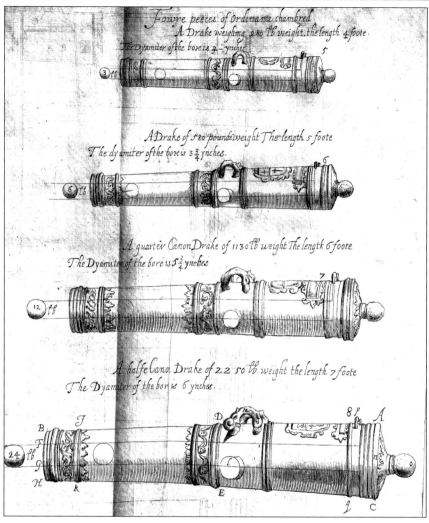

Fowre peeces of Ordinance chambred.
A Drake weighing 280 ℔ weight, the length 4 foote.
The Dyamiter of the bore is 3¼ ynches.

A Drake of 580 pound weight The length 5 foote.
The dyamiter of the bore is 3¾ ynches.

A quarter Canon Drake of 1130 ℔ weight The length 6 foote.
The Dyamiter of the bore is 5¾ ynches.

A halfe Canon Drake of 2250 ℔ weight the length 7 foote.
The Dyamiter of the bore is 6 ynches.

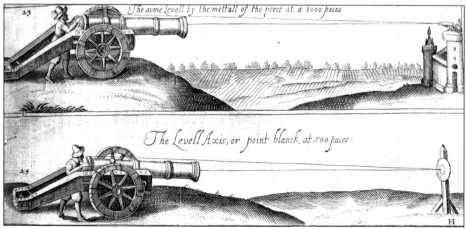

The avme levell by the mettall of the peece at a 1000 paces

The Levell Axis, or point blanck at 500 paces

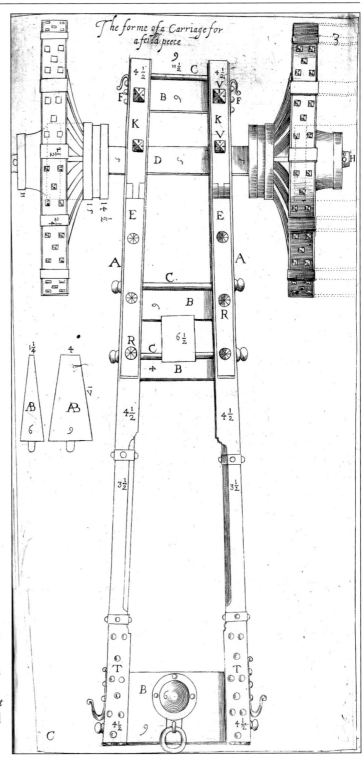

Figures 26 A, B, and C Contemporary illustrations of field artillery from Henry Hexham's *Principles of the Art Military.* (© Royal Armouries RAL. 08487)

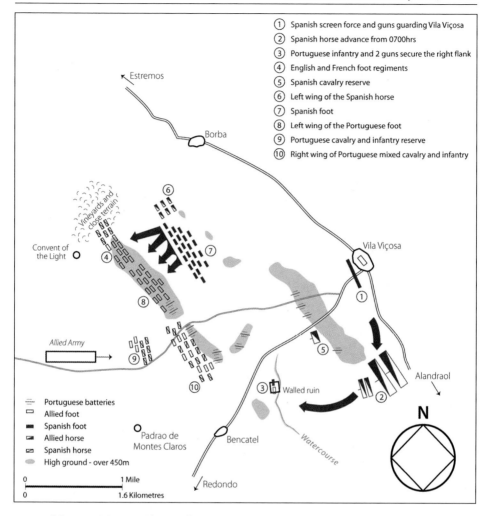

① Spanish screen force and guns guarding Vila Viçosa
② Spanish horse advance from 0700hrs
③ Portuguese infantry and 2 guns secure the right flank
④ English and French foot regiments
⑤ Spanish cavalry reserve
⑥ Left wing of the Spanish horse
⑦ Spanish foot
⑧ Left wing of the Portuguese foot
⑨ Portuguese cavalry and infantry reserve
⑩ Right wing of Portuguese mixed cavalry and infantry

Estremos

Borba

Vineyards and close terrain

Convent of the Light

Vila Viçosa

Allied Army

Alandraol

Portuguese batteries
Allied foot
Spanish foot
Allied horse
Spanish horse
High ground – over 450m

Padrao de Montes Claros

Walled ruin

Bencatel

Watercourse

N

0   1 Mile
0   1.6 Kilometres

Redondo

Map 15 Montes Claros, the opening moves, 07.00 to 10.00, 7 June 1665.

at Vila Viçosa, probably to speed the movement of his army. The Portuguese guns were deployed to fire in enfilade from high ground across the line of approach of the Spanish horse.

There are two illustrations of the battle that are close to being contemporary. One is a depiction on tiles in the Battle Room of the Palace of Fronteira in Lisbon; the other is an Italian engraving. Both are highly formalised affairs: the Italian engraving in particular gives few clues to the conduct of the battle other than the positioning of the Portuguese guns and their reserves; the rest is merely representative blocks of troops. The tile illustration is more helpful on the detail of combat in the 17th century: the tactics of the horse, the formations adopted by the foot, cavalry-on-cavalry action, the taking of prisoners, the drift of the faint-hearted away from the back of each army, the effect of heavy fire on a close formation – and even the attack by the English using clubbed muskets are all

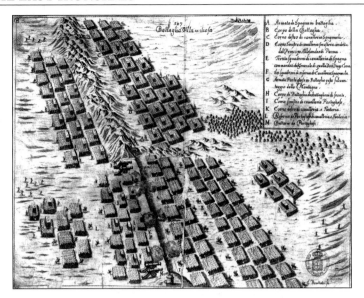

Figure 27 A contemporary illustration of the opening phase of
the battle of Montes Claros. (Author's collection)

there to be seen. The painters had either themselves been present at the battle or had been talked through the work of painting by others who had.

Caracena placed his command post on the Sierra de Vigario, which cannot now be identified from modern mapping and place names but it seems likely to have been the parallel ridge close to Vila Viçosa, where the road from Rio dos Moinhos crossed it. After leaving his screen force at Vila Viçosa, he fielded 13,000 foot and 7,000 horse. He opened the action not, as might have been thought, with his strongest and most manoeuvrable arm, the horse, but on his right, the Portuguese left, with a mass attack by Swiss and German infantry and the Spanish *tercios* of Castilla, the Armada and Guadalajara,[18] to clear the difficult terrain on the high ground above and among the vineyards. This attack met and at first drove back the English and French regiments and the auxiliary *tercio* of Évora which deployed with them. It was reported that the attack 'drove off some of Schomberg's French Regiment [i.e. most likely the German turncoats from Valencia de Alcantara] whom they had paid to run, but Lord Schomberg brought forward Portuguese foot from the reserve to take their place.' The remaining regiments rallied and the fighting was fierce for control of the stone walls that lay between the two forces, to the extent of throwing rocks and struggling at close quarters with sword and pike. Once again, the imperial troops could not tolerate the English way of using their discharged muskets as clubs at close quarters. According to the memoirs of d'Ablancourt, Schomberg's regiment faced a body of Swiss foot in desperate close combat, and in the push of pike the Swiss colonel killed the English lieutenant-colonel, to be himself killed by the English major, Netmore, 'overthrowing him with such a Blow as the other had given Lieutenant-Colonel Shelton … whereupon the English battalions at his example falling upon the Switzers with mighty shoutings, beat them back to their second line; which sustaining vigorously the attack, restored the fight.'[19] Schomberg had succeeded to the colonelcy of Moore's Regiment and the dead lieutenant-colonel was therefore William Sheldon, royalist veteran of both Civil Wars and many battles in England; the major could not however have been Wetmore (rather than Netmore), since he had been killed at Valencia de Alcantara, but Lawrence Dempsey.

The first line of the Spanish horse was now ordered to attack the centre and right wing of the allied army, seeking to cut Schomberg's foot from the horse and destroy the army in detail. Schomberg at once saw Caracena's intention and ordered the two detached companies of Portuguese horse from left flank to reinforce the main body of the horse. He also rode among the Portuguese infantry, spoke to the soldiers, encouraged them and even demonstrated how best to employ the pike against cavalry.[20] Maynard reported that:

> The English horse and three regiments of French commanded by the younger Schomberg [i.e. Frederick], the Conde de Maria and Monsieur Brickmore [i.e. Briquemaut] … could hardly come to our ground before our first two lines [of horse] were routed – the first were Portuguese commanded by the Conde de St John's, and Lord Schomberg's Life Guard … came back in great disorder and confusion and some fled as far as Estremos.

This was the action by the Imperial Cuirassiers of Rabat, eight full squadrons strong, supported by the Italian regiments of Chalais and Fabri and the *trozo* of Extremadura, which pushed back the Portuguese first line of horse who broke and fled along the road towards Estremos. They were followed by much of the Portuguese second line, some of whom rallied behind the infantry. More than 1,000 Portuguese horse were thus dispersed by the shock of the Spanish attack, telling all as they went that the battle was lost and precipitating the flight of the baggage train back to Estremos.

> The first onset the Spaniards gave was so home, that they beat the first and second line into the rear; in such disorder, that divers of them never stayed till they came to Estremos, and gave the field for lost.[21]

What was not known until afterwards was that in spite of the success of the Spanish attack, the colonel commanding the *trozo* of Rabat had been killed. Fortunately for the allies, the Portuguese infantry held its ground where the horse had fled and the Spanish cavalry could not pierce its pike squares. This provided time for what remained of the allied cavalry to counter-charge the Spanish and restore the position. Heading this charge were the English, divided into three troops each of about 100 men 'all in buff coats,' led by Schomberg's son Frederick: 'After which that division where the English were, charged the Spaniard, and beat them back to their first ground, keeping also what they had gotten'.[22] Schomberg also ordered the two regiments of Maret and Briquemaut (re-formed after their mauling the year before), which were to the right and left of the English horse, to fall on the flanks of the enemy's cuirassiers, while the English took on their centre: 'no man could or would have charged with greater courage than they did, against one of those regiments that was Prince Rupert's when he served in Germany, their colours given by him were taken.'[23]

The English and French, and such Portuguese horse as had held together, found themselves under heavy pressure. One account describes repeated attacks by squadrons of Spanish horse, riding up and firing, retiring while new squadrons appeared from the smoke and fired in their turn.[24] The Spanish horse actually succeeded in penetrating the third line at one point, even sending bodies of horse to pursue the fleeing Portuguese for a time, but then they rallied at a trumpet call and rejoined their infantry: a manoeuvre which astonished the Portuguese by its discipline and timing. However it was the very success of the Spanish cavalry attack by the regiments of Rabat, Extremadura, Chalais and Fabri which ironically was the cause of the battle being lost, by depriving the Prince of Parma of the means to break the resistance of the rest of the Portuguese line which

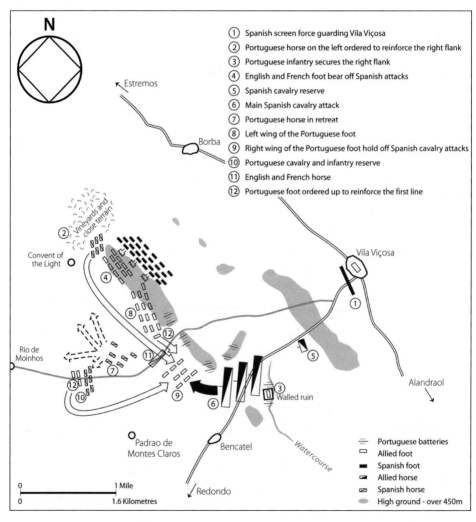

N

① Spanish screen force guarding Vila Viçosa
② Portuguese horse on the left ordered to reinforce the right flank
③ Portuguese infantry secures the right flank
④ English and French foot bear off Spanish attacks
⑤ Spanish cavalry reserve
⑥ Main Spanish cavalry attack
⑦ Portuguese horse in retreat
⑧ Left wing of the Portuguese foot
⑨ Right wing of the Portuguese foot hold off Spanish cavalry attacks
⑩ Portuguese cavalry and infantry reserve
⑪ English and French horse
⑫ Portuguese foot ordered up to reinforce the first line

Estremos

Borba

Convent of the Light

Vineyards and close terrain

Vila Viçosa

Rio de Moinhos

Alandraol

Padrao de Montes Claros

Bencatel

Walled ruin

Watercourse

Redondo

0   1 Mile
0   1.6 Kilometres

Portuguese batteries
Allied foot
Spanish foot
Allied horse
Spanish horse
High ground - over 450m

Map 16 Montes Claros, the attritional phase, 10.00 to 15.00, 7 June 1665.

still resisted. The force ratio between the foot of the two armies was far more even than that of the two bodies of horse and a combined arms attack by the Spanish against the Portuguese or allied foot might well have been enough to turn the tide – as it was, there was near stalemate in the centre and north of the position – the Portuguese left – and a success that could not be exploited in the south.

To restore matters in the south, his right, Schomberg ordered up a reinforcement of four companies of infantry held in reserve under the Conde de Ericeira, along with his own guards and the Comte de St-Jean's guards. These troops, joining what remained of the Portuguese infantry on the right, provided just enough strength to re-form the line. The Portuguese generals who commanded in the centre, meanwhile, grew anxious and ready to break off the action: a number had already fled with the horse and were spreading alarm as far as Estremos. Marialva sent word to Schomberg that his troops could no longer endure the Spanish fire; to which Schomberg replied that he now intended to attack the depleted Spanish cavalry, whose momentum had been halted and, once it was broken, the defeat of their infantry would be an easy matter.[25]

It was now about 3 o'clock in the afternoon and after seven hours of hard fighting the allies had begun to gain the upper hand. The Portuguese and allied front consisted of, from left to right, the English and French foot; the bulk of the Portuguese foot; and those *terzos* of foot that had remained after the flight of the Portuguese horse, reinforced by the reserve companies and the guards. Behind them on the right were six companies of Portuguese horse and the English and French horse: barely two lines in the accepted sense of a battlefield layout of the day. These two lines were ordered forward together. What was left of the first line of the Spanish horse, commanded by the Duke of Parma, was so closely engaged that the second line under Don Diego Correa had to be committed to its support, but Schomberg kept up the pressure company by company, regiment by regiment. With much of the Spanish horse neutralised, Schomberg was able to make a penetration between them and the bulk of the Spanish infantry. By wheeling the main body of his Portuguese *terzos* to the left, pivoting on the English and French foot, and supported by the fire of the powerful Portuguese artillery, carefully sited on high ground as it was, he was able to do what Caracena had sought to do, but had failed – that is, split his enemy and destroy the different parts of Caracena's army in detail as it lost its cohesion and its ability to receive and execute the orders of its commander.

The Spanish reserve cavalry, which had been held back near Caracena's command post, now tried to make its way forward along the road through a narrow valley among olive groves at the foot of Montes Claros, 'with order and resolution'. This was an intelligent move, as they would have fallen on the exposed right flank of the Portuguese foot as they wheeled. Seeing this, Schomberg ordered the four detached companies on the right to rejoin their *terzos* in the centre to strengthen the line and then turned his cavalry, under Don Denis de Mello, to fall on the rear of the Spanish horse as they came forward. The shock of this attack was so sudden and unexpected, that it transformed the advance of the Spanish horse into a disorderly rout. The attack was led by the English and French horse which according to the official report:

> so encouraged the rest, that they came again with a fresh body, as at first, with other French battalions, and then the English charged again with the same success

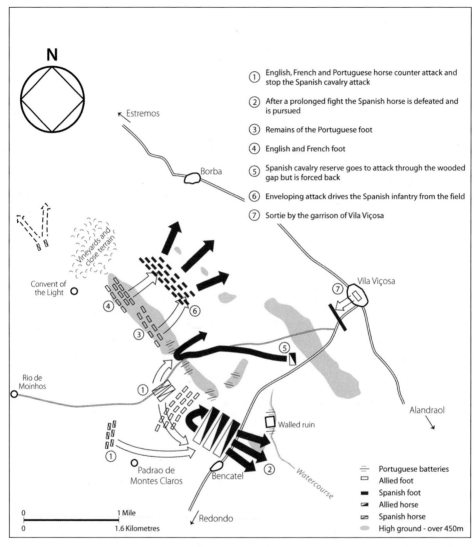

N

① English, French and Portuguese horse counter attack and stop the Spanish cavalry attack

② After a prolonged fight the Spanish horse is defeated and is pursued

③ Remains of the Portuguese foot

④ English and French foot

⑤ Spanish cavalry reserve goes to attack through the wooded gap but is forced back

⑥ Enveloping attack drives the Spanish infantry from the field

⑦ Sortie by the garrison of Vila Viçosa

Estremos

Borba

Vineyards and close terrain

Convent of the Light

Vila Viçosa

Rio de Moinhos

Alandraol

Walled ruin

Padrao de Montes Claros

Bencatel

Watercourse

Portuguese batteries

Allied foot

Spanish foot

Allied horse

Spanish horse

High ground - over 450m

0   1 Mile

0   1.6 Kilometres

Redondo

Map 17 Montes Claros, the decisive phase.

as before, and forced the enemy to clear the field. Major Trelawny had the fortune to charge the Prince of Parma, who was in the head of his own battalia, killed most of his men, and brought off his standard, which is sent to Lisbon.[26]

This attack led by the English caused complete disorder. Correa himself was unhorsed and captured. Schomberg's horse was shot from underneath him; one account says that he engaged in personal combat with the Prince of Parma and was in imminent danger of being killed, however the prince's sword was shattered on the cuirass he wore under his uniform coat. This may however be more romance than reality.

There was nothing now to prevent the envelopment of the Spanish foot. Some units retreated into the parkland of Vila Viçiosa, where Colonel Chauvet and Major Francis Moreneur, who had stepped up to take Apsley's place, followed with their regiments, cutting the fleeing troops to pieces, and taking forty-five Colours.[27] At that moment, the garrison of Vila Viçosa made a sudden sortie against the Spanish troops left by Caracena to mask the fortress, seizing the Spanish guns around the town and taking many prisoners. Four *tercios* who had concentrated in the closer terrain of the Spanish right flank were surrounded and surrendered. The rest of the Spanish army disintegrated and as it broke up and fled in disorder, it abandoned all its artillery and many dead, wounded and prisoners: the captives included twenty-one grandees and senior officers, fifty-nine junior officers, sixty-two sergeants, eighteen adjutants and quartermasters, two surgeons, forty-two reformadoes and 6,000 soldiers.[28] When the 4,000 dead were added, the total Spanish losses in killed, wounded and prisoners amounted to 10,000 men in total, or half the force, along with fourteen guns and two heavy siege mortars and the staggering total of 600 carts and 200 wagons, loaded with quantities of powder and shot, muskets and pikes.[29] The Spanish also lost 3,500 valuable horses, which were then distributed to various commands around Portugal; and finally eighty infantry Colours and fourteen cavalry Standards. On the following day, 8 June, 'all the captured Colours, Standards and spontoons of the officers were placed as a trophy before Schomberg's tent and he was woken with shouts of victory and the noise of drums, cymbals and trumpets.'[30] As one newspaper put it: 'This victory is much greater than that two years since, the general of the horse being taken, and divers other general officers, with 5,000 prisoners, and 3,000 killed, all their baggage, seven guns, and 3,000 mules.'[31]

Caracena managed to make good his own escape to Jerumenha with what remained of the horse. This remnant was only saved from annihilation by the fact that the Portuguese and allied army was so exhausted by more than seven hours of battle that it was in no state to pursue its beaten enemy.[32] Even the planned naval manoeuvre against Lisbon turned out to have been a failure, as the fleet had not been able to sail in time – it did sail, but did not reach Lisbon until after the defeat at Montes Claros became known and was immediately recalled.[33]

The Portuguese army suffered about 1,500 dead and wounded. The English casualties were bad but not catastrophic, but the cumulative total of their losses during the course of the war was now such that according to Maynard, 'the English [foot] are not 800 fighting men.'[34] In Schomberg's Regiment of Foot, the dead included Lieutenant-Colonel William Sheldon, Captain Francis Stansby, Lieutenant John Jones, Ensign Watkins and fifty-four soldiers. The wounded included Colonel Francis Moore, Captain John Sandys, Lieutenant Sherwood, Lieutenant George Sandys, Ensign Emerson and sixty soldiers. In Pearson's Regiment, those killed included Captain Heathfield, Captain Charles Serres and Ensign Summers, along with forty-eight soldiers. The wounded included Captain-Lieutenant Newsome, Ensign Berry and fifty soldiers. Losses were lighter in the horse, with only Captain John Rust, three corporals and ten men killed; Cornet Samuel Sharpe and twenty men were wounded.

Lavish praise was again heaped on the English brigade, for it was believed that their example had saved the day when many Portuguese officers had been slinking back to Estremos. Maynard, the English consul, wrote that:

The Conde [Castelo Melhor] fair promises that they shall speedily have some monies, and I believe if the Conde knew where to procure it, he would not keep it an hour from them, being, he tells me every day, that never did soldiers deserve to be better paid than the English troops. The Marquis de Marialva told me about a week since, that no prince in the world had so stout men in the field, nor so civil in their garrisons, as the English in the service of this Crown. Their gallant comportment hath induced the King of Portugal to desire recruits from his Majesty to fill up the two foot regiments, which orders the Ambassador carries with him.[35]

This was just as well, for in spite of Clarendon's threat to withdraw them, life for the English had not changed much for the better in the past year: Thomas Maynard had written that 'The soldiers are very much discontented and ... declare against this service.' Pay was still seven months in arrears and there was no food for the horses but 'rotten shipp wheat'.

*   *   *

Shortly after the battle of Montes Claros, the Portuguese re-entered the liberated Vila Viçosa, where a council of war was convened. Schomberg proposed marching immediately to catch the remnants of the enemy as they passed the Guardiana and thus complete their destruction,[36] but his advice was rejected on the excuse that there was insufficient food and transport to sustain the advance. The majority demanded a move to Estremos: the heat of summer was now coming on and this effectively prevented another movement until September; moreover the Comte de St-Jean was sent back to Beira with his contingent, which significantly reduced the combat power of the army.

The war was still not over, but it was now effectively won: Montes Claros therefore deserves the much-misused title of decisive battle. Decisive battles fall into two broad categories: first, there are battles that mark the end of an era in warfare. Such battles usually bring the termination of a campaign and with it, the end of a period of total war, war from which only one side can expect to emerge with its political system, or its territory, or its economy – or a combination of these – intact. In the aftermath of such a battle, both sides recognise that a decision has been reached and agree on the resolution of the conflict – usually on terms favourable to the victor. Battles that bring cease-fires, or treaties that temporarily settle disputes, again cannot be classed as decisive in this way. It would be tempting to see Montes Claros in this guise – tempting, but wrong: for Imperial Spain did not cease to exist as a result of its defeat by Portugal.

Secondly, there are battles which, on their conclusion, and probably with the benefit of hindsight, either mark the point at which a campaign changes direction, or mark the passing of the initiative from one side to the other, as one side reaches its culminating point. From this point onwards, the side holding and maintaining the initiative moves towards its inevitable victory. These battles tell us at least something about the changing dynamic between the decision to make war, battle, and conflict termination or resolution: it is in this class of decisive battles that Montes Claros belongs:[37] for it is not enough that a battle merely achieves operational objectives – like Ameixial – that alone does not make it decisive. The other side of this coin is the Pyrrhic victory, a battle won at such cost that it may cause the winners to seek compromise, or otherwise modify their objectives. Thus the context of a decisive battle is not only its place within a campaign, but its relation to strategy, which can be defined very simply as the attainment of national or alliance objectives using all such ways and means as are available, appropriate and legal. It is about a state's external political objectives, its relations with other powers, and the coupling of security issues with the organisation of the state in all its facets to ensure that its objectives can be met either through its own exertions or else through alliance.

The effect on the Spanish brought about by the defeat of Montes Claros, or Vila Viçosa as it was known in Spain, was cataclysmic. Philip IV received the news in a state of shock, shame and grief on 20 June, a state from which he never recovered. He died on Thursday 7 September 'having been sick but four days of a flux and a fever.'[38] His young son Carlos was immediately proclaimed king.

10

Taking the War into Spain, Autumn 1665

'Within cannon shot'

When the news of King Philip's death arrived in Lisbon in early September, Schomberg determined to exploit the confusion and inertia that was bound to follow, keeping up the pressure on the Spanish armies in order to retain the initiative he had gained at Montes Claros. He therefore assembled a force at Campo Maior, which consisted of 1,500 horse, including the English; Pearson's Regiment of Foot with two companies from Moore's Regiment – those of Captains Charles Love and Andrew Maynard; and the whole of the French brigade. Given the size of the force, this was more of a large-scale raid than a campaign. Schomberg marched for the Spanish border just north of Badajoz, which he by-passed, before rejoining the main eastward road through the village of Talavera and on to the town of Merida, the provincial capital of Extremadura.

On the Spanish side, Caracena had remained in command on the frontier in Extremadura after the defeat of Montes Claros, presumably because there was no other general either able or willing to take his place. Even so his health, after a lifetime of campaigning, was not good: he died in Madrid of an old wound in 1668.[1] At about the same time that Schomberg and his troops entered Spain, Caracena had sent the Prince of Parma with 1,800 men on a raid to Barbacena, near Elvas. The two expeditions passed each other at some distance and only subsequently learned of each other's presence. Caracena immediately halted Parma, reinforced him with his own regiment of horse guards, formed into ten companies, and ordered him to intercept Schomberg's likely withdrawal route back across the Xévora River to Campo Maior, on the border between Portugal and Spain. Schomberg had sent out two reconnaissance parties, one of which brought him accurate news and he was therefore able to avoid the planned ambush: the little allied army made a forced march back to the river and had barely completed the crossing when the Spanish horse appeared.[2] However, the Spanish foot were some way behind and there was considerable disagreement among the senior Spanish officers about whether to attack or not. Sensing their lack of resolution, Schomberg formed his troops and attacked first, throwing the Spanish horse into confusion and then falling on the infantry as they came up but before they could deploy from the line of march. 300 Spanish horse and most of the infantry surrendered and were brought into Elvas; the remainder fell back to the fort of St Christopher, one of the outworks of Badajoz, pursued by the English and French horse. After a short skirmish on the perimeter, the pursuit was broken off.[3]

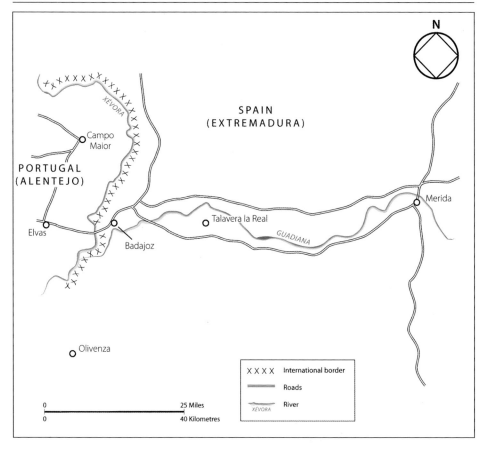

Map 18 Schomberg's raid into Extremadura, Autumn 1665.

*   *   *

Meneses too was determined not to waste the opportunity provided by the victory of Montes Claros and the death of Philip of Spain, for the Spanish field army had all but ceased to exist and the Portuguese could, for the first time, move to an offensive operational posture. Schomberg was ordered back to Lisbon for a council of war and here, the Conde de Prado,* governor of the northern province of Minho, laid out a proposal to take the war across the northern frontier of Portugal, into Spanish Galicia. The proposed objective was the fortified town of Tuy, on the Minho River opposite the Portuguese town of Valença. Tuy had been fortified since the 12th century and although

---

* Luis de Sousa, 4th Conde de Prado and 2nd Marquis de Mines (1644–1721) was a Portuguese general and later Governor-General of Brazil.

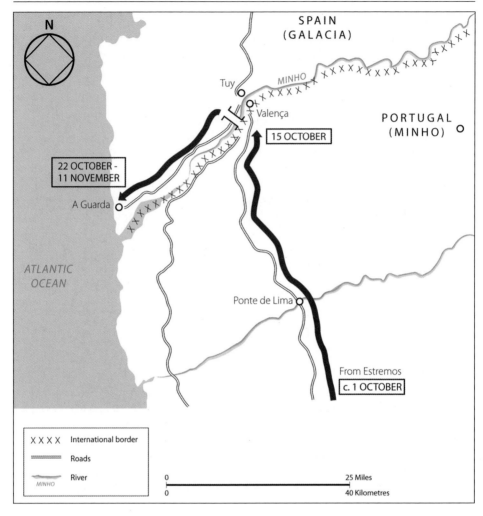

Map 19 Schomberg's campaign in Galicia, autumn 1665.

its fortifications had not been extensively modernised, the walls were thick and the castle well garrisoned. The armies in Alentejo and Beira were to be assembled for this purpose: 'In the custom of Portugal, the governor had the right to command all troops in his province but he was unable to get anything done,'[4] and therefore the command again devolved on Schomberg, who objected to the proposed plan: Tuy, he believed, was far too strongly held.[5] However political pressure carried the day and the expedition went ahead.

This campaign would require a considerable effort of marching, and of logistic support for the troops. On campaign, unburdened men in small parties could comfortably cover 32 kilometres (20 miles) per day, although the averages on the Spanish Road, for example, were rather less.[6] Cavalry could move faster of course, from 40 to 48 kilometres

(27 to 31 miles) per day on raids or forced marches. However for large bodies of troops accompanied by wagon and artillery trains, 12 to 15 kilometres (7 to 9 miles) was more usual. An army of up to 30,000 people including its baggage train and camp followers, moving on one road, would form a column about eight miles in length, and take about six hours to march past a single point. It was thus the pass time that really determined how far the army would march each day without becoming too strung out or having to re-assemble in the dark rather than the speed that the infantry or cavalry could achieve.[7] Of course the army could march dispersed, on several routes, to move more quickly and make better use of forage. However, in Europe generally and in Portugal in particular, roads were few and bad and more than one route just might not exist. Moreover an army that marched dispersed before the days of radio communication risked being brought to battle dispersed – and therefore on unfavourable terms.

A major difficulty for commanders in these marches was the losses from straggling and desertion. Even in the early 19th century, James Dunnigan in his work on Leipzig,[8] for example, calculated that a Napoleonic corps could lose 80 percent of its fighting strength over a period of months through sickness, disease, desertion, and straggling without firing a shot. Since the human body did not undergo any evolutionary change between 1600 and 1800, we can assume these figures are transferable. This problem was compounded by the troops' urge to take leave of absence – armies had no regular leave system at this period and permits for leave were issued only to officers or reformadoes. In The Spanish Army of Flanders, for example, between 1582 and 1586 only 854 leave passes were issued, while the total losses were 11,570 – the balance either died or deserted.[9] In Iberia, desertion was an endemic problem as both sides relied on locally recruited forces and militias: these soldiers were far more interested in remaining at or near home to defend their families and farms and take part in harvest, than in undertaking expeditionary operations. Even foreign troops were prone to desertion if pay was not forthcoming – as the English troops had demonstrated in 1662 and early 1663.

The further an army marched from its ports or bases, the longer the line of supply and the more reliant it became on local resources. The acreage for foraging cited earlier assumes that the army kept moving: the problem came when movement stopped and the army reached its intended destination, for example to undertake a siege, or when it went into winter quarters. Here, the first resource to be exhausted would be fodder and this explains why armies dispersed widely when in quarters and if possible, exported the problems and costs of feeding an army by living off the enemy's territory. The logistic requirements of the army of Alentejo, for example, were 20,000 ration loaves per day and 6,000 portions of barley for the horses and mules. Over a period of thirty days, the cost of this would be 116,550 *cruzadoes*; when the pay of the troops was added, the total requirement was 213,928 *cruzadoes* per month.[10]

Schomberg sent word to Estremos for the two English regiments of foot, the German regiment of Clairin and all the available troops of English and French horse, to assemble and march north. It is 340 kilometres (200 miles) from Estremos to the northern frontier, or about fifteen days' march. It was 19 October before Schomberg's force reached the Minho River and there he made rendezvous with the Portuguese army in the north, under Prado, bringing the total strength of the army to 13,500 – 'betwixt 10 and 11000 Foot, and 2500 Horse, of the best Troops in the Kingdom.'[11] The river at that time was not bridged and was too deep to ford – the usual method of crossing was by ferry. Schomberg therefore established a pontoon bridge. This was Roman river-crossing technology, using tethered boats with a plank walkway built across them, which was still in use and is still used today, for only since the Second World War has technology developed mechanical alternatives to this tried and tested method. The chosen crossing site was four leagues (20 kilometres or 12 miles) downstream from Tuy,[12] well out of sight of the place and far enough away so as not to expose the force to an attack from the town as it crossed: for as Schomberg had predicted, the Spanish were strongly established in the town under the command of the Captain-General of Galicia, Don Luis Podrigo (or Poderico), who had 6,000 foot in the fortress and 1,500 horse quartered nearby.

Podrigo had decided not to try to seek battle, but to hold his position and therefore made no serious move to interfere with the river crossing. He did send out two squadrons of horse, which were chased back into Tuy by Prado's men. Prado then called a council of war and, having considered the relative strengths of the forces, the supply situation and the time of year, decided not to attempt a siege. Schomberg straightaway decided, in order 'that the Trouble and Expences of the Expedition might not altogether be in Vain',[13] he would invade the country anyway and capture La Baionia, from where he could threaten the major port of Vigo, whose defences were in such poor condition that it could be taken in a siege of only three or four days. If Vigo were taken, the army could be supplied by sea directly from France thus avoiding the long haul by wagon trains across the mountainous country of northern Iberia.

Schomberg therefore decided to leave a guard force at his bridging site – probably made up chiefly of the horse – to secure his line of communication and mask Tuy. The remainder of the army marched through the valleys of Rozal and Mignora. On the fourth day, they passed within a mile of La Baionia and two days later, camped 9 kilometres (6 miles) from Vigo. That night, Schomberg took 500 of the horse and the same number of foot and made an armed reconnaissance to the outskirts of the port, where they plundered several ships containing sugar, spices, cloth and silver ingots.[14] Pushing on to Vigo itself, he found it even more dilapidated than had been reported. When he returned to the camp, he asked for the council of war to be assembled to confirm that Vigo should be seized: the Spanish were sitting tight in Tuy and in any case they were preoccupied with the death of their king. There was no risk. The Conde de Prado, however – the man who had in the first place urged the expedition – had made up his mind that the thing was too difficult. He put forward a string of objections, in spite of which the army actually began to march on Vigo. Even as they marched, Prado continued his objections: there was no bread, the roads were bad, there was not enough artillery, and the draught animals were worn out. In disgust, the officers of the English regiments offered to take the place unsupported but Prado, who in the last analysis held the command as governor of Beira, insisted that the army be diverted to the Spanish supply base of Poligono in order to replenish the food supply for the army. On arrival, however, it was found that the garrison of Tuy had already stripped the place bare. Schomberg considered marching further north, to Pontevedra, about 8 kilometres (12 miles) away, where as well as gathering a large store of plunder, an insurrection might have been ignited which would detach Galicia from Spain and join it to the Crown of Portugal. However Prado, again, could not summon up the courage and withdrew his troops back in to Portugal.

Schomberg could not in honour leave Galicia without accomplishing something. He therefore proposed that he would capture the town of A Guarda and its castle of Santa Cruz, sited on a height 350 metres (1,000 feet) above the town. A Guarda is located at the extreme south-western tip of Galicia where the Minho River reaches the Atlantic Ocean, controlling river traffic upstream and providing a sheltered harbour for resupply by sea. The fortifications had been rapidly modernised during 1663 by two German engineers in the Spanish service, Carlos and Fernando Grunemberg, and certified as complete by Podrigo on 12 May 1664.[15] The place was held by 2,400 Spanish troops under the command of its governor, Jorge de Madureira. Of these, about 500 were local auxiliaries and the rest, regular Spanish troops. Grudgingly, Prado agreed.

On 22 October, the little allied army was 'within cannon shot' of A Guarda and the siege was begun at once.[16] Although the fortifications were in good condition and the garrison at a reasonable strength, the supply situation inside the castle was not good. Madureira wrote to Don Luis Podrigo:

> I asked repeatedly for what was necessary for the place: troops, ammunition, guns and other necessities ... all I received was a small amount of powder and ball, so that by November 11th, I had only one hundred and forty pounds of powder [i.e. enough for seventy men for a single day's fighting at normal rates of expenditure, using the figures cited in Chapter 3] and a small quantity of shot ... by night I had ordered parties to search for spent bullets from the enemy's fire which had fallen in the streets and squares, for which I paid cash, thus melting down the lead and making a few artillery shells and musket balls.[17]

On the sixth day of investment, 28 October, the English foot regiments with the Portuguese *terzo* of the Conde de Athalias were ordered to storm the outworks in the vanguard of the army; this they did with little loss – not surprising given the evident lack of ammunition among the defenders – the Spanish garrison having abandoned the town along with all the women and children to the mercy of the attackers – 'whom the English, as much as lay in their power, protected from all kinds of Injury'[18] – and retreated into the Castle of Santa Cruz. On 7 November, the English were ordered to storm the castle, 'which they performed with all imaginable gallantry', but without being able to break in. Schomberg, realising that this was too tough a nut to crack, called off the attack[19] – hardly surprising given the defences of the castle and the fact that Schomberg had neither siege guns nor engineers. The English lost Captain Charles Langly, Lieutenant Senhouse and Ensign Berry – who had been wounded at Montes Claros – and twenty-seven soldiers killed; Captain Love and twenty soldiers were wounded.

Mining operations were stepped up, however, and four days later, on 11 November, the Spanish garrison asked for a parley. After another two days, the castle surrendered.[20] The garrison marched out with honours of war, most of the regulars went to La Baionia, but the governor, 600 regulars and 500 auxiliaries were escorted to Tuy,[21] leaving all their 200 horses in Schomberg's hands. Two persons were allowed to be masked, indicating that they were probably Portuguese renegadoes who feared reprisal. A Guarda remained in Portuguese hands for the next three years and the northern frontier on both sides of the Minho River was secure: for the Spanish evacuated the garrison of Tuy, which was in danger of being encircled. Schomberg's troops withdrew, having 'sacked and burned 24 towns and many gentlemen's houses':[22] the description 'towns' probably included a good many villages and large farms.

While Schomberg's troops were away in the north, Caracena was able to raid into Alentejo by way of Vila Viçosa and his troops captured the town of Moura on the southern border of Alentejo, which he garrisoned. From there he burned farms and villages, including Veiros and Fronteira further north. Once word was received that the Army of Alentejo was returning, Caracena evacuated the province carrying a great deal of booty – but far less than that taken in Galicia – for in any case the coming of the winter rains made further campaigning impractical. Once Schomberg and the allied troops had returned, Moura was retaken after only four days.[23]

* * *

Meanwhile, the English ambassador to both courts, Sir Richard Fanshawe, had for some time been engaged in negotiations for a general settlement with the Spanish government. In January 1666 he had even agreed terms for a treaty of peace between England and Spain and a truce of thirty years between Spain and Portugal – this being subject to signature and ratification by all the parties involved including England. However Lady Fanshawe was convinced that Clarendon hated her husband and was determined to oust him and replace him with the Earl of Sandwich. English ministers, she said, had had the papers submitted by her husband for five months and that far from demurring, they were determined to conclude the war but that 'room was left in the league' to amend the draft.[24] Whatever the truth, the proposed terms of this treaty brought disfavour on Fanshawe on the grounds that various clauses were detrimental to English trade interests. His recall was mooted: surely a shameful episode after his long and devoted efforts in Iberia, but in the end nothing was done to bring matters to a head due to the outbreak of the great plague in London.

Throughout Fanshawe's negotiations, the Spaniards had stubbornly resisted any recognition of Portuguese independence until December, 1665. However the Portuguese and allied victories during 1665 no doubt contributed strongly to the Spanish change of face; but no doubt, too, the decision to come to terms was prompted by the death of Philip IV and alarm at Louis XIV's intentions towards the Spanish Netherlands once she declared war on England in accordance with her treaty to support the Dutch Republic. Spain could no longer afford the drain of the Portuguese war – especially because it looked certain that it was a lost war. On 6 January 1666, Fanshawe left Madrid for Portugal, returning on 8 March. When he returned to Lisbon he found Sir Robert Southwell, Secretary of State for Ireland – who had arrived on 16 January having been appointed as the personal envoy of Charles II to the courts of Spain and Portugal – charged with negotiating a final peace settlement.[25] Fanshawe had many friends at the Spanish court, who trusted his ability to bring about a resolution to the war, and the arrival of Southwell was not well received by them. But it was now the turn of the Portuguese to be obstinate. With French support, the Portuguese rejected Fanshawe's proposals and to break the deadlock, on 26 March 1666 Clarendon announced of the appointment of the Earl of Sandwich as extraordinary ambassador to Spain. He arrived in Madrid on 18 May 1666, with letters revoking Fanshawe's embassy.[26] On 5 June, Fanshawe fell ill and on 16th he died, just fifteen days before he was to return to England.[27]

11

The Campaigns of 1666–1667

'disgusts betwixt them and the Court'

War, as Karl von Clausewitz later remarked in a much mis-quoted passage, is not merely an act of policy but a true political instrument, a continuation of political intercourse, carried on with the addition of other means.[1] He was clear that political dialogue through diplomacy never ceased during hostilities, but interacted with them. 150 years earlier, Castelo Melhor had already been busy proving that this was a timeless principle. In early 1666 he made a further attempt to realise the long-cherished Portuguese dream of establishing an alliance with France, by arranging for Alfonso VI to marry Marie de Nemours,* the younger daughter of Charles Amadeus, Duke of Nemours,† a French soldier who had served in the Fronde and in Flanders. However, this marriage did not long endure: a year later, Marie Françoise petitioned for an annulment of her marriage on the grounds of the king's impotence, a petition which was granted by the Holy See – the papacy being still less inclined to favour Portugal than either France or Spain.

As if matters were not already complicated enough, there were developments between Portugal's allies England and France; and between England and Spain with Portugal's enemy, the Dutch Republic, all of which had an impact on the war in Iberia. In England the Secretary of State, Sir Henry Bennet, Lord Arlington,‡ who had been the king's envoy to Madrid during his exile and who had usurped somewhat the place of Clarendon in Charles II's favour, began moves in cooperation with James, Duke of York, the Lord High Admiral, aimed at war with the Dutch – from which both expected great personal gain. In particular James, as head of the Royal African Company, was intent on seizing the possessions of the Dutch West India Company. They were supported by the English ambassador in The Hague, the Anglo-Irish soldier and diplomat Sir George Downing,§ who hated the Dutch and told James that the monarchist Orange faction would collaborate with the English in case of war against the republican, mercantile, States faction. Arlington planned not only to defeat the Dutch militarily, but also to occupy the key Dutch cities of Amsterdam and Rotterdam. As enthusiasm for war rose among the

---

* Marie Françoise Élisabeth de Nemours (1646–1683), Princess of Savoy, daughter of Charles Amadeus and Élisabeth de Bourbon.
† Charles Amadeus, Prince of Savoy, Duke of Nemours (1624–1652).
‡ Sir Henry Bennet KG PC, Baron Arlington (1664) and later 1st Earl of Arlington (1618–1685), became Secretary of State in 1662.
§ Sir George Downing, 1st Baronet (1623–1684). Downing Street in London is named after him. He was largely instrumental in the acquisition of New Amsterdam – later New York – by the English.

English navy and the general population, English privateers began to attack Dutch ships. To provoke open war, James sent Admiral Sir Robert Holmes,* of the Royal African Company, to capture Dutch trading posts and colonies in West Africa. On 14 June 1664, the English also attacked and captured New Holland (later New York) in North America. The Dutch fleet under Michael de Ruyter,† however, recaptured their African trading stations, took most of the English posts there and then crossed the Atlantic for a punitive expedition against the English in America. In December 1664, the English made an unsuccessful attack on the Dutch Smyrna trading fleet. The fleet was again attacked outside Calais on 16 January 1665 by a squadron of seven ships under Captain Thomas Allin,‡ which sank two Dutch ships and captured another two from a fleet of three men-o'-war and eleven merchantmen.[2] On the following 21 February 1665, Charles II formally declared war.

The Dutch were ready: after their defeat in the First Anglo-Dutch War, the Dutch had constructed new, heavy warships with professional captains. In early 1664, when war threatened, still heavier ships were built. Upon the outbreak of war, the Dutch possessed four new ships of the line and were building at a faster rate than the English, for although their population was smaller, their economy was far stronger. The outbreak of war was followed ominously for the English by the coming of plague and then by the Great Fire of London, which virtually brought England to its knees. The only way to finance the war now was to capture the Dutch trading fleets and their immensely valuable cargoes. As an example of the value of these cargoes, the prizes captured by the French in 1693 from a combined English and Dutch fleet amounted to forty ships with a total sale price of 30 million *livres*. This equated to £2,250,000, or at today's prices, the truly staggering figure of £600,000,000.

The war was largely fought at sea, beginning with the English victory at Lowestoft on 3 June 1665. At about the same time, pressure increased on the Dutch on land when the Prince-Bishop of Münster, Bernhard von Galen, invaded the Republic. Diplomatic efforts were also stepped up in order to make peace between Spain and Portugal, in order to release Spanish troops for an invasion of the Dutch Republic. Louis XIV, England's ally in Portugal, was obliged by his 1662 treaty to assist the Republic in case of war with England, but had so far held off; however the attack from Münster and the prospect of an English–Spanish coalition was too alarming. Louis feared that a collapse of the Dutch Republic and its subjugation to Spain would create a serious threat on his northern border. He therefore planned to send a French army; French envoys were sent to London to open negotiations under the threat of French intervention.

---

*   Sir Robert Holmes (c. 1622–1692) was an English admiral of the Restoration Navy. He took part in the Second and Third Anglo-Dutch Wars, both of which he is, by some, credited with starting. Holmes is chiefly remembered for his exploits on the cruise to Guinea (1664) for the Royal African Company and for the so-called Holmes's Bonfire of 1666.

†   Michiel Adriaenszoon de Ruyter (1607–1676) was the most famous and one of the most skilled admirals in Dutch history. He fought the English and French and scored several major victories against them, the best known being the raid on the Medway. The pious De Ruyter was very much loved by his sailors and soldiers, who called him *Bestevaêr,* or 'grandfather'.

‡   Later Admiral Sir Thomas Allin, 1st Baronet (1612–1685). Allin had served Charles I and Charles II during the Civil Wars and later during the Second and Third Anglo-Dutch Wars.

Unsurprisingly these events caused uproar in the English court: the Dutch Republic would end up as either a Habsburg possession or a French protectorate: either of these outcomes would be strategically dangerous for England. Clarendon, who had been opposed from the outset to 'this foolish war', was brought back to centre stage and begged by Charles II to make peace with the Dutch as soon as possible, without French mediation or intervention. However in November, after a thwarted Orangist coup, the Dutch States-General promised Louis never to conclude a separate peace with England.

* * *

Little wonder, then, that there were no available reinforcements for the English Brigade in Portugal under its French commander. Even as far away as they were and with communications uncertain, the growing political and military friction between France and England must have been felt to some degree among the officers on the ground. They might do their best to put higher political considerations aside, since they were jointly servants of a master other than their own monarch and, moreover, faced with the far more immediate prospect of battle and death; but even so, human nature and loyalty being what they are, there must have been at least a measure of cooling between the allies.

As the 1666 campaigning season approached, Maynard wrote despairingly to Arlington of the state of the English Brigade:

> The English soldiers are discontented, being they are about six months in arrears. I do what I can to prevent disgusts betwixt them and the Court. The worst is they are constrained to straggle abroad to get provisions … which hath cost the lives of many of them of late, and if they escape the fury of the country people, they fall under the severity of their officers who endeavour to preserve the reputation of civil men.[3]

Castelo Melhor's assurances after the battle of Montes Claros had clearly, once again, been empty promises. The horse still numbered 300, but the two foot regiments could muster only 700 men between them and a third of these were foreigners – probably Irish and German deserters from the Spanish army – who had been drafted into the ranks. At least a thousand replacements were urgently required and a good number of these needed to be experienced men, not raw recruits. However, no recruits, raw or seasoned, arrived and in consequence the two foot regiments were amalgamated into one: even this was well below the usual strength of 1,000. Pay was seven months behind and altogether the brigade was in a very sorry state. Maynard once more wrote that the English contingent was so reduced 'that no considerable service can be expected of them, although they should all lay down their lives for the honour of their King and country.'[4]

* * *

The Portuguese government was very much inclined to continue the offensive operational posture that had been followed since Montes Claros; indeed with few Spanish troops available to oppose them this made sense, for they were in a position to threaten major centres like Badajoz and even Seville.[5] Castelo Melhor's inclination was to extend the

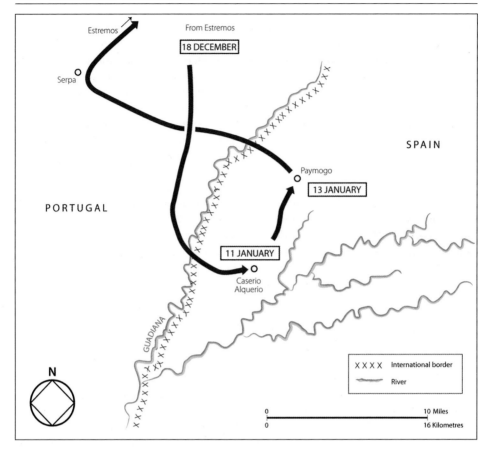

Map 20 The Campaign in Andalusia, December 1665–February 1666.

previous year's operations in Spanish Galicia for the province was sandwiched between Portugal's northern border and the Bay of Biscay; and to annex the province and secure it to the Portuguese crown appeared attractive, at the very least as a bargaining chip in the now-inevitable peace negotiations. This was exactly what Schomberg's proposed seizure of Vigo in the previous autumn would have provoked, had it been allowed to go ahead – but the opportunity had been squandered.

The alternative objective was the rich agricultural province of Andalusia with its capital, Seville. Schomberg was in favour of resurrecting the plan proposed by him and d'Ablancourt in 1664, but he was still not able to persuade Castelo Melhor to consider this – probably because of the intrigues in progress between the king's party and that of his brother Pedro.[6] Schomberg therefore took matters into his own hands and with a small field army of 4,000 men, marched first to Serpa. The army crossed the Guadiana River into Andalusia very early in the season, on 18 December 1665, with the objective of disrupting the winter quarters of the Spanish army in the county of Niebla, or Huelva, which adjoins Portugal.[7] A move this early was only possible because of the milder climate and more developed agriculture in the south of Andalusia. On 11 January

1666, after a night march, the horse – the advanced guard of the army – arrived at a town referred to in most accounts as Algueria de la Puebla, a market town. There is no place with that name now, but there are two contenders within the county: first, Puebla de Guzman, the home of the deposed Queen-Regent of Portugal, Luiza, about 15 kilometres (10 miles) across the border and about 80 kilometres (50 miles) from Estremos – about five days march therefore in good weather, but probably more in winter, hence the long time-lag in the dates between leaving Estremos and arriving at the objective.

The alternative, and more likely objective since it was a stronger fortification and thus better able to withstand a Spanish counter-attack once garrisoned, was Caserio Alqueria de la Vaca, about 8 kilometres (5 miles) west of Puebla de Guzman. The army surrounded the place at dawn and summoned the garrison to surrender. The troops in the town consisted of four troops of the Cuirassier Regiment of Rabat, whom the English and French knew well from the battle of Montes Claros, supported by 700 auxiliaries ('armed peasants,')[8] whose commander declined the offer, saying that he 'had not been sent hither to surrender.'[9] For the rest of the day of 11 January, Schomberg blockaded the gates of the town with his cavalry, awaiting the arrival of the slower infantry which marched in around midnight. At dawn, the town was attacked from two sides and the garrison forced back into their entrenchments around the church. Here, they mounted a fierce and determined defence, to the extent that the cuirassiers were allowed to march out with the honours of war – although without their horses. Four Standards were taken, which were sent to the king and the town was given over to plunder, which 'was very great'. The next day, the army marched 15 kilometres (10 miles) north to Paymogo which was taken after three hours of skirmishing, even though it was well fortified. The inhabitants had already heard word of the sack of Alqueria and wanted none of the same treatment. The garrison were taken prisoners and the horses of the troop of cavalry confiscated, although the governor was given leave to depart with a small escort. Schomberg left a garrison in the town under Major Solomon of his own regiment of French horse; Paymogo remained in Portuguese hands for the rest of the war.

But in spite of expectations, at this season it proved impossible for the army to live off the land even in the milder weather and richer agriculture of Andalusia; and the logistic demands were far greater than the commissariat could deal with. The want of food for men and particularly horses therefore obliged Schomberg to break off his campaign and return to Estremos, through Serpa and Moura, arriving on 24 February. Schomberg rejoined the court at Salvaterra de Magos, just south of Lisbon, where he was laid up for

Figure 28 A view of the town of Sanlucar from the sea; the Castle of Santiago is clearly visible. (Author's collection)

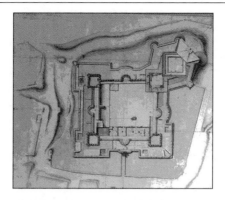

Map 21 The Castle of Santiago in Sanlucar,
contemporary map. (Author's collection)

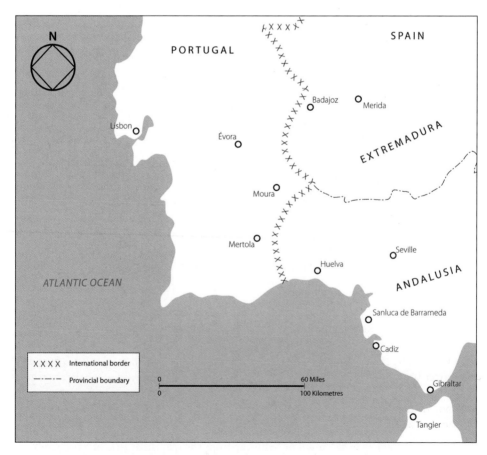

Map 22 The Spring campaign in Andalusia, April–May 1666.

some time with a mysterious and unidentified illness: this could have been malaria which was endemic in the marshy areas of the Guadalquivir. On making a good recovery, he left Lisbon about the middle of April 1666 and rejoined the field army. Here, he ordered the assembly of 4,000 foot, 1,200 horse, four pieces of artillery and fifteen days of provisions, enough for a raid if not a campaign. About half the foot and two-thirds of the horse were made up of the English and French brigades.

Schomberg once again crossed the Guadiana River into Andalusia on or about 1 May and made for Sanlucar de Barrameda on the southern coast of Andalusia, within striking distance of the great naval base of Cadiz. This was a place of symbolic importance as well as dangerous to Cadiz: it was the seat of the family of the Duke of Medina-Sidonia, the governor-general and principal nobleman of Andalusia; and also the place from which both Ferdinand Magellan and Christopher Columbus had set sail. The town was 160 kilometres (100 miles) from Moura, about eight days' march, and therefore at the limit of what was logistically sustainable unless the army could live off the land. The town was situated on a high hill above the river, with three great towers on the river side and two bastions covered with two demi-lunes on the landward side.

Although much of the foot and the supply and siege trains were delayed by the state of the roads, Schomberg nonetheless set his engineers to work straight away, on or about 10 May. After only three days, even before the heavy guns had been brought up, the Castle of Santiago capitulated and the garrison was given leave to march out with its arms and baggage but without its six guns – two 24-pdrs and four smaller pieces.[10]

Castelo Melhor had not, however, approved this action and reinforcements of neither men nor supplies were made available to exploit the victory; the army was in consequence left in great want of food. The English and French horse were sent to raid as far as the outskirts of Seville and then westwards along the coast, taking and burning the towns of Gibraléon, at the mouth of the Odiel River, and Trigueros – 'one of the finest Places of the Province';[11] plundering shipping on the river; and capturing two Standards after an encounter between troops commanded by Meinhard von Schomberg and the cuirassier regiment of Rougemont, which lost 100 men in the fight. The effect of these actions was to persuade most other towns and castles in the area to open their doors and deliver suitable contributions – to the delight of the English and French troops.[12] The inhabitants of the region were now thoroughly panicked, having never before seen so many foreign troops, so that several towns and villages ransomed themselves with payments of money or food to escape plunder. The booty was all treated as prize and distributed among the officers and men.

When the news of the capture of Sanlucar and the domination of one of Spain's richest provinces, reached Lisbon, the significance of this achievement was downplayed at court – probably deliberately so in order to save Castelo Melhor's face. Schomberg had intended to demonstrate that it was now easy to expand the frontiers of Portugal, as well as to divert Spanish troops away from Extremadura and Alentejo to defend Andalusia. Moreover the possession of ports on the south coast of Iberia would allow direct supply to the army from France or from Tangier – but Castelo Melhor took the view that it was not in the interest of Portugal to expand the war further into Andalusia, 'Which Arguments smelt as little of the Politician as of the Soldier.'[13] Schomberg's patience was close to exhaustion: he ordered up supplies of food and ammunition from Mertola to Sanlucar, left a garrison of 400 Portuguese foot and a squadron of horse in Sanlucar and marched off on 25 May 1666 for Estremos, retiring into summer quarters in mid-June. The precise activities of the English brigade in these operations in Andalusia are nowhere detailed; however there appear to have been few if any casualties. The most likely losses, if any, would have come from straggling, given the considerable marching distances undertaken by the troops from December to May.

*   *   *

The new queen arrived in Lisbon in August 1666 and Schomberg was among those who greeted her. He remained there throughout September and October while the army stayed in quarters around Estremos. Caracena meanwhile had stepped up the level of cross-border raids, probably in response to Schomberg's incursions in Andalusia. In early September, 4,000 Spanish horse and 2,000 musketeers made a feint towards Serpa to draw the attention of the Portuguese while Caracena marched deep into Portugal, plundering Veiros and other places. A counter-move by John da Silva with 1,200 Portuguese horse came to grief when he encountered the Prince of Parma, for although the preliminary skirmishes cost the Spanish dearly in casualties, a determined engagement resulted in the loss of 400 Portuguese killed, wounded and taken prisoner. These raids ceased as November drew in; however Caracena's plunder had been considerable and had cost the Portuguese around 1,000 horses that they could ill afford to lose. Meanwhile in Lisbon, intrigues deepened in the court in Lisbon between the three political factions attached to the king, the queen and Don Pedro.[14] Schomberg, vexed both at Caracena's boldness and the Portuguese losses against the Prince of Parma, returned to Alentejo.

In Estremos, Schomberg kept abreast of the progress of the court intrigues but, rather than become embroiled, fixed his attention on the task which had brought him to Portugal: its independence through victory against Spain. Having extended Portuguese territory into Andalusia, he switched his focus back to Extremadura, not least to repay Caracena for the damage his raids had done. At the beginning of January 1667 he began to plan a surprise attack against the town and fortress of Albuquerque, about 20 kilometres (12 miles) north of Badajoz and within easy reach of his bases in Estremos and Campo Maior. Although they would not arrive in time, he petitioned Arlington for up to 400 more recruits for the English brigade; Pearson supported him in this and sent his Lieutenant-Colonel, John Rumsey, home with a detailed account of how many recruits were needed and why, as well laying out the need to keep up the pressure for the troops to be paid as they were once again seven months in arrears.[15] Even Southwell was induced to join in the clamour, writing in support of reinforcements – even though the troops already in Portugal remained unpaid – and commending Rumsey.[16]

Albuquerque lies to the south of Valencia de Alcantara and was described by Southwell as being 'on the Spanish frontiers, and has a strong and high castle, within the towne and suburbs without.'[17] The various levels of the town are clearly visible in the illustration below which, although published in 1684, shows the town as it was in 1664. The lower town was surrounded by a medieval wall with towers, enclosing the usual maze of narrow, winding streets.[18] The garrison in the lower town consisted of a Spanish *trozo* of horse – that of Extremadura;[19] and an Irish regiment of foot. This 'regiment' was probably several detached companies of the regiment of Colonel Shean, or John Morphy, which had been sent to Spain from Flanders with Caracena – Morphy appears to have been a

Figure 29 This is a contemporary view of the town and fortress of Albuquerque from the north side of the town and shows the concentric lines of medieval fortification which had not been modernised to take cannon. (Author's collection)

client or follower of Caracena and his regiment had been raised in 1667 for Alexander MacDonnell, 3rd Earl of Antrim.[20] The medieval castle or citadel rose about 300 metres (1,000 feet) above the town and had also not been modernised – but it was a formidable objective for an attacking force and although not improved, it was far larger and stronger than Valencia de Alcantara. It was held by a garrison of four Spanish companies from the territorial *tercio* of Extremadura along with four companies of Catalan infantry.

Intelligence reports from spies and the interrogation of prisoners and deserters, as reported by Southwell, gave out that the walls of both the upper town and of the castle were in a ruinous state, partly collapsed, and further damaged by the heavy rains of that

Figure 30 A modern photograph of Albuquerque. (A.M. Goulden)

year; only very short scaling ladders would be needed to get over the defences. Moreover with the Guadiana running in spate, the garrison did not fear an attack and had, it was said, grown lax. Schomberg assembled a force of 3,000 foot in four regiments: the English regiment, the French regiments of Maret and Briquemaut, along with the Portuguese regiment of the Marquis of Noirmontier; and 1,500 English and French horse: 'some to make ye attacque, and others to prevent supplyes' (i.e. reinforcement of the garrison).[21] The army marched from Estremos early on the morning of on 24 February 1667.

The advance continued all day and all night, without a break, during which the troops had to ford the upper Ouguela and the Xévora, both of which, although not large rivers, were in full spate, in order to force the lower town by a surprise attack at dawn on 25 February. The total distance was over 60 kilometres (38 miles). The English foot led the assault, as Maynard reported, 'With a great deal of trouble our forces got within musket shot of Albuquerque without being discovered and shortly became masters of the outworks [i.e. the outlying picquets and earthworks protecting the lower town] without loss'.[22] They pressed on into the lower town, carrying two petards to blow in the gate to the fortified upper town. The petard was an early version of the shaped charge and provided the besieger with a noisy but simple means of breaking open a gate. A hollow, bell-shaped metal container would be filled with well-rammed charges of powder and fastened to a large, iron-bound wooden beam. The device would be carried up to the gate under cover of darkness or supporting fire and fixed to the gate, bell end against

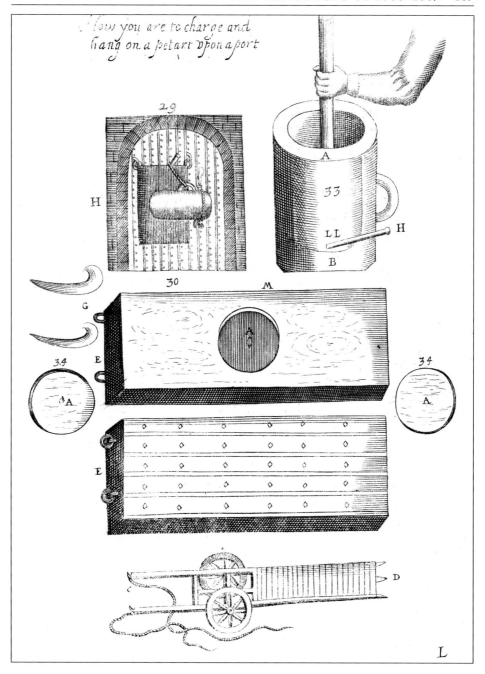

Figure 31 The preparation of a petard, from Henry Hexham's *Principles of the Art Military.* (© Royal Armouries RAL. 08487)

the target. The petardier then ignited a fuse in the base of the bell and ran for cover. The charge would go off, sending the bell backwards and propelling the beam through the gate. By the late seventeenth century the petard had all but disappeared, not least because of the very high incidence of death among petardiers.

The intelligence was, however, faulty. The garrison was alert and standing to arms. New pallisadoes had also been erected around the gates into the town and 'when Coll Pearson marcht with his Regiment up to ye wall and planted their ladders of 15 foote, they found them by halfe and more too short … neither was the petar yet come which should have forced the gate.'[23] The Irish infantry lined the walls and their fire was so effective that, as Maynard reported, 'being deceived in their intelligence and finding no places where the soldiers could breach the walls, they were constrained to draw off with the loss of about 150 men, and 60 more wounded.'[24] The assault did not penetrate the upper town wall, never mind approach the citadel. Many of the losses were in the English regiment, which here had made what was to be its last assault: Pearson lost sixteen men killed including one un-named ensign, probably Emerson, since there is no subsequent record of him; and twenty wounded including two un-named lieutenants who cannot be identified – there are at least a dozen potential candidates. The English horse had no loss as the regiment did not take part in the assault. The Marquis of Noirmontier, a popular figure with the army, was reported to be also among those killed.[25] It was said that he had been leading a Portuguese regiment which had been ordered to assault the opposite side of the town from the English, where the same problems had been encountered. Noirmontier was shot under the eye and fell. His regiment ran, except for a few stalwarts who remained to shield him. Three French reformadoes brought him off the field but would have been obliged to leave him had not a file of English musketeers arrived and carried him away.* Southwell remarked tartly in his account, derived from reports of those who had been present, that 'The Portuguese Regiment … and ye French lost more in plundering the [lower] towne than fighting, a French Captain-Lieut. with 50 soldiers I heare of killed, besides severall wounded.'[26]

After looting a nearby town, probably Benevente as this lies directly on the line of retreat, and a poor place as it turned out, Schomberg was forced to retire back into Alentejo with all the haste his troops could make: 'vex'd at this disappointment, but ye fault was in the bad Intelligence.'[27] He made off with haste, for intelligence suggested that the Spanish intended a further invasion of Alentejo with 'a strong army of horse and foot as soone as the season of the yeare will suffer them to take the field. We are making all possible preparations'.[28] However the casualties at Albuquerque had reduced the English foot to 600 effectives, who were still eight months adrift in pay and although full of fight, were hungry and ragged. Southwell reporting that 'our men doe very bravely on all occasions, and yet I am every month at daggers drawn with this Court over their pay'.[29] While Maynard wrote that the English regiments had never been so weak as now and would be hard pressed should the Spanish come on as they had before and were reported

---

*   Although cited by several sources including d'Ablancourt (p. 303) and in letters quoted in the references to this chapter, the identification of Noirmontier, or Noirmoutier, is highly dubious. The only candidate is Louis II de la Trémoille (1612–1666), who had been on the wrong side during the Fronde and then, with his brother, served the Spanish king. He died almost a year before this episode.

as preparing to do – especially with their superiority in horses and equipment. Recruits were urgently needed, as the brigade was 'so faire mouldred away that it is impossible for them hereafter to subsist in three Regiments.'[30] But before any further efforts could be made to secure recruits and funs, events outside the theatre of war moved the situation in quite another direction.

12

The Last Acts, 1667–1668

'those which survived left it as full of poverty and necessity'

On 26 January 1667, in accordance with his obligations to the Dutch Republic, Louis XIV of France declared war on England, his ally in the Portuguese Restoration War. In February, Frederick III of Denmark did the same after he had received a large subsidy from Louis. Then Brandenburg threatened to attack England's client, Münster, from the east: Prince-Bishop Von Galen made peace with the Republic in April. A seriously alarmed Charles II of England put out new peace feelers in February, but without enough substance to be accepted and the Second Anglo-Dutch War dragged on. During 1666, the inconclusive Four Days' Battle and then the Dutch victory in the St James' Day Battle at sea had turned the tide towards the Dutch Republic. By late 1666/early 1667, the English financial position was desperate: most pressing for the king's government was that the exchequer lacked the funds to keep the fleet seaworthy, so it was decided in February 1667 that all the heavy line-of-battle ships would be laid up in ordinary at Chatham. In the wake of this measure, Clarendon told Charles that he had only two options: either to make substantial concessions to Parliament at home in order to raise money, or to begin peace talks with the Dutch on their terms. In March 1667, talks were opened at Breda.

Charles, however, had already decided to try to a third option: to become a secret ally of France in order to obtain money and out-manoeuvre the Dutch. On 18 April he concluded his first secret treaty with Louis, stipulating that England would support a French conquest of the Spanish Netherlands. In May the French invaded, starting the War of Devolution; meanwhile Charles hoped, by spinning out the negotiations at Breda, to gain enough time to ready his fleet in order to coerce the Dutch. Before the English fleet could be got ready, however, the Dutch navy entered the Medway and burned much of it at anchor. On 2 July, 1,500 Dutch marines were landed on the Essex coast and attacked Landguard Fort, which was garrisoned by 400 men of the Duke of York and Albany's Maritime Regiment of Foot under Captain Nathaniel Darrell, 'a malignant papist and incompetent', according to one source, but who turned out to be anything but incompetent, whatever his religious beliefs. To add insult to injury, the Dutch were led by Colonel Thomas Dolman, an Englishman who had served with the Anglo-Dutch Brigade and refused the order to return to England on the outbreak of war. He and enough of the brigade had taken the oath to the Dutch Republic to form a regiment of foot. The attack on Landguard was beaten off, but the Dutch naval success was a serious physical and psychological blow to England, just a year after the Great Fire. Charles came as close as he ever did to facing another rebellion and Clarendon ordered the English envoys at Breda to sign a peace rapidly, whatever the cost to English prestige.

On 21 July 1667, the Treaty of Breda sealed peace between the two nations.[1] The loss of face was such that it brought about the eclipse and fall of Clarendon, who fled to exile in France and was replaced by his rival, Arlington.

Not long afterwards, on 29 August 1667, the political landscape of Portugal was also dramatically transformed. Alfonso VI, Castelo Melhor, and his Francophile party were overthrown by the king's younger brother, Pedro, Duke of Beja, who, backed by a considerable faction of the Portuguese nobility and bourgeoisie which was unable to stomach the conduct of the court any longer, installed himself as his brother's regent. It was some time, however, before the transfer of power was completed and there was a good deal of turbulence in Lisbon throughout the following months. Although he would have preferred to remain aloof, Schomberg could see which way the wind was blowing and reluctantly, he threw in his lot with Don Pedro. Marialva had changed all the guards within the city for soldiers under his control and set about raising money to pay the rest of troops, thus ensuring their loyalty,[2] but it was Schomberg's control of the field army in Alentejo that was the key in frustrating Castelo Melhor's attempts to employ it on behalf of Alfonso. Schomberg 'dispersed into the uttermost Borders of Alentejo the Troops of that Province' until word arrived that the coup was complete.[3] Southwell also reported that 'the English Officers from Elvas acquaint me, that as first there went private orders from my Lord Schomberg, to let no man enter from Badajoz',[4] in other words, to ensure that peace negotiations were delayed until they could be concluded by the new government. Marialva, meanwhile, frustrated Alfonso's bid 'to draw down with him the forces of Lisbon unto Alcantara, for that he had a mind to go there, and would have the soldiers with him.'[5]

Once firmly in control of the reins of power, Pedro consigned Alfonso to exile in the islands of the Azores, on the very reasonable ground that he was incapable of governing. Castelo Melhor fled abroad: ironically, he chose to live in England. Pedro, who eventually became King Pedro II in 1683, took immediate steps to repair the damage caused to relations with the French by marrying his brother's former queen; he also moved quickly to restore the primacy of the English political alliance, now reconcilable with the desire for friendship with France after the conclusion of peace at Breda. This alliance would continue to be the bedrock of Portuguese foreign policy for the next 250 years and result in two further British military interventions in Iberia in 1705 and 1808 as well as the assistance given in the civil war of 1831–1832.

Although it had never been in contemplation that there would be serious fighting during 1667,[6] the English brigade took part in one final short expedition. Schomberg advanced against the castle of Hertara de Alcantara on the upper Tagus (or Tejo) River, 'the Garrison of which extreamly incommoded the Country.'[7] This, it will be recalled, had been mooted as a subsequent objective after the capture of Valencia de Alcantara in 1664 but not followed up. The place surrendered with little resistance as soon as the attacking force appeared and the garrison became prisoners of war. Schomberg ordered the English and French horse to exploit as far as Brozas, keeping the foot regiments in place to hold the crossing of the Tagus for the safe return of the horse, after which the troops marched back to Elvas with their considerable plunder. Maynard reported that the English troops had again distinguished themselves; the plunder was no doubt welcome as pay was now nine months in arrears.[8]

The political landscape had, however, been transformed to a greater degree than even Pedro suspected. In May 1667,[9] a treaty between England and Spain had been concluded and a secret article bound the signatories not to assist one another's enemies.[10] This alone spelled the end of English intervention on Portugal's behalf and realised a key objective of Spain's foreign policy. But from the other side, the decisive act had already been put into effect when the great goal of a Franco-Portuguese treaty was at last realised. This treaty, signed on 31 March 1667, provided for a league 'Offensive and defensive against Castile'[11] that would restore Portuguese independence and last for ten years, but would not prejudice Portugal's relations with England: Article 1 declared that as soon as peace was signed between England and France, that France would immediately declare war against Spain. Under Articles 3 and 4, the King of France would grant the King of Portugal an annual subsidy of 600,000 *cruzadoes*, while under Article 8, French troops would invade either Catalonia or the Basque region to divert Spanish forces away from Portugal. In return, the Portuguese would put into the field each year 'a considerable Army' of 12,000 foot and 5,000 horse, which would be prepared to invade Spain as well as defend Portugal and which would mount two campaigns each year, before and after the summer heat. This it would do on four equally-resourced 'inroads', or axes of attack. The treaty also contained the provision in Article 14 for France to mediate between Portugal and the Dutch and under Article 15 gave the King of Portugal the right to raise mercenary regiments in France and Alsace.[12]

Faced with the prospect of a renewed assault by enemies on two fronts, Spain finally agreed to recognize Portugal's independence with the help of English mediation by the Earl of Sandwich, in the Treaty of Lisbon, signed on 3 February 1668 by the representatives of both monarchs.[13] Maynard gave the credit for this to Southwell,[14] but Pepys reported in his diary that 'all the court is full of good news of my Lord Sandwich's having made a peace between Spain and Portugall; which is mighty great news, and above all to my Lord's honour more than any thing he ever did.'[15] By the terms of this treaty, Portugal kept all of its remaining overseas colonies, with the exception of Ceuta on the North African coast, which had never recognized the Braganza dynasty and which remained Spanish. The near-dictatorship of Castelo Melhor was replaced by government in the hands of the old hereditary nobility rather than royally appointed officials. Lisbon became once again a powerful, wealthy, mercantile centre thronged by English and Dutch ships. But the empire overseas, which had been the real source of Portuguese wealth, was in decline and outside the immediate environs of Lisbon, prosperity never took root.

* * *

On 19 May 1668, its mission completed, the French contingent was embarked on fifteen merchant ships acting as transports and four frigates;[16] Schomberg himself embarked on 20 May and the whole convoy departed for La Rochelle on 21 May, arriving there fourteen days later. Schomberg was still owed 10,000 *cruzadoes* in arrears of pay by the Portuguese but had clearly decided that he had had enough of their country. Southwell reported that, in keeping with earlier reports of the French soldiers' tendency towards plundering and indiscipline, 'The Portuguese were exceedingly rejoiced at this deliverance, for ye many Insolencys committed by these troops, from the frontier to their very embarquing.'[17] On their arrival at La Rochelle the French regiments were immediately disbanded and the Germans given rations and passage to the frontier at Strasbourg.

The English brigade, or what was left of it, had been placed under the command of Schomberg's son Frederick who remained in Portugal after his father left. With the war over, it might be assumed that the troops were free to return to England – or were they? There were at most 1,000 of the original brigade and its subsequent reinforcements – a total of 3,730 men – still standing. At first, it was suggested that 'My Lord of Sandwich will endeavour to make good conditions for them, with Spaigne if his Majesties be pleased to let them serve that Crowne, soeth the souldiers are willing to doe, if they have recruits from England to fill up their regiments, and security for their pay.'[18] Ultimately this scheme of maintaining an English brigade in Spanish service was dropped because English foreign policy was moving towards a French alliance. While their fate was decided, most of the officers and men of the English brigade remained in their garrisons and quarters around Estremos, although some of the officers applied for leave to depart almost immediately: Robert Boone, for example, secured a lieutenancy in the Earl of Manchester's Regiment in 1667.[19]

Before any final evacuation could be effected, however, there were prolonged negotiations lasting a year over the payment of the full arrears of pay to the troops from the seriously depleted Portuguese treasury; and the settlement of numerous petty disputes between soldiers and civilians. The troops were, as Maynard reported, 'extreamly neglected being eleven months in arrears; and none of the ministers will take cognizance of their complaints, but I hope that when these great businesses [i.e. the peace negotiations] are settled they will consider of their condition, and not let so many of His Majesties subjects to perish, that have done this Countrie such Remarkable Service.'[20]

The Portuguese treasury still owed nearly 1 million *cruzadoes* to Charles II for the unpaid portion of the queen's dowry and 3 million to the Dutch government. In addition, more than 2 million *cruzadoes* a year were needed to pay for the army and revenues ran short by at least 250,000 *cruzadoes*.[21] Against this background of debt, many Portuguese towns were at least reluctant and in many cases downright unwilling to pay their war taxes; while revenues from the empire and from trade continued to be depressed because of the conflict with the Dutch. News of the change of government in Portugal had already prompted Charles II to issue instructions to Sir Robert Southwell, in November 1667, to press for the payment of the arrears of the queen's dowry.[22] This was again stressed in Southwell's detailed instructions from the king on 31 May 1668;[23] and in June, Arlington instructed Southwell to 'make one last effort for the recovery of the remaining portions of Her Majesties Dowry', before he returned home. He was instructed to make his way via Tangier in order to be able to report on the state of defence of the fortress and the progress of construction of the harbour mole.[24]

Throughout the winter of 1667 and well into 1668, the brigade remained quartered and around Estremos. Discipline in general seems to have held up well, although there was at least one fatal duel between officers of the brigade. Writing to Joseph Williamson, Sir Robert Southwell described how 'It seems the [English] Party have many differences among themselves and Coll. Moore hath in a Duel killed Capt. Shanon, one of the compleatest brave men in ye whole Party. I will not name you the occasion till I reach Lisbone, because it is mentioned to the Consull's disadvantage and perhaps it may be true.'[25] What the cause of the duel was is now not known: perhaps religion or nationality, or old loyalties, for Moore was a former Parliamentarian soldier and a Protestant Englishman, while Shanon was an Irish Catholic and likely a Royalist. However it seems that Maynard ('the Consull') was in some way involved: Southwell's instructions had contained the order that he should 'acquaint Our Consull Thomas Maynard with the many Complaints which have been here made against him both from the Court at Lisbon, and the Merchants'.[26] Although nothing explicit can be determined on the basis of these few scraps of information, there is still a whiff of corruption around this affair.

Southwell and Maynard meanwhile worked to secure the conditions necessary for the return home of the brigade. There were persistent rumours that Maynard was to be replaced, but Schomberg, Dempsey and Trelawney all petitioned Arlington to leave him in post 'until all the outstanding military accounts are cleared through him.'[27] The actual sums owing to the English brigade were themselves in dispute and before any payment could be made, these had to be agreed. Once this had been overcome, repeated promises were made by the Portuguese authorities to settle the debt – there are letters to that effect in February, March, April, July and early August. A Portuguese Royal decree of 13 August 1667 removed lingering fears of prosecution from the English by announcing that no English subject in Portugal should be arrested or brought to trial without the consent of the Judge-Conservator, other than in undeniable circumstances of *flagrante delicto*. To settle the arrears, an initial payment of 30,000 *cruzadoes* had been made in August 1667 and another 30,000 were made available from the unpaid portion of the queen's dowry in the following March.[28] Critically, in May 1668, the *Cortez*, or Parliament, voted Pedro half a million *cruzadoes* a year to settle military expenditure, this to be raised by a land tax.[29] Considerable resistance continued, however, from many Portuguese towns to paying war taxes now that there was peace with Spain and collecting the money took time.[30]

It was not until 7 August, therefore, that Southwell was at last able to report that he had succeeded in securing the full arrears of pay for the troops, amounting to 140,000 *cruzadoes*:[31] there was still one last-minute hitch to be overcome when the Queen of Portugal insisted on retaining 40,000 *cruzadoes* from this sum. On 5 September, however, the troops were paid their full arrears 'to their great satisfaction.'[32] Sir Robert Southwell's successor as minister in Portugal, Sir Francis Parry, wrote to Sir Joseph Williamson, who had succeeded Arlington as Secretary of State and Lord Chamberlain to Charles II, extolling 'the great difficulties overcome by Southwell in obtaining payment for the English troops, and the great esteem in which he is held at court.'[33]

Directions were therefore issued from London for the dispersal of the English troops.[34] Any officers who so wished were permitted to remain in the Portuguese service, but there are no known examples of any who took advantage of this offer, which is hardly surprising given the treatment of the brigade by the Portuguese during the war. The most obvious solution to the problem of what to do with the soldiers, from the point of view of the English government, was to send some of the men to Tangier,[35] whose garrison was seriously undermanned. They were, after all, soldiers of the Protectorate who had been sent to Portugal in the first place to remove them from the British Isles – nothing had changed in that respect. If a small number remained after that, especially if they were Royalists or even Catholics, then they might safely be embarked for service in England. At a council of the court held in Whitehall on 5 May 1668, the Duke of York had already ordered that 400 men from Portugal, with officers, should be sent to Tangier:[36] 200 to bring the regiments there up to strength and 200 to permit a similar number to return home – the only documented relief of the entire English occupation of Tangier between

1662 and 1684.[37] Royal Instructions were sent to Southwell on 31 May 1668 warning him of this and also directing that a further 100 men were to be contracted as labour to work on the construction of the great harbour mole at Tangier,[38] although it is doubtful that these men were actually employed in this way for there are no other references to the matter; the remainder were to be returned to England. Lieutenant-Colonel John Rumsey, of Pearson's Regiment, agreed to take the men to Tangier, expressing satisfaction at Southwell's 'great and successful efforts to obtain all that was due to them.'[39] But the prospect of service in Tangier was, unsurprisingly, not greeted with wild enthusiasm by the troops – even though for many, it seemed better than starvation at home.[40]

In the event, 130 of 'the very worst men of the garrison' of Tangier were sent away on the arrival of the contingent from Portugal. The situation of the colony and the course of the war in Iberia had always been intertwined since the original treaty of accession; and an important element of the negotiations carried on by Fanshawe, which eventually resulted in the peace between Spain and Portugal, had been freedom of trade between Spain and Tangier – without which Tangier had to be supplied directly from England. The Spanish in return had tried to negotiate the cession of Tangier to them.[41] The Anglo-Dutch war had made supply from England even more difficult than usual and the result was very short rations for the garrison with little in reserve for emergencies. Sir Palmes Fairborne, a soldier who had fought as a volunteer against the Turks and who had served in Tangier from the time it was first occupied by the English until his death fighting the Moors while acting governor in 1680, wrote that 'Tangier never was in worse condition than at present. I hope some care is taken to remedie this, or else the Lord have mercy upon us.'[42]

The garrison of Tangier had originally consisted of five regiments of foot and a troop of horse, the horse being new-raised in England from veterans. The foot consisted of two old Protectorate regiments from Dunkirk (Harley's in 1661 and Rutherford's in 1663); a new regiment raised in 1661 in England (Peterborough's); two Irish regiments from Dunkirk that had originally been in the Spanish service, but had later served Charles II in exile (Farrell's and Fitzgerald's); and finally elements of Roger Allsopp's Regiment which arrived with Rutherford's after the sale of Dunkirk to France in 1663.[43] This explosive mix of former enemies – similar in kind to that found in the force for Portugal – had been reduced by 1664 to two regiments, one English and one Irish – or twenty companies. Disease, drink, and fighting the Moors had depleted the strength of the garrison, not least when a grand forage by the garrison was ambushed by the Moors, resulting in the deaths of the Governor, Andrew Rutherford Earl of Teviot, eighteen officers, fifteen volunteers and gentlemen, and nearly 400 men. Only nine men survived to recount what had happened.[44] The two foot regiments had subsequently been reorganised again, into nineteen weak companies, and the new acting Governor, John Fitzgerald, was told to remove the national distinctions between the English and Irish regiments. Fitzgerald was an experienced officer who had commanded an Irish regiment in the service of Charles II in exile in the Low Countries and led it at the battle of the Dunes in 1658. Pepys records that Fitzgerald was a great favourite of the Duke of York, who wished to promote him, but Norwood, Bridge, and Peterborough were all hostile and so the Privy Council blocked his preferment. He was deputy governor, and then acting governor of Tangier 1664–1666. He was made Governor of Yarmouth in 1672 and given command of a regiment for sea service. He was later promoted to major-general but died, in 1680, before this could be gazetted. As Governor of Tangier he would have been listed among the colonels of the Governor's Regiment, later the 2nd or Queen's Royal Regiment of Foot. However being Irish and a Catholic, subsequent history air-brushed him out, in common with many of those who took part in the expedition to Portugal.

Those veterans of the war in Portugal who were now shipped to North Africa for service in Tangier had to all intents and purposes been issued with a death sentence. On 7 September 1668, 400 of the foot, 'very brave men', under the command of Lieutenant-Colonel John Rumsey, embarked at Lisbon in four English frigates.[45] They arrived at Tangier five days later. The ships dropped anchor under the shelter of the incomplete harbour mole, which was being built at enormous expense and technical difficulty, to provide a sheltered haven from the north Atlantic storms. Here they found but a cold welcome from the old Royalist soldier and Lieutenant-Governor, Sir Henry Norwood,* who was standing in until a successor to Belasyse could be found. Norwood found a large body of new troops inconvenient because of the difficult supply situation by sea that has already been outlined, but also because foraging, after the great ambuscade of 4 May 1664, was no longer practicable. Reinforcement from Portugal, even though it increased the effective fighting strength of the garrison, meant more mouths to feed in what was a beleaguered outpost:

> Sir William Jennings arrived yesterday with the Mermaid in his company and brought 400 men for the service of the garrison of those who served so well in Portugal. I wondered that so many should be consigned to this place since half the number would have completed the last establishment, but [I] learn by Sir Robert Southwell it was considered in Council that it would much encourage those who serve here to make place for the reception of the whole number by allowing an equal number of the supernumeraries to garrison their country, and upon that precedent design they were sent.
>
> It is a sad paradox to tell your Lordship that I am sorry these men are come here at this juncture but I must tell your Lordship that much I have often repeated to the Lord Commander by their office (viz, that the victuals sent in April last [when our stores were utterly drained]) is wholly spent and that since the middle of this instant September here has been no flesh in the stores but what I have borrowed of Sir Thomas Allen or procured upon my proper credit, much bad meat has been rejected of that which should have served the 6 months, in so much that if the weakness of the garrison had not retarded our necessity we had been truly put [?] ere this; but now that more months fall upon us as then the establishment, and no supply from England to help us out, our case is deplorable and a very great allay to the arrival of these brave men. I will use all importunity to persuade Sir William Jennings to take our old desperate men which if I please it will some ease for us besides this want of victuals and stores, to repair the walls and quarters, the arrears due unto the garrison is almost insupportable the 9th of September next, a complete year the account thereafter will make God send his Majesty's Exchequer to [succour?] us.[46]

---

*   Sir Henry Norwood (1615–1689) was active in the Royalist cause at he outbreak of the Civil Wars in England. In 1649, after the killing of Charles I, he fled to Virginia rather than compound with the Republic, where his cousin Sir William Berkeley was Governor. In 1658 he made his way to the Netherlands and from thence to England where he was active in the Restoration.

But there was worse to come, for having left one station where pay was always long in arrears, the men from Portugal arrived in Tangier to find that the garrison there was twelve months behind in its pay.[47] Sir Hugh Cholmeley, who served briefly as governor, remarked that:

> the poor soldier, being sometimes six or sometimes nine months without his pay, when he gets a flood of money spends it all in a week … and when he comes to help himself he hath no money because that is spent, or credit because his pay is not till six months afterwards … I have been told many have died for want of twelve pence to relieve him.[48]

The casualty list continued to grow: less than a year after the arrival of the veterans from Portugal, the garrison, which on their arrival had been at a strength of 1,900 men, besides officers, NCOs and supernumeraries, was reduced to one regiment of twelve companies – 1,440 men. Few, if any, would have survived the rigours of fighting the Moors and working on the great mole during the increasingly severe conditions of the occupation, before its final evacuation twelve years later in 1684.

The remaining 500 soldiers sailed for England with their officers on 7 September 1668. Seventy soldiers but no officers from the foot were taken into the Portsmouth garrison by the governor, Sir Philip Honeywood, and the captain of the garrison there, George Legge, later Lord Dartmouth and Master-General of the Ordnance. The remainder marched to London, where they were disbanded in October, 1668;[49] it seems that a considerable number – among them probably most of the surviving soldiers of the regiment of horse – were taken into the Life Guards and the Royal Horse Guards, while what remained of the foot after the Portsmouth garrison had had their pick joined the thirty companies of the King's Guards: the king himself, it is said, expressed himself pleased with the men and ordered them to be taken into the ranks.

We know more details of the officers than of the ordinary soldiers, and for them there were serious difficulties in England. Their arrival coincided with the disbandment of the army after the Second Dutch War, so there were no vacancies on the reduced

Figure 32 *A View of Tangier from the East* – that is, from the anchorage – in 1669, by Wencelaus Hollar. This is the view that the troops arriving from Portugal would have had from their transports, including the mole, still under construction, to the right of the picture. (Author's collection)

home establishment. Sir William Salkeld was lucky, obtaining a lieutenancy in the Royal Horse Guards.[50] Even the most senior officers – Pearson, Moore, Trelawney and Rumsey – had to petition Arlington for employment,[51] as did Sharpe, Farrell and – before his death – Shanon,[52] while Schomberg himself had to petition Charles II for a commission for his son Frederick.[53]

In the wake of a series of plots, both real and supposed, against the king, Parliament had obliged the Privy Council to purge the army of Catholic officers by enforcing the Oaths of Supremacy and Allegiance, along with the Corporation Act which debarred non-Anglicans from any public office: forty-three Catholic soldiers were dismissed from three companies of the King's Guards in 1667, most of them Irish and the sons of Catholic gentlemen.[54] Many of the English and Irish officers from Portugal were Catholics and would thus have found it impossible to get places. A typical petition in December 1667 by thirteen officers and thirty-six soldiers asked 'for a livelihood, till they can be employed in some foreign country; have served faithfully, but are recalled from Portugal as incapable of bearing arms, because they are Roman Catholics.'[55] Those named (no ranks are given), as far as the entry is legible, include John Glaisey, Charles Bullocke, Charles Burns, Charles Dayley, Dominic Horby, Timothy Fox, Robert Lodwidge, Garret Frost, Caspar Rochford, Robert Haines, Arthur Horolan, Dempsey, Patrick Snaith, Christopher John, William Ryan, Thomas Dyer, Thomas Owen, Hugh Konady (or Kennedy), Darby Maghee, Laughlan Cowper, Timothy Hogan and Cornelius O'Brian. Dempsey may be Captain Lawrence Dempsey, but no others can be safely identified and it is likely from their names that most were Irish soldiers – possibly men who had been either recruited in Ireland, or else taken to Portugal from Tangier, or even taken on as deserters from the Spanish service in 1666. Given the date, these appear to be officers and men who had managed to leave Portugal ahead of the main evacuation – perhaps forgoing their arrears of pay in order to do so.

As the petition indicated, usually the only recognition of the service of Catholic officers and men was a licence to seek further employment with a foreign prince.[56] Another petition came from '11 underwritten officers for relief to bear their charges to foreign service, there being no hope for them here; served with satisfaction in Portugal though not made equal to others who were not Catholics.'[57] They included Captains Charles Farrell, John Roche and James Lee of the Foot; Lieutenants Francis Trelawney and Charles Bullocke of the Horse, John Harbord, Charles Love, Nicholas Habyne and Charles Bourke of the Foot; and Ensign John Burke of the Foot. Most, from their names, were probably Irish. Indeed, Farrell, Harbord, Roche and the two Bourke's had all served in Tangier with one of the two Irish regiments there, before going to Portugal: Bourke in Farrell's Regiment and the others in Fitzgerald's.[58] Farrell, along with Dempsey, had been commended to Lord Arlington by Sir Robert Southwell when they left Portugal – but to little effect.[59]

Even for the Protestant officers from Portugal the outlook was bleak; after petitioning the king for having been 'recalled home and dismissed their employment', twenty-four of the field officers, captains and junior officers, as well as an unknown number of soldiers, were admitted into the Life Guards, three in each troop,[60] where necessary by turning out incumbents:[61] one undated petition from those thus turned out in 1668 came from 'the gentlemen excluded from the troops of Life Guards of Horse in 1667 and some reformed officers. Beg him to find them bread; spent their youth and blood and underwent all hardships short of death for his Majesty and his father.'[62] It is likely however that they were taken on as reformadoes rather than as commissioned officers, for there is no record in the commission registers of them; but the remainder had to wait until vacancies occurred and then petition for them. John Rumsey and Edward Trelawney petitioned the Privy Council in October 1669 for employment or relief and, surprisingly perhaps, they were granted £200 a year each;[63] Rumsey was later lieutenant-colonel of Sir Henry Goodrick's Regiment in 1678, in which he found a place for John Turner as an ensign;[64] while Trelawney is possibly the man who was captain-lieutenant in the Duke of Monmouth's Regiment in 1678.[65]

The later expansion of the army for the Third Dutch War and the expedition to France provided opportunities for many of the remaining officers and men,[66] although usually in lower ranks than those they had held in Portugal. Pearson, for example, was only a major in an Irish regiment in 1672.[67] Theodore Russell was still a major in 1678: he was granted a commission in Lord Worcester's Regiment for the Third Dutch War but then transferred to the Duke of York's Regiment of Horse.[68] South, John Sandys, Robert Sutton and Richard Sandys found places as captain, lieutenants and ensign respectively in the Earl of Ogle's Regiment.[69] William Armstrong gained a lieutenancy in the Queen's Regiment of Horse in 1678, in which Sir Thomas Armstrong – doubtless a relative – was the lieutenant-colonel;[70] Richard Hill, by then a captain, was appointed quarter-master in the troop of horse raised by Captain William Wind in 1678;[71] Andrew Maynard, William Littleton and James Baxter found places in John Fitzgerald's Regiment in 1672 as captain and lieutenants respectively;[72] Henry Morgan may be the man who raised a company to defend Plymouth in 1672;[73] Nicholas Cusacke went to the Earl of Inchiquin's Regiment in Tangier in 1672:[74] not the same earl as had originally been in command of the brigade in Portugal, but his son, William. Francis Thomson was still an ensign when he joined Lord John Belasyse's Regiment in 1673, presumably using the family connection from Portugal.[75]

Lists of the officers of the two regiments of foot were compiled in 1676 and of the eighteen listed there as still living, ten were in the army, six still in the rank of ensign:[76] Samuel Lord and Thomas Tesman both in Lord John Frescheville's troop of horse at York, Edward Tomes in Sir Thomas Armstrong's troop of the Duke of Monmouth's Regiment of Horse Guards; Boys in the Earl of Oxford's own troop of the Royal Horse Guards; Richard Towneley and Thomas Coningsby in Major Windham's troop of the same regiment; Towneley was later captain-lieutenant in Sir John Talbot's Regiment of Dragoons.[77] Captain John Middelton and Captain-Lieutenant John Sherrard (or Sherwood) were also in the household troops: Middleton in The Duke of Monmouth's troop of the Life Guards and Sherrard in Sir Howard Compton's troop; while John Wharton was in Sir Phillip Howard's troop of the Life Guards and later in the Earl of Carlisle's Regiment.[78] Lieutenant-Colonel John Rumsey was in the Bristol garrison. The remainder – Captains Henry Boade, Adam Bolton and Richard Sandys, Lieutenants Robert Wattson and William Ash, Quarter-Master William Reines and Secretary George Barnadiston – were all listed as living privately 'in the country'. However for some, their period of unemployment may have been temporary: Boade is listed elsewhere as a major in the Earl of Peterborough's Regiment in 1673, then with the Holland Regiment from 1677 until at least 1684:[79] Bolton is listed as a lieutenant in the Earl of Carlisle's Regiment in 1673;[80] William Ash was a captain in the Marquis of Worcester's Regiment in 1673 and transferred to the Irish Establishment in 1674;[81] and Robert

Wattson was a lieutenant in George Legge's Regiment of Foot in 1678.[82] At least one rose to high rank in later years: Edmund Mayne, for example, who was a cornet in Portugal, was major in the Duke of Monmouth's Horse in 1678, then major in the Royal Horse Guards and lieutenant-colonel in Lord Gerard's Horse in 1679. He was eventually a brigadier of horse and Governor of Berwick.[83] An unusual posterity awaited one long survivor: the Irish officer Lawrence Dempsey, who it will be remembered had served in Spain between 1657 and 1661. He had been sent to Portugal as captain of horse, was promoted first to major and later to lieutenant-colonel by Schomberg; and after the return of the brigade he had received a pension. He was still serving in Colonel Thomas Dongan's Regiment on the Irish Establishment in 1678, along with Theobald Byrne, whom he had commended to Schomberg after the Battle of Ameixial in 1663.[84] At the so-called Glorious Revolution Dempsey was commissioned as lieutenant-colonel of Lord Galmoy's Horse in James II's Irish Army where Charles Farrell, or Carroll, John Roach and Nicholas Cusacke also transferred their allegiance. They were all soon in action against Schomberg, his old commander. Dempsey died of wounds received in a skirmish on 22 June 1690, just before the Battle of the Boyne, where Schomberg himself lost his life.[85]

*   *   *

The intervention in Portugal was one of the few successful episodes of the Restoration government's foreign policy. As Pepys said in his diary, London was full of the news of the victory at Ameixial; the diarist took particular satisfaction in the high reputation the English foot had earned.[86] With the benefit of hindsight, weakening Spain to strengthen France may not seem a sound basis for foreign policy but in 1662 the threat was not obvious; and anyway, the economic advantages of trade in the Far East, South America and Africa appeared to outweigh more nebulous strategic considerations.

The numerous accounts in the State Papers and personal accounts cited during this story testify to the hardships of the soldiers in the Portuguese service and to the poverty of the discharged veterans. Charles Croke summed matters up in a way that cannot be bettered. Speaking of the regiment of horse, he wrote that:

> I verily believe, there was never a more gallant party went out of *England* upon any design whatever, than were that regiment of horse ... of six hundred, there were at least four hundred of them Gentlemens Sons; they came into the Country full of money and gallantry, and those which survived left it as full of poverty and necessity: But they startled the *Portuguees*, and made that proud people confess, that few Princes in Christendom, but must vail their Bonnet to *Britains* King.[87]

The bravery of the English between 1662 and 1668 was a recurring theme in later military interventions. On the eve of the War of the Spanish Succession, in which English troops were again sent to the Peninsula, the English translator of d'Ablancourt's account of the Portuguese War of Independence said that:

> Nothing can be more fit than the reading of these memoirs to make the officers who are to serve in Portugal acquainted with the genius and manners of their friends

and enemies, the Portuguese and Spaniards, with their ways of fighting, with the situation and strength of the forts and places of those countries; and in a word with everything that 'tis necessary they should know.[88]

Even more striking was the tribute paid in 1807, when an account of Schomberg's Portuguese campaigns was published for the express purpose of inspiring the Portuguese to throw off Bonaparte. Again the historic precedent was emphasised: on the victory at Ameixial, for example: '*L'action du Colonel Dungan et de la cavalerie Angloise est heroique. On y reconnoit les vainqueurs de Maida.*'[89] Schomberg's campaigns are said to have been studied by the great duke, Wellington, himself. But since then, the English intervention in Portugal has become a forgotten war. Perhaps, however, posterity can give the honour to those unnamed soldiers that they earned in their lifetimes, but never received. As Monck's biographer, Chaplain Thomas Grumble said of them, 'What excellent soldiers these were, two thousand of them demonstrated (in Portugal) to all Europe, where they saved that kingdom, and made the Spaniards glad to make peace.'[90]

Annex A

Army Lists of the Brigade in Portugal, 1662–1668

These lists have been compiled from John Child's book *The Army of Charles II* supplemented by other sources quoted in the bibliography. No army lists or muster rolls have survived, and so the names have been gleaned from casualty returns, petitions and letters. The date after an officer's name indicates the first year in which he is mentioned in any source. It is impossible to give dates for any of the commissions as officers on foreign service stations were commissioned on the spot by the local commander-in-chief, whose own commission authorised him to appoint officers in the king's name.

GENERAL OFFICERS COMMANDING THE BRIGADE

Name and Rank	Dates	Notes
Murrough O'Brien, 1st Earl of Inchiquin	1662	Old Royalist, Irish, See his entry in Chapter 2.
Frederick, 1st Duke of Schomberg	1662	See his entries in Chapter 2 *et seq.* Later in the English service under William III as Master-General of the Ordnance. Killed at the Boyne in 1690.
Major-General Sir Thomas Morgan	1662	Protectorate officer. See his details in Chapter 2.
Major-General Christopher O'Brien	1663	Brother of Inchiquin, old Royalist. See his details in Chapters 2 and 3; dismissed by court-martial on charges of collusion with the Spanish, but later cleared.
Major-General Sir John Talbot	1662	Old Royalist veteran of the Civil Wars; left Portugal in the first year.
Frederick Schomberg	1667	Son of the Duke; assumed command of the brigade when the Duke returned to France after the peace.
George Barnadiston, Secretary to the Commanding General	Not known	Listed in C.S.P.D. Addenda in 1676.

THE REGIMENT OF HORSE

Name and Rank	Dates	Notes
Lieutenant-Colonel Michael Dongan	1662	Old Protectorate officer, served in Dunkirk. Killed at Ameixial.
Lieutenant-Colonel John Belasyse	1662	Old Royalist, brother of Lord Fauconberg. Had been a captain in the garrison of the Hull garrison in 1661. Wounded at Ameixial. In 1665, captain in the troop of horse at Tangier.
Major Thomas Hunt	1664	Old Royalist, promoted to lieutenant-colonel vice Apsley, 1664; killed at Valencia de Alcantara.
Captain Henry Boade	Not known	Listed in C.S.P.D. Addenda in 1676.
Captain Francis Kelly	1662	Wounded at Ameixial. Given £264 in 1667 for having taken his troop to Portugal. Captain then major in the Duke of Albemarle's Regiment of Foot 1673–1674.
Captain William Littleton	1662	From Dunkirk garrison, member of a Royalist family. Wounded at Ameixial. Lieutenant in John Fitzgerald's Regiment in 1672.
Captain John Middleton	Not known	Wounded at Ameixial. Listed in C.S.P.D. Addenda in 1676 as being in the Duke of Monmouth's troop of the Life Guards.
Captain Richard Mill	1662	From Harley's Dragoons; old Protectorate officer. Wounded at Ameixial and possibly dismissed following the mutiny after Ameixial.
Captain Guy Molesworth	1662	Old Royalist from Prince Maurice's Horse, wounded at First Newbury. Dismissed in 1663. Captain in Colonel Richard Norton's Regiment until disbanded and then major in Lord Alington's Regiment in 1667. Later colonel of the Duchess of York's Regiment. Knighted in 1680.
Captain — Paulinge	1663	Killed at Ameixial.
Captain Theodore Russell	1664	Possible old Royalist. Major in Lord Worcester's Regiment in 1673.
Captain John Rust	1665	Killed at Montes Claros.

Name and Rank	Dates	Notes
Captain Sir William Salkeld	1662	Had been a captain in Sir Robert Harley's Regiment in Dunkirk. Old Royalist, knighted in 1660. Brother of Colonel John Salkeld. Granted a commission in the Major's troop of the Horse Guards under Sir Francis Wyndham in 1667 and retired as a captain 1 Nov 1667. Elected as MP for Old Sarum in October 1669.
Captain Robert Sutton	1662	Probable old Royalist, relative of Lord Lexinton? Wounded at Ameixial. Retired from Portugal at the end of 1663. Later lieutenant in the Earl of Ogle's Regiment.
Captain — South	1662	Wounded at Ameixial. Captain in the Earl of Ogle's Regiment in 1673.
Captain Edward Trelawney	1662	Old Royalist? Family known to Clarendon. Wounded and then promoted to major after Ameixial. Captured the Prince of Parma's standard at Montes Claros. Lieutenant-colonel commanding the horse in 1667. Granted a pension in 1668; possibly captain-lieutenant to the Duke of Monmouth in his regiment in 1678.
Lieutenant William Armstrong	1668	Later lieutenant in The Queen's Horse, 1678.
Lieutenant William Bullocke	1667	Petitioned the king on return in 1668; ensign in Viscount Townshend's Regiment?
Lieutenant William Grant	1662	
Lieutenant Richard Gwynne	1668	Of a Welsh Royalist family from Gwempa, Llangyndeyrn, in Carmarthenshire. Was later High Sherriff in 1671.
Lieutenant William Osborne	1668	
Lieutenant John Wetmore	1662	Protectorate officer, from Morgan's Regiment? Wounded at Ameixial. To Moore's Regiment as major after Ameixial; killed at Valencia de Alcantara.
Lieutenant — Pollen	1663	Wounded at Ameixial; killed at Évora
Lieutenant Charles Croke	1662	Former Royalist officer. Deserted.
Cornet John Crossman	1662	Wounded at Ameixial. Possibly dismissed following the mutiny after Ameixial.
Cornet Hugh Firman	1668	
Cornet Samuel Sharpe	1665	Wounded at Montes Claros.

Name and Rank	Dates	Notes
Cornet Francis Trelawney	1664	Relative of Captain Edward Trelawney? Lieutenant in 1667. Petitioned the king on return in 1668.
Cornet John Philipps	1668	
Cornet Richard Hill	1668	Quarter-master in the troop of horse raised by Captain William Wind in 1678.
Cornet William Soulon	1668	
Cornet Edmund Mayne	1668	Major in the Duke of Monmouth's Horse in 1678, then in the Horse Guards, lieutenant-colonel in Lord Gerard's Horse in 1679. He was eventually a brigadier-general and governor of Berwick.
Cornet John Wharton	1663	Wounded at Ameixial; rose to captain in Moore's Regiment. Listed in C.S.P.D. Addenda in 1676 in Sir Philip Howard's troop of the Life Guards; later in the Earl of Carlisle's Regiment.
Cornet Robert Meakinge	1663	Died of wounds at Ameixial.
Quarter-Master David Dunbar	1668	
Quarter-Master Richard Rogers	1668	
Quarter-Master John Hersman	1668	
Quarter-Master Thomas Smythe	1668	

HENRY PEARSON'S REGIMENT OF FOOT

Name and Rank	Dates	Notes
Colonel Henry Pearson	1662	Old Protectorate officer. Wounded at Valencia de Alcantara. Major in Lord de Poer's Regiment in 1672.
Lieutenant-Colonel Henry Belasyse	1662	Old Royalist, cousin of John Belasyse of the Horse, son of Sir Richard Bellasyse of Ludworth, Co. Durham. Went on to Tangier as captain of a company in 1665 and then attached to a troop of horse under the Duke of Buckingham in 1667. Died in 1717 aged 70.

Name and Rank	Dates	Notes
Lieutenant-Colonel John Rumsey	1664	Rose from Cornet to Lt-Col in Portugal. To Tangier in 1668 and later in Sir Allen Apsley's Regiment of Foot; later still Sir Henry Goodrick's Regiment of Foot. Listed as being in the garrison of Bristol in 1676.
Lieutenant-Colonel William Sheldon	1664	Royalist, formerly of Prince Maurice's Regiment with Molesworth, so brought by his influence? From the King's Life Guard. Killed at Montes Claros.
Captain Adam Bolton	Not known	Listed in C.S.P.D. Addenda in 1676. Lieutenant in the Earl of Carlisle's Regiment in 1673.
Captain Lawrence Dempsey	1662	Irish Catholic; promoted to major after Ameixial, 1663. Petitioned the king on return in 1668 and granted a pension. Lt-Col of Colonel Thomas Dongan's Regiment of Foot, raised for service with Louis XIV of France in 1678; later Lt-Col of the Earl of Ardington's Regiment of Horse in 1686. Later killed in Ireland fighting for James II as Lt-Col of Lord Galmoy's Regiment of Horse against William of Orange and Schomberg.
Captain Edward Witham	1662	From Morgan's Protectorate Regiment; Killed at Valencia de Alcantara.
Captain — Heathfield	1665	Killed at Montes Claros.
Captain Theobald Byrne	1663	Commended by Dempsey and Schomberg for his conduct at Ameixial; later served with Dempsey in Colonel Thomas Dongan's Regiment in 1678.
Captain Charles Langley	1665	Killed at A Guarda.
Captain John Turner	1663	Cornet in Prince Maurice's Horse with Molesworth so brought by his influence? Wounded at Valencia de Alcantara. Went with John Rumsey to Sir Henry Goodrick's Regiment in 1678.
Captain-Lieutenant – Newsome	1665	Wounded at Montes Claros.
Lieutenant John Jones	1665	Killed at Montes Claros.

Name and Rank	Dates	Notes
Lieutenant William Ash	Not known	Listed in C.S.P.D. Addenda in 1676. Captain in the Marquis of Worcester's Regiment in 1673 and transferred to the Irish Establishment in 1674 as captain of a company in Connaught. Later captain in the Irish Foot Guards in 1680 and later still in Viscount Mountjoy's Horse.
Lieutenant Charles Serres	1662	Captain after Ameixial; killed at Montes Claros.
Ensign — Berry	1665	Wounded at Montes Claros; killed at A Guarda.
Ensign — Boys	Not known	Listed in C.S.P.D. Addenda in 1676 as being in the Earl of Oxford's troop of the Royal Horse Guards.
Ensign Richard Coningsby	Not known	Listed in C.S.P.D. Addenda in 1676.
Ensign — Summers	1665	Killed at Montes Claros.
Ensign Thomas Tesman	1668	In Lord Frescheville's troop of the Life Guards in 1676.
Ensign Richard Towneley	Not known	Listed in C.S.P.D. Addenda in 1676 in Major Wyndham's troop of the Royal Horse Guards with Salkeld, later captain-lieutenant in Sir John Talbot's Regiment of Dragoons.
Surgeon Don John Leadger	1665	
Quarter-Master William Reines	Not known	Listed in C.S.P.D. Addenda in 1676.

FRANCIS MOORE'S REGIMENT OF FOOT

Name and Rank	Dates	Notes
Colonel Francis Moore	1662	Old Parliament officer. Wounded at Montes Claros. No details found after the end of the war; perhaps disgraced after killing Captain Shanon.
Lieutenant-Colonel James Apsley	1662	Captain in Prince Maurice's Horse; POW at Naseby along with Molesworth so brought by him? Lieutenant-colonel of the horse after Ameixial then to Moore's Regiment; killed at Montes Claros.
Major Francis Moreneur	1665	

Name and Rank	Dates	Notes
Captain Charles Farrell (also referred to as 'Carroll' or 'Farroll').	1664	Irish Catholic, from Farrell's Regiment at Tangier; commended to Lord Arlington by Southwell in 1668. Petitioned the king on return in 1668. Lt-Col of Lord Galway's Horse in James II's Irish Army, 1689.
Captain Charles Love	1665	Wounded at A Guarda. Petitioned the king for relief on return in 1668.
Captain Richard Sandys	1664	Wounded at Valencia de Alcantara and again at Montes Claros. Lieutenant in the Earl of Ogle's Regiment in 1673?
Captain Dominic Shanon	1667	Petitioned the king for employment in February 1668 but was later killed in a duel with Col Moore.
Captain Andrew Maynard	1665	Brother of the English Consul-General in Lisbon. Wounded at Valencia de Alcantara. Captain in John Fitzgerald's Regiment in 1672.
Captain Francis Stansby	1665	Wounded at Valencia de Alcantara; killed at Montes Claros.
Captain John Roach (Roche)	1663	Irish Catholic, from Fitzgerald's Regiment at Tangier. Wounded at Valencia de Alcantara. Petitioned the king on return in 1668. Captain in the Earl of Tyrconnel's Horse in James II's Irish Army in 1689.
Captain William Moore	1663	English Catholic; killed at Valencia de Alcantara. Not to be confused with an officer of the same name who was in Lord Falkland's Regiment at Dunkirk in 1661 and then went to Tangier.
Captain John Wharton	1664	Former Cornet of the Horse – see above.
Captain-Lieutenant Richard Mill	1662	Possible Royalist, relative of Sir John Mill? Not to be confused with Richard Mill in the Regiment of Horse.
Lieutenant George Sandys	1665	Relative of Captain Richard Sandys? Wounded at Montes Claros. Ensign in the Earl of Ogle's Regiment in 1667.
Lieutenant John Sherwood, or Sherrard	1665	Wounded at Montes Claros. Rose to be Captain-Lieutenant. Listed in C.S.P.D. Addenda 1676 in Sir Howard Compton's troop of the Royal Horse Guards.
Lieutenant — Senhouse	1665	Killed at A Guarda.

Name and Rank	Dates	Notes
Ensign — Emerson	1664	Former Protectorate officer, had been a Captain in Sir Robert Harley's Regiment in Dunkirk, then in Peterborough's Regiment at Tangier. Wounded at Montes Claros. Probably killed at Albuquerque.
Ensign Samuel Lord	Not known	Listed in C.S.P.D. Addenda in 1676 in Lord Frescheville's troop of horse at York.
Ensign Edward Tomes	Not known	Listed in C.S.P.D. Addenda in 1676 in Sir Thomas Armstrong's troop of the Royal Horse Guards.
Ensign — Watkins	1665	Killed at Montes Claros.
Ensign Robert Wattson	Not known	Listed in C.S.P.D. Addenda in 1676. Lieutenant in George Legge's Regiment of Foot in 1678.
Quarter-Master George Chapse	1662	

FOOT OFFICERS WHO SERVED IN EITHER PEARSON'S OR MOORE'S

Name and Rank	Dates	Notes
Captain — Atkinson	1663	Killed at Ameixial.
Captain John Birch	1664	
Captain — Sandys	1664	Wounded at Valencia de Alcantara and again at Montes Claros. Captain in the Earl of Ogle's Regiment in 1672.
Captain — Fitzpatrick	1664	Irish Catholic, from Fitzgerald's Regiment at Tangier. Killed at Valencia de Alcantara.
Captain James Baxter	1664	Wounded at Valencia de Alcantara. Lieutenant in Fitzgerald's Regiment in 1672.
Captain Charles Bourke (Burke)	1664	Irish Catholic, from Fitzgerald's Regiment at Tangier. Petitioned the king for relief on return in 1668.
Captain James Lee	1667	Petitioned the king on return in 1668.
Captain Gregory Noland	1664	Killed at Valencia de Alcantara.
Captain — Goudinge	1663	Killed at Ameixial.
Captain Henry Travers	1664	Killed at Valencia de Alcantara.
Captain Nathaniel Hill	1664	Wounded at Valencia de Alcantara.
Lieutenant — Ashton	1665	Murdered in Lisbon.

Name and Rank	Dates	Notes
Lieutenant Henry Morgan	1664	Nephew of Sir Thomas Morgan. Captain of a company at Plymouth in 1672?
Lieutenant Robert Boone	1665	Lieutenant in the Earl of Manchester's Regiment in 1667.
Lieutenant — Mulberry	1664	
Lieutenant Nicholas Cusacke	1664	Nephew of the Earl of Tyrconnel. Later lieutenant in Inchiquin's Regiment at Tangier in 1678. Colonel in James II's Irish Army in 1689.
Lieutenant — Terry	1664	
Lieutenant Pollen	1663	Killed at Évora. Not to be confused with Pollen, officer in the Regiment of Horse.
Lieutenant — Fitzherbert	1664	Irish Catholic.
Lieutenant Nicholas Habyne	1667	Petitioned the king for relief on return in 1668.
Ensign John Burke	1664	Irish Catholic, from Farrell's Regiment at Tangier. Petitioned the king for relief on return in 1668. Served in Thomas Dongan's Regiment in 1678 with Dempsey and Byrne. Captain in the Earl of Clanricarde's Regiment of Foot in James II's Irish Army in 1689.
Ensign John Harbord	1664	From Fitzgerald's Regiment at Tangier. Lieutenant in 1666. Petitioned the king on return in 1668.
Ensign — Pettybons	1664	Possibly captured at Valencia de Alcantara.
Ensign Francis Thomson	1664	Ensign in Lord John Belasyse's Regiment in 1673?
Chaplain — Cargill	1663	

Annex B

Rates of Pay

Throughout the period the pay of both officers and soldiers remained constant. The amounts given in the tables below represent the full daily pay as given for service in England, before any deductions were made. Off-reckonings were subtracted from this sum and the balance paid as subsistence money. To gain some idea of comparative worth, a calculator in widespread use[1] gives the value of one shilling in 1660 as the equivalent of £5.40 today using the retail price index. The second figure is the amount in Portuguese *cruzadoes* paid for service in Portugal, at the rate of four to the pound sterling:[2]

THE HORSE

Colonel as Colonel*	12s 0d, Cr 48.00
Lieutenant-Colonel as Lieutenant-Colonel*	7s 0d, Cr 30.00
Major	5s 0d, Cr 23.00
Captain	14s 0d (10s 0d pay+2 horses at 2s 0d each); Cr 56.00
Lieutenant	10s 0d (6s 0d pay+2 horses at 2s 0d each); Cr 40.00
Cornet	9s 0d (5s 0d pay+2 horses at 2s 0d each); Cr 36.00

* *Colonels, lieutenant-colonels, and majors were captains of companies as well as field officers. They received pay for both offices.*

Quarter-Master	6s 0d (4s 0d pay +1 horse at 2s 0d); Cr 20.00
Corporal	5s 0d; Cr 20.00
Trumpeter	2s 8d; Cr 10.80
Private Trooper	2s 6d; Cr 9.96

The Off Reckonings for the horse amounted to 6d per man per day, leaving 'subsistence' of 3s 6d for the Life Guard and 2s 0d for all other troopers. From this money the soldier had to care for both himself and his horse.

THE FOOT

Colonel as Colonel	12s 0d, Cr 48.00
Lieutenant-Colonel as Lieutenant-Colonel	7s 0d; Cr 28.00
Major as Major	5s 0d; Cr 20.00
Captain	8s 0d; Cr 35.00
Lieutenant	4s 0d; Cr 16.00
Ensign	3s 0d; Es 12.00
Chaplain	6s 8d; Cr 26.00
Adjutant	4s 0d; Cr 16.00
Surgeon	4s 0d (+2s 6d for a horse to carry his chest); Cr 26.00
Quarter-Master/Provost	4s 0d (performed by the same officer); Cr 26.00
Sergeant	1s 6d; Cr 4.00
Corporal	1s 0d; Cr 4.00
Drummer	1s 0d; Cr 4.00
Private Soldier	10d; Cr 3.00

The private infantryman suffered off-reckonings of 2d a day. This left subsistence money 8d. Deductions from full pay applied only to private soldiers and non-commissioned officers. All commissioned ranks received their full pay.

Notes

CHAPTER 1

1   Stanley G. Payne, *A History of Spain and Portugal* (The Library of Iberian Resources [online]), vol. II, p. 392.
2   David Birmingham, *A Concise History of Portugal* (2nd edn, CUP, 2003), p. 33.
3   Geoffrey Parker, *The Army of Flanders and the Spanish Road, 1567–1659* (CUP, 1972), p. 35.
4   James Maxwell Anderson, *The History of Portugal* (London, 2000), p. 131. See also Birmingham, p. 51 *et seq.*
5   For a full account see J.H. Elliott, *The Revolt of the Catalans: A Study in the Decline of Spain 1598–1640* (2nd edn, CUP, 1984).
6   Jorge Penim de Freitas, *A Cavalaria na Guerra da Restauração* (Lisbon, 2005), p. 15.
7   Gabriel Espírito Santo, *Montes Claros 1665: A Vitória Decisiva* (Lisbon, 2005), p. 39.
8   Parker, p. 274.
9   Espírito Santo, *Montes Claros 1665*, p. 40.
10 The ducat became a standard gold coin throughout Europe, especially after it was officially imperially sanctioned in 1566. Its weight is 3.4909 grams of .986 gold, which is 0.1107 troy ounces. The ducat remained sanctioned until 1857. There was also a silver ducat minted in many European countries. The Royal Dutch Mint still issues silver ducats with a weight of 28.25 grams.
11 See especially J.H. Elliott, 'The Decline of Spain', T. Aston (ed.), *Crisis in Europe 1560–1660* (London, 1965), p. 176.
12 J.H. Elliott, 'The Decline of Spain', p. 178.
13 John Childs, *Warfare in the Seventeenth Century* (London, 2003), pp. 110–111.
14 Lorraine White 'The Experience of Spain's Early Modern Soldiers: Combat, Welfare and Violence', *War in History*, 9:1 (January 2002), p. 34.
15 Jurgen Brauer & Hubert Van Tuyll, *Castles, Battles & Bombs: How Economics Explains Military History* (London, 2008), p. 119.
16 Philip II's instructions, 5 June 1558, cited in Parker, p. 129.
17 Childs, *Warfare in the Seventeenth Century*, p. 77.
18 David Maland, *Europe in the Seventeenth Century* (London, 1991), p. 227.
19 De Freitas, *A Cavalaria na Guerra da Restauração*, p. 44.
20 For more details see, for example, Glenn Joseph Ames, 'Renascent Empire?: the House of Braganza and the Quest for Stability in Portuguese Monsoon Asia c.1640–1683', review by M. N. Pearson., *The International History Review*, 23:3 (September 2001), pp. 657–659.

CHAPTER 2

1   Violet Shillington, 'The Beginnings of the Anglo-Portuguese Alliance', *Transactions of the Royal Historical Society* (London), New Series, XX (1906), pp. 109–132.
2   See George Chalmers, *A Collection of Treaties Between Great Britain and Other Powers* (2 vols., London, 1790), vol. II for a summary, especially the Portuguese treaty of 1642.
3   Clyde L. Grose, 'The Anglo-Portuguese Marriage of 1662', *The Hispanic American Historical Review*, 10:3 (August 1930), p. 314.
4   Grose, 'The Anglo-Portuguese Marriage of 1662', p. 316.

5   L.G. Davidson, *Catherine of Braganza* (London, 1908), p. 15.

6   C.R. Boxer, 'Marshal Schomberg in Portugal, 1660–1668', *History Today*, 26:10 (October 1976), p. 654.

7   Bishop Burnet, *History of His Own Time* (London, 1906), p. 64. The suggestion was made by Father Russell, de Mello's interpreter and chaplain, to Monck's agent, William Morice. Sir Robert Southwell when he became Ambassador to Lisbon got his account of the negotiations from Russell who continued to be the conduit throughout the process.

8   Colonel John Davis, *History of the Second Queen's, now the Royal West Surrey Regiment* (London, 1887), vol. I, p. 9.

9   Villaret to Clarendon, 26 April 1661, C.C.S.P., 1660–1726, ed. F.J. Routledge (Oxford, 1974), vol. V, p. 94.

10   Davidson, p. 44.

11   Grose, 'The Anglo-Portuguese Marriage of 1662', p. 316.

12   Ibid., p. 317.

13   Birmingham, p. 25.

14   Davison, p. 47.

15   Grose, 'The Anglo-Portuguese Marriage of 1662', p. 320.

16   Davidson, p. 48.

17   Grose, 'The Anglo-Portuguese Marriage of 1662', p. 321.

18   Burnet, p. 64.

19   Ibid., p. 64.

20   Keith Feiling, *British Foreign Policy 1660–1672* (London, 1972), p. 48.

21   Samuel Pepys, *The Diary of Samuel Pepys*, ed. H.B. Wheatley, (8 vols., London, 1904–1905), 30 September 1661.

22   *A True Relation of the Manner of the dangerous dispute and bloody conflict between the Spaniards and the French, etc* (London, 1661); Feiling, p. 43

23   Davidson, pp. 51–52; Grose, 'The Anglo-Portuguese Marriage of 1662', p. 328.

24   Grose, 'The Anglo-Portuguese Marriage of 1662', p. 330.

25   *Journals of the House of Lords*, vol. II, pp. 243–244.

26   Chalmers, pp. 257–295.

27   For a full account of the English occupation of Tangier see E.M.G. Routh, *Tangier: England's Lost Atlantic Outpost 1661–1684* (London, 1912).

28   According to his wife's account, *The Memoirs of Ann Lady Fanshawe* (London, 1908), they arrived in Lisbon on 4 September 1662.

29   Feiling, p. 61.

30   Grose, 'The Anglo-Portuguese Marriage of 1662', p. 335.

31   Davidson, p. 65.

32   Burnet, p. 67.

33   Ibid.

34   Davis, vol. I, p. 13. See also Statement by Duerte da Silva, 19 July 1662, H.M.C. Heathcote MSS, Series 50 (Norwich, 1899), p. 30.

35   Feiling, p. 51.

CHAPTER 3

1   Childs, *Warfare in the Seventeenth Century*, p. 88.

2   V.G. Kiernan 'Foreign Mercenaries and Absolute Monarchy', T. Aston (ed.), *Crisis in Europe 1560–1660* (London, 1965), pp. 132–133.

3   P. Sagnac and A. De Saint-Léger, *La Prépondérance française: Louis XIV (1661–1715)* (2nd edn, Paris, 1944), p. 232.

4   Antichel Grey, *Debates in the House of Commons 1667–1694,* (London, 1763), vol. VIII, p. 357.

5   See the summary in the Spanish Correspondence, TNA S.P.D. Charles II, vol. X, p. 185, dated 9 August 1660.

6   Edward Hyde, *The Life of Edward, Earl of Clarendon* (London, 1857), vol. I, pp. 277–278.

7   12 Charles II, cap. 9.

8   William A. Shaw, *Calendar of Treasury Books: 1661–1668* (Institute of Historical Research, 1916), vol. VII.

9   TNA S.P.D. Charles II, vol. XXXIV, p. 567.

10 Burnet, p. 66.

11 Francis Grose, *Military Antiquities respecting a history of the English Army* (London, 1786–1788), vol. II, pp. 180–181.

12 Orders-in-Council, 14, 17 and 28 September 1660.

13 Shaw, *Calendar of Treasury Books,* vol. VII.

14 Thomas Babington 1st Baron Macaulay, *The History of England from the Accession of James II* (1848), vol. I, p. 154.

15 *House of Commons Journal,* 7 April 1659.

16 Childs, *Warfare in the Seventeenth Century,* p. 106.

17 C.F.D. Dumouriez, *Campagnes de Maréchal Schomberg en Portugal, 1662–1668* (London, 1807), p. 61: This extract and all that follow translated from the original French by the author; H.M.C. Seventh Report, p. 381.

18 Dumouriez, p. 7.

19 De Freitas, *A Cavalaria na Guerra da Restauração,* p. 46.

20 D'Ablancourt, p. 86.

21 Dumouriez, p. 62.

22 Burnet, p. 65.

23 Ibid., p. 67.

24 Sir Charles Firth and G. Davies, *Regimental History of Cromwell's Army* (2 vols., Oxford, 1940), vol. II, p. 561.

25 John Aubrey, *Brief Lives,* ed. Richard Barber, (Woodbridge and New York, 1975), vol. II, p. 87; see also *The Dictionary of National Biography* (London, 1961).

26 Aubrey, *Brief Lives,* vol. II, p. 88.

27 Major General Morgan's *Memoirs,* 1657–1658 in the Harleian Miscellany, vol. III.

28 Firth and Davies, vol. II, p. 409.

29 Ibid., p. 496.

30 *Mercurius Publicus,* 8–15 May 1662, pp. 292–293.

31 Firth and Davies, vol. II, pp. 558–559.

32 Ibid., p. 509.

33 Ibid., p. 518.

34 Firth and Davies, vol. I, p. xxxiv.

35 C.S.P.D., 1661–1662, p. 251; C.C.S.P., vol. V, p. 192.

36 *Dairy of Public Transactions,* p. 367, cited in Firth and Davis, vol. II, p. 499.

37 C.S.P.V., 1661–1664, 3 March 1662.

38 John Childs, *The Army of Charles II* (London and Toronto, 1976), Annex A.

39 P.R. Newman, *The Old Service: Royalist regimental colonels and the Civil War, 1642–1646* (London, 1993), pp. 114–116, 284. See also Richard W. Cotton, *Barnstaple and the Northern Part of Devonshire during the Great Civil War, 1642–46* (London, 1889), pp. 353, 441, 443–444; H.M.C. Pepys MSS at Magdalene College (London, 1911), pp. 209, 214, 241, 274, 280; Bulstrode Whitelocke, *Memorials* (Oxford, 1853), vol. III, 297–298. Apsley was reduced to forging signatures to Navy Office documents until given his command in Portugal; *Notes which Passed at Meetings of the Privy Council between Charles II and the Earl of Clarendon,* ed. W. D. Macray, (London, 1896), p. 82.

40 Firth and Davies, vol. II, pp. 491–496; *Journals of the House of Commons*, vol. VII, 763.

41 Charles Dalton, *English Army Lists and Commission Registers, 1661–1714* (6 vols., London, 1894–1904), vol. I, p. 51.

42 J.P. Riley, 'Continuity in the English Army, 1658–1668' (Unpublished M.A. Thesis, Leeds, 1989), p. 94.

43 *Mercurius Publicus*, 18–25 October 1660, p. 675; Firth and Davis, vol. II, p. 314.

44 Childs, p. 170; C.S.P.D. 1666–1667, p. 320.

45 Dalton, vol. I, pp. 137,162.

46 Riley, 'English Army 1658–1668', p. 95.

47 On the decision to send the Irish to Portugal, see H.M.C. Portland MSS (London, 1894), vol. III, p. 254.

48 Firth and Davies, vol. II, p. 671; Thurloe Manuscripts (Rawlinson A Volumes 1–67), vol. 65, ff. 91, 106, 143.

49 Lockhart to Cromwell, Thurloe Manuscripts, vol. VII, f. 201.

50 Ibid., f. 274.

51 TNA SP 44/2, pp. 27, 302, 308; Dalton, vol. I, pp. 17, 25, 27; Firth and Davies, vol. II, p. 676.

52 Dalton, vol. I, p. 17.

53 Ibid., p. 25.

54 TNA SP 44/2, p. 301.

55 *The Kingdom's Intelligencer*, 23–30 June 1662, p. 411.

56 TNA SP 44/2, p. 27; H.M.C. Heathcote MSS, p. 29; C.S.P.D., 1661–1662, pp. 331, 344.

57 Firth and Davies, vol. I, p. 162.

58 Monck's Letter-Book, Sir William Clarke MSS, 1662–1664.

59 Charles Croke, *Fortune's Uncertainty, or Youth's Unconstancy* (London, 1667; reprinted Oxford, 1959), p. 51; H.M.C. Heathcote MSS, pp. 84, 98.

60 Newman, pp. 103–104.

61 'A List of Officers Claiming to the £60,000' (London, 1663), col. 95; *Virginia Magazine of History and Biography*, XII (1904), p. 205; H.M.C. Seventh Report (London, 1879), p. 146; C.S.P.D. 1666–67, p. 403; *JSAHR*, XXXV (1957), p. 12.

62 Newman, pp. 95, 106, 186–187, 215, 229, 234, 239, 281.

63 *Intelligencer*, 25 August–1 September, 1662; Thomas Shipman, *Carolina: or Loyal Poems* (London, 1683), pp, 91–93.

64 TNA SP 29/249, f. 80; TNA SP 44/29, ff. 21–30.

65 John D'Alton, *Illustrations, Historical and Genealogical: Of King James's Irish Army List (1689)* (Dublin, 1855) p. 416.

66 Davis, vol. I, p. 67.

67 *Intelligencer*, 23–30 June 1662; H.M.C. Heathcote MSS, p. 29.

68 T. H. Lister, *Life and Administration of Edward, First Earl of Clarendon* (London, 1837), vol. III, p. 516; H.M.C. Heathcote MSS, pp. 75–77.

69 C.S.P.I., 1660–1662, p. 51; C.S.P.D., 1661–1662, pp. 335, 344.

70 De Freitas, *A Cavalaria na Guerra da Restauração*, p. 48.

71 D'Alton, p. 8.

72 Childs, *Army of Charles II*, Annex A; Newman, pp. 240–241.

73 See Chapter 8.

74 John Miller, 'Catholic officers in the later Stuart Army', *English Historical Review*, LXXXVIII: CCCXLVI (January 1973), pp. 42 cites the war-time strength for a troop of horse as 60 with 3 officers and 4 NCOs; and a regiment of foot as 800 in ten companies, with 3 officers and 5 NCOs per company and 3 regimental officers.

75 Childs, *Warfare in the Seventeenth Century*, p. 106.

76 C.H. Firth, *Cromwell's Army* (London, 1921), p. 280.

77 Childs, *Warfare in the Seventeenth Century*, p. 106; Parker, p. 12.

78 Paul Hardacre, 'The English Contingent in Portugal, 1662–1668', *Journal of the Society for Army Historical Research*, 38 (1960), p. 117.

79 *Memoirs of the Sieur d'Ablancourt* (London, 1703), p. 135.

80 *Intelligencer*, 28 March, 19 December, 1664; *Memoirs of the Sieur d' Ablancourt* (London, 1703), pp. 135, 143.

81 TNA SP 89/7, f. 49.

82 Richard Bagwell, *Dictionary of National Biography* (London, 1961) vol. XV, pp. 320–327.

83 E. Settle, 'The Character of a Popish Successor' (1681), *State Tracts* (London, 1689), pp. 149–157; Miller, 'Catholic officers in the later Stuart Army', p. 53.

84 Miller, p. 50.

85 Ibid., p. 38.

86 TNA PC 2/59 pp. 206–207; C.S.P.D., 1667, pp. 196, 206–207; Pepys, *Diary*, 13–14 June 1667.

87 Routh, *Tangier*, pp. 304–305.

88 See especially G.N. Clark, *War and Society in the Seventeenth Century* (Cambridge, 1958), p. 61 *et seq.*

89 In particular, for details of how national contingents operated on both sides and indeed changed sides, see Sir Roger Williams, *The Actions of the Low Countries* (New York, 1985).

90 Parker, p. 52.

91 See especially Brendan Jennings, *Wild Geese in Spanish Flanders, 1582–1700* (Dublin, 1964), pp. 32–43.

92 *An Historical Account of the British Regiments employed since the Reign of Queen Elizabeth and King James I in the formation and defence of the Dutch Republic, particularly of the Scotch Brigade* (London, 1795), p. 6.

93 Childs, *Army of Charles II*, p. 162.

94 Wienand Drenth, *The Regiments of the Modern British Army 1660–1714: From the Beginnings through the end of the War of the Spanish Succession* (unpublished).

95 Firth and Davies, vol. II, pp. 499–500; C.S.P.V., 1661–1664 pp. 141, 152.

96 *Intelligencer*, 26 May–2 June 1662; *Mercurius Publicus*, 31 July–7 August 1662, p. 505 and 21–28 August 1662, p. 570.

97 *Mercurius Publicus*, 8–15 May 1662 p. 310; 'The Journals of Sir Thomas Allin, 1660–1678', ed. R. C. Anderson (Navy Records Society, 1939–40), vol. I, pp. 76–85. See also the report of Francisco Giaverina, C.S.P.V., 9/19 May 1662.

98 *Intelligencer*, 23–30 June 1662, p. 411; Luiza, Queen of Portugal to King Charles II, 22 June 1662, H.M.C. Heathcote MSS, p. 29; C.S.P.V., 9/19 June 1662.

99 Croke, p. 52.

CHAPTER 4

1 The lyrics of this song place it firmly in the reign of Queen Anne, a whole generation on from the Restoration War; however there is a strong element of inherited and shared experience in soldiers' songs and this one seems to capture the memory of the English brigade forty years before. See Lewis Winstock, *Songs and Music of the Redcoats: A History of the War Music of the British Army, 1642–1902* (London, 1970), pp. 35–37.

2 *The Memoirs of Ann Lady Fanshawe* (London, 1908), p. 116.

3 Lorraine White, 'Strategic Geography and the Spanish Habsburg Monarchy's Failure to Recover Portugal, 1640–1668', *The Journal of Military History*, 71:2 (April 2007), p. 379.

4 Inchiquin to Clarendon, 30th June/10th July, Bodleian Library, MS Clarendon 77, ff. 31–32; C.S.P.D., 1661–1662, p. 440.

5 TNA SP 89/7, f. 299.

6 31 October 1662, TNA SP 89/6, f. 44.

7 TNA SP 89/7, f. 299.

8 *Mercurius Publicus*, 31 July–7 August, 1662, p. 506; C.S.P.D., 1661–1662, p. 344.

9   Croke, pp. 52, 57; *Mercurius Publicus*, 31 July–7 August 1662, p. 506.

10   Schomberg to Fanshawe, 7 May 1663, H.M.C. Heathcote MSS, p. 84.

11   Dempsey to Sir Richard Fanshawe, 4 January 1662, H.M.C. Heathcote MSS, pp. 55–56.

12   Maynard to Clarendon, 28 July 1662, MS Clarendon, ff. 90–91.

13   H.M.C. Heathcote MSS, p. 32. See also the account by Paul Hardacre in *JSAHR*, 38, pp. 111–125.

14   Fanshawe to Charles II, 6 February 1662, TNA SP 89/6, ff. 7–10.

15   Pepys, *Diary*, p. 132.

16   Fanshawe to Clarendon, 11 December 1662, H.M.C. Heathcote MSS, p. 51.

17   H.M.C. Heathcote MSS, pp. 40–5, 71.

18   H.M.C. Heathcote MSS, pp. 65–66; Lister, *Life of Clarendon*, vol. III, p. 516.

19   C.C.S.P., vol. V, pp. 242–243.

20   Firth, *Cromwell's Army*, p. 494.

21   A.S.P. Woodhouse, *Puritanism and Liberty: Being the Army Debates (1647–9) from the Clarke Manuscripts with Supplementary Documents* (London, 1938), pp. 16–18. See also the remarks in *Memoirs of Ann Lady Fanshawe*, p. 166.

22   See Riley, 'English Army 1658–1668' for more detailed information. See also Miller, 'Catholic Officers in the Later Stuart Army'.

23   Grey, *Debates*, vol. VIII, pp. 4, 21.

24   See Routh, *Tangier* and Riley, 'English Army 1658–1668' for details.

25   Don Miguel de Salamanca to the Secretary of State in Madrid, 11 May 1647, cited on p. 44.

26   Pepys, *Diary*, 25 May 1661.

27   Dumouriez, p. 5.

28   Alfonso, King of Portugal, to King Charles II, 21 June 1662, H.M.C. Heathcote MSS, p. 29; Thomas Carte, *The History of the Revolutions of Portugal, From the Foundation of that Kingdom to the year MDCLXVII: With Letters of Sir Robert Southwell During his Embassy there, to the Duke of Ormond; Giving a particular Account of the deposing of Alfonso, and placing Don Pedro on the Throne* (London, 1760), p. 178.

29   TNA SP 89/7, f. 350.

30   Inchiquin to Clarendon, 10–20 June, MS Clarendon 76, ff. 361–362.

31   For the details of this affair, see the article '"God forbid it should come to that": the feud between Colonel Molesworth and Major-General O'Brien in Portugal, 1663', *The Seventeenth Century*, 26:2 (2011), pp. 346–367.

32   Articles against Colonel Guy Molesworth, 19–23 February 1663, TNA SP 89/6, f. 23.

33   Ibid.

34   TNA SP 89/6, f. 35.

35   TNA SP 89/5, f. 162.

36   H.M.C. Heathcote MSS, pp. 68, 72, 84, 86; C.S.P.I., 1663–1665, f. 205.

37   TNA SP 89/6, ff. 35, 59, 70, 73, 116, 127.

38   O'Brien's Petition to Charles II, TNA SP 89/5, f. 159.

39   Sir Henry Bennet to Fanshawe, 12 May 1663, H.M.C. Heathcote MSS, p. 86.

40   Fanshawe to Schomberg, June 1663, H.M.C. Heathcote MSS, p. 113.

41   Molesworth's Petition to Charles II, TNA SP 29/186, f. 78.

42   David J. Appleby, '"God forbid it should come to that": the feud between Colonel Molesworth and Major-General O'Brien in Portugal, 1663', *The Seventeenth Century*, 26:2 (2011), p. 359.

43   Dalton, vol. I, p. 80.

44   Riley, 'English Army 1662–1668', p. 91–92.

45   *Mercurius Scoticus*, 18–21 February 1651.

46   Clarendon to Fanshawe, 12 April 1663, H.M.C. Heathcote MSS, p. 76.

47   Dumouriez, p. 6.

48   H.M.C. Heathcote MSS, p. 74; Hardacre, p. 117.

49 *Memoirs of the Sieur d'Ablancourt, Containing a general history of the court and kingdom of Portugal* (Translated from the French, London, 1703), p. 4.
50 Dumouriez, p. 9.
51 Fanshawe to Bishop Russell, 11 February 1663, H.M.C. Heathcote MSS, p. 62.
52 Glazier, p. 60.
53 D'Ablancourt, p. 33.
54 Dumouriez, pp. 11–12.
55 D'Ablancourt, p. 38.
56 Ibid., p. 39.
57 De Freitas, *A Cavalaria na Guerra de Restauração*, pp. 20–21.
58 Dumouriez, p. 21; d'Ablancourt, p. 55.
59 Dumouriez, p. 22
60 Ibid., p. 24.
61 Ibid., p. 23.
62 Ibid., p. 29.
63 D'Ablancourt, p. 82.
64 Ibid., pp. 83–84.
65 Fanshawe to Clarendon, 6 November 1662, H.M.C. Heathcote MSS, p. 41.
66 To Clarendon, 12 March 1663, H.M.C. Heathcote MSS, p. 64.
67 Schomberg to Fanshawe, June 1663, H.M.C. Heathcote MSS, p. 98.
68 D'Ablancourt, p. 30.
69 TNA SP 89/7, f. 350.
70 D'Ablancourt, p. 31.
71 Ibid., p. 87–88.
72 Dumouriez, p. 34 citing d'Ablancourt.
73 Schomberg to Clarendon, 10 October 1661, C.C.S.P., vol. V, p. 149.

CHAPTER 5

1 D'Ablancourt, p. 95.
2 Ibid., p. 96.
3 Fanshawe to Clarendon, 4 December 1662, H.M.C. Heathcote MSS, p. 52.
4 Schomberg to Fanshawe, 13 May 1663, H.M.C. Heathcote MSS, p. 83.
5 Schomberg to Fanshawe dated 7 May 1663, H.M.C. Heathcote MSS, p. 84.
6 D'Ablancourt, pp. 40–41.
7 Dumouriez, p. 13.
8 Ibid., p. 10. See also a similar description in d'Ablancourt, p. 30.
9 Dumouriez, p. 15.
10 D'Ablancourt, p. 94.
11 Dumouriez p. 35.
12 Christopher Duffy, *Fire and Stone: The Science of Fortress Warfare 1660–1860* (New Jersey, USA, 1975), p. 11.
13 Brauer and Van Tuyll, p. 129.
14 Geoffrey Parker, *The Army of Flanders and the Spanish Road, 1567–1659* (CUP, 1972), pp. 11–12.
15 Childs, *Warfare in the Seventeenth Century*, p. 113.
16 White, 'Strategic Geography', p. 383.
17 Ibid., p. 401.
18 Ibid., p. 385.
19 Ibid., p. 380.
20 Ibid., p. 393.
21 Parker, p. 28.

22 Jonathon Riley, *Napoleon as a General* (London, 2007), p. 118.
23 Winstock, pp. 38–39.
24 See the calculations in Martin Van Crefeld, *Supplying War* (CUP, 1977), Chapter 1.
25 Childs, *Warfare in the Seventeenth Century*, p. 153.
26 White, 'Strategic Geography', p. 391.
27 Ibid., p. 381.
28 *Memoirs of Ann Lady Fanshawe,* pp. 161, 165.
29 D'Ablancourt, p. 20.
30 White, 'Strategic Geography', p. 382.
31 Conde de Clonard, *Historia Orgánica de las Armas de Infantería y Caballería,* vol. VIII (Madrid, 1851–1862), pp. 258–311; *Mercurius Publicus,* 31 July–7 August 1662, p. 500.
32 Alvaro Melendez, 'The Recovery of Extremadura and Spanish Military Memory' [online] (2011); Giancarlo Boeri, José Luis Mirecki and José Palau, *The Spanish Armies in the War of the League of Augsburg (Nine Years' War, 1688–1697)* (Madrid, 2002).
33 Account of Colonel James Apsley, H.M.C. Heathcote MSS, p. 101.
34 De Freitas, *O Combatente na Guerra da Restauração,* p. 148.
35 White, 'Strategic Geography', p. 387.
36 D'Ablancourt, p. 96.
37 The descriptions of the ground are drawn from the author's personal detailed reconnaissance on foot in January 2012.
38 Fanshawe to Sir Henry Bennet, 11 May 1663.
39 White, 'Strategic Geography', p. 404.
40 D'Ablancourt, pp. 96–97.
41 Schomberg to Fanshawe, 7 May 1663, H.M.C. Heathcote MSS, p. 84.
42 Don Antonio de Sousa de Macedo to Schomberg, 9 May 1663, H.M.C. Heathcote MSS, p. 85.
43 Apsley to Fanshawe, H.M.C. Heathcote MSS, p. 102.
44 Fanshawe to Sir Henry Bennet, 20 May 1663, H.M.C. Heathcote MSS, p. 92.
45 Dumouriez, p. 39; d'Ablancourt, p. 104.
46 *Memoirs of Ann Lady Fanshawe*, p. 111.
47 Croke, p. 60.
48 D'Ablancourt, p. 99.
49 Schomberg to Fanshawe, H.M.C. Heathcote MSS, p. 98.
50 Apsley to Fanshawe, H.M.C. Heathcote MSS, p. 102.
51 White, 'Strategic Geography', p. 396.
52 D'Ablancourt, p. 104.
53 Ibid., p. 105.
54 Schomberg to Fanshawe, 31 May 1663, H.M.C. Heathcote MSS, p. 109.
55 Apsley to Fanshawe, H.M.C. Heathcote MSS, p. 102.
56 Ibid.
57 Hardacre, p. 118.
58 D'Ablancourt, p. 107.
59 Ibid., p. 106.
60 Apsley to Fanshawe, H.M.C. Heathcote MSS, p. 103.
61 Schomberg to Fanshawe, 31 May 1663, H.M.C. Heathcote MSS, p. 109.
62 Apsley to Fanshawe, H.M.C. Heathcote MSS, p. 103.
63 White, 'Strategic Geography', p. 394.
64 Ibid., p. 395.
65 Apsley to Fanshawe, H.M.C. Heathcote MSS, p. 103.
66 Dumouriez, p. 40.
67 D'Ablancourt, p. 107.

CHAPTER 6

1 The descriptions of the ground result from the author's detailed reconnaissance on foot during January 2012.

2 Dumouriez, p. 41.

3 Schomberg to Fanshawe, 30 May 1663, Heathcote MSS, p. 97.

4 Apsley to Fanshawe, H.M.C. Heathcote MSS, p. 103.

5 D'Ablancourt, p. 109.

6 White, 'Spain's Early Soldiers', p. 11.

7 Ibid., p. 15.

8 D'Ablancourt, p. 109.

9 Edward McMurdo, *The History of Portugal: From the Reign of D. Joao II to the Reign of D. Joao V* (London, 1889; facsimile reprint London, 2010), vol. III; Livermore, H.V., *A New History of Portugal* (CUP, 1969); Dauril Alden, *The Making of an Enterprise: The Society of Jesus in Portugal, Its Empire, and Beyond, 1540–1750* (Stanford, USA, 1996), p. 115; William C. Atkinson, *A History of Spain and Portugal* (London, 1961), p. 190.

10 Dumouriez, pp. 44–45.

11 D'Ablancourt, p. 111.

12 Apsley to Fanshawe, H.M.C. Heathcote MSS, p. 104.

13 Dumouriez, p. 54.

14 Hardacre, p. 119.

15 Dumouriez, p. 54.

16 Ibid.

17 Dumouriez, p. 50.

18 Apsley to Fanshawe, H.M.C. Heathcote MSS, p. 104.

19 *Intelligencer*, 22–29 June, 1663; Bodleian Library, MS Rawlinson C. 808, 'Militarie Occurrences in Portugal: The Spring Campagne A.D. 1663'; John Colbatch, *An Account of the Court of Portugal* (London, 1700), pp. 127–140; d'Ablancourt, pp. 106–116.

20 Dumouriez, p. 51.

21 Apsley to Fanshawe, H.M.C. Heathcote MSS, p. 104.

22 English prisoners to Fanshawe, 13 June 1664, H.M.C. Heathcote MSS, p. 168.

23 C.S.P.D. Addenda, 1676 and TNA SP 29/4442, f. 301.

24 See the discussion in Jonathon Riley, *Decisive Battles* (London, 2010), Chapter 1.

25 Schomberg to d'Ablancourt, H.M.C. Heathcote MSS, p. 109.

26 *Memoirs of Ann Lady Fanshawe*, p. 112.

27 Croke, p. 61; H.M.C. Heathcote MSS, pp. 106, 113–115.

28 *A Relation of the Great Success the King of Portugal's Army had upon the Spaniards, the 29th of May (Engl. Stile) 1663* (London, 1663), p. 9.

29 D'Ablancourt, p. 113.

30 Gabriel Maura G Gamazo, *Carlos II y su corte* (Madrid,1911), vol. I, p. 186.

31 Schomberg to Fanshawe, 30 May 1663, H.M.C. Heathcote MSS, p. 97.

32 Schomberg cited in Boxer, p. 658.

33 John Pitt to Samuel Pepys, 7 June 1663, TNA S.P. 29/75, f. 33.

34 Fanshawe to Bennet, 5 June 1663, H.M.C. Heathcote MSS, p. 111.

35 Croke, pp. 61–62.

36 Schomberg to Fanshawe, 7 May 1663, H.M.C. Heathcote MSS, p. 84.

37 Croke, p. 62.

38 Pepys, *Diary*, 25 June 1663.

39 Ibid., 4 July 1663.

CHAPTER 7

1   Apsley to Fanshawe, H.M.C. Heathcote MSS, p. 116.
2   Schomberg to Fanshawe, 31 May 1663, H.M.C. Heathcote MSS, p. 106.
3   Schomberg to d'Ablancourt, 30 May 1663, H.M.C. Heathcote MSS, p. 106.
4   10 Feb 1662/3, H.M.C. Heathcote MSS, p. 58.
5   Sir Henry Bennet to Fanshawe, 12 May 1663, H.M.C. Heathcote MSS, p. 86.
6   Fanshawe to Sir Henry Bennet, 17 June 1663, H.M.C. Heathcote MSS, p. 111.
7   D'Ablancourt, p. 116. He gives 'Piniers' for the Portuguese village of Espinheiro.
8   Apsley to Fanshawe, H.M.C. Heathcote MSS, p. 116.
9   *Mercurius Publicus*, 2–9 July 1663.
10 Fanshawe to Sir Henry Bennet, 19 June 1663, H.M.C. Heathcote MSS, p. 119.
11 Schomberg to Fanshawe, 12 June 1663, H.M.C. Heathcote MSS, p. 114.
12 Ibid.
13 Apsley to Fanshawe, H.M.C. Heathcote MSS, p. 116.
14 Schomberg to Fanshawe, H.M.C. Heathcote MSS, p. 115.
15 28 May 1663, H.M.C. Heathcote MSS, p. 109; d'Ablancourt, pp. 124–126, 135; de Freitas, *A Cavalaria na Guerra da Restauração*, p. 47.
16 For a fuller discussion see Riley, *Decisive Battles*, Chapter 1.
17 For a detailed look at medical care in Iberia at this time see White, 'Spain's Early Soldiers', pp. 20–27.
18 H.M.C. Heathcote MSS, undated. TNA SP 89/6, ff. 257–258.
19 Tom Brown (ed.), *Miscellanea Aulica* (London, 1702), pp. 332–333, 339–340; C.S.P.I., 1663–1665, pp. 362–363, 366–368, 382.
20 See Chapter 8.
21 C.S.P.D., 1663–1664, pp. 315, 553; *Original Letters and Negotiations of Sir Richard Fanshaw* (London, 1724), vol. I, p. 49.
22 H.M.C. Heathcote MSS, pp. 153–154, 163; *The Newes*, 20 June 1664; *Intelligencer*, 8 August 1664.
23 Burnet, p. 117.
24 TNA E351/344.
25 <ww.eh.net/ehresources/howmuch/poundq.php> (accessed 2011).
26 Routh, *Tangier*, p. 29 citing a figure of £837,777 per annum from the Calendar of Treasury Books, vol. I.
27 Riley, 'English Army 1662–1668', pp. 59, 64.
28 Ibid., p. 90.
29 See the lists of names by regiment in Jennings.
30 D'Alton, p. 87.
31 He is mentioned and recommended in Southwell to Arlington, 4 February 1667, TNA SP 89/9, f. 39.
32 Riley, 'English Army 1662–1668', p. 82.
33 Dalton, vol. I, p. 9; Riley, 'English Army 1662–1668', p. 82.
34 Riley, 'English Army 1662–1668', p. 90.
35 Schomberg to Fanshawe, June 1663, H.M.C. Heathcote MSS, p. 115.
36 <www.eh.net/ehresources/howmuch/poundq.php> (accessed 2011).
37 Childs, *Warfare in the Seventeenth Century*, pp. 96–97.
38 White, 'Spain's Early Modern Soldiers', p. 4.
39 Ibid., p. 5.
40 Parker, p. 209.
41 H.M.C. Heathcote MSS, p. 161. See also Woodhouse, pp. 21–22, 396–399.
42 9 March 1663, TNA SP 89/7, ff. 25–26.

43 Boxer, p. 659.
44 'Mr Peter's Message' (1646), cited in Woodhouse, p. 387.
45 D'Ablancourt, pp. 106–116.

CHAPTER 8
1 *Memoirs of Ann Lady Fanshawe*, p. 126.
2 *Intelligencer*, 16 May 1664.
3 Maynard to Fanshawe, 24 February 1663, H.M.C. Heathcote MSS, p. 142.
4 Maynard to Fanshawe, 23 May 1664, H.M.C. Heathcote MSS, p. 163.
5 Dumouriez, pp. 63–64; d'Ablancourt, p. 140.
6 D'Ablancourt, p. 140.
7 The descriptions of the town and the terrain are drawn from the author's detailed reconnaissance on foot in January 2012.
8 Sebastian Alonso Planchuelo, 'Journal of the Defense of the town of Alcantara, armed siege of the rebel army, 13 to June 25, 1664', *Historical Issues of Alcantara*, (1) (1986).
9 D'Ablancourt, p. 142.
10 Planchuelo *op cit*, no page numbering.
11 Ibid.
12 Childs, *Army of Charles II*, p. 168.
13 Planchuelo *op cit*, no page numbering.
14 Maynard to Fanshawe, 29 July 1664, H.M.C. Heathcote MSS, pp. 160–161.
15 Ibid.
16 Ibid.; Colbatch, pp. 150–152; d'Ablancourt, p. 142; Hardacre, p. 121; Dumouriez, p. 66.
17 D'Ablancourt, p 142.
18 H.M.C. Heathcote MSS, pp. 160–161; Colbatch, pp. 150–152; d'Ablancourt, p. 142.
19 Planchuelo *op cit*, no page numbering.
20 D'Ablancourt, p. 144.
21 Boxer, p. 660.
22 Maynard to Fanshawe, 29 July 1664, H.M.C. Heathcote MSS, pp. 160–161.
23 C.C.S.P., vol. V, pp. 410–411.
24 Childs, *Army of Charles II*, p. 165.
25 Maynard to Fanshawe, 29 July 1664, H.M.C. Heathcote MSS, pp. 160–161.
26 Clarendon to Schomberg, January 1663, MS Clarendon 83, ff. 59–60; Hardacre, p. 122.
27 Clarendon to the English officers in Portugal, 7 February 1663, MS Clarendon 83, f. 48.
28 D'Ablancourt, p. 143.
29 Maynard to Arlington cited in Boxer, p. 660.
30 Ângelo Ribeiro, *História de Portugal: A Restauração da Independência-O início da Dinastia de Bragança* (Lisbon, 2004), p. 96.
31 1 July 1664, TNA S.P. 89/6, f. 293.
32 Firth and Davies, vol. I, p. 312.
33 Clarendon to Schomberg, 18 August 1664, MS Clarendon 82, ff. 61–62; Colbatch, pp. 150–152.
34 C.C.S.P., vol. V, pp. 442–443.
35 C.S.P.D., 1660–1661, p. 445; C.S.P.D., 1661–1662, pp. 508, 577; C.S.P.D., 1664–1665, p. 199.
36 D'Ablancourt, p. 144.
37 *Original Letters of Fanshawe*, vol. I, pp. 114, 254, 258; C.S.P.D., 1660–1661, pp. 87, 151, 303, 320, 347; Hardacre, p. 121.
38 D'Ablancourt, pp. 146–147.
39 Maynard to Arlington, 2 November 1664, TNA SP 89/6, f. 301.
40 Schomberg to Clarendon, 6 December 1664, C.C.S.P., vol. V, p. 445.
41 Maynard to Arlington, 1 February 1664, TNA SP 89/6; Dumouriez, p. 68.

CHAPTER 9

1   *Memoirs of Ann Lady Fanshawe*, p. 174n.
2   Espírito Santo, *Montes Claros 1665*, p. 53.
3   Conde de Clonard, *Historia Orgánica de las Armas de Infantería y Caballería* (Madrid, 1851–1862), vol. VIII, pp. 258–311.
4   TNA SP 89/7, f. 46.
5   D'Ablancourt, p. 161.
6   Maynard to Clarendon, TNA SP 89/7, f. 46; Espírito Santo, *Montes Claros 1665*, p. 53.
7   Dumouriez, p. 70.
8   De Freitas, *A Cavalaria na Guerra da Restauração*, p. 47.
9   'A Relation of last summer's Campaign in the Kingdom of Portugal, 1665', by le Conde de Castelmelhor, transcribed by Maynard, TNA SP 89/7, ff. 48–52.
10 TNA SP 89/7, f. 46.
11 TNA SP 89/7, ff. 48–52.
12 The descriptions of the ground are drawn from the author's detailed reconnaissance on foot in January 2012.
13 Dumouriez, p. 72.
14 Espírito Santo, *Montes Claros 1665*, p. 65.
15 D'Ablancourt, pp. 162–163.
16 Dumouriez, p. 72.
17 TNA SP 89/7, ff. 48–52.
18 Clonard, vol. VIII, p. 32.
19 D'Ablancourt, p. 164.
20 Ibid., p. 165.
21 *Intelligencer*, 11 July 1665.
22 Ibid.
23 TNA SP 89/7, ff. 49–51.
24 Ibid.
25 D'Ablancourt, pp. 167–168.
26 *Intelligencer*, 11 July 1665.
27 D'Ablancourt, p. 169. He mentions Maynard in place of Moreneur, which makes no sense, Maynard being a captain.
28 TNA SP 89/7, ff. 49–51; McMurdo, pp. 424–425.
29 TNA SP 89/7, ff. 48–52; Thomas Maynard to Arlington, 14 June 1665, TNA SP 89/7, f. 46; Dumouriez, p. 78. Five officers killed, 11 officers wounded, 150 other ranks killed and wounded.
30 Dumouriez, p. 79.
31 *Intelligencer*, 11 July 1665.
32 D'Ablancourt, p. 169.
33 *Memoirs of Ann Lady Fanshawe*, p. 174n.
34 TNA SP 89/7, f. 49.
35 Maynard to Bennet, 3 August 1665, TNA SP 89/7, f. 63.
36 Dumouriez, p. 81.
37 For a more detailed discussion see Riley, *Decisive Battles*, Chapter I.
38 *Memoirs of Ann Lady Fanshawe*, p. 176.

CHAPTER 10

1   *Memoirs of Ann Lady Fanshawe*, p. 174.
2   D'Ablancourt, p. 172.
3   Ibid., p. 173; Dumouriez, p. 82.
4   Dumouriez, p. 82.

5   Hardacre, p. 123.

6   Parker, p. 87.

7   See for example: Monique Sommé, 'L'Armée bourgognienne au siége de Calais de 1436', *Guerre et société en France, en Angleterre et en Bretagne XIV–XV siècle,* ed. P. Contamine, C. Giry-Deloisin, M. Keen (Lille, 1991), pp. 197–219; Parker, pp. 96–98.

8   James F. Dunnigan, *Leipzig* (Simultaneous Publications War-game, 1971).

9   Parker, p. 209.

10 TNA SP 89/7, f. 299.

11 D'Ablancourt, p. 174; *Oxford Gazette,* 14–18 December 1665.

12 D'Ablancourt, p. 175.

13 Ibid.

14 *Oxford Gazette,* 14–18 December 1665; D'Ablancourt, pp. 176–177.

15 José Antonio Uris Guisantes, 'Castelo de Santa Cruz' [online], A Guarda-Foros, <https://www.xenealoxia.org> (accessed 2011).

16 Maynard to Clarendon, 10 October 1665, TNA SP 89/7, f. 82.

17 Guisantes, 'Castelo de Santa Cruz'.

18 *Oxford Gazette,* 14–18 December 1665.

19 Ibid.

20 Maynard to Clarendon, 4 December 1665, TNA SP 89/7, f. 82.

21 Guisantes, 'Castelo de Santa Cruz'.

22 Maynard to Clarendon, 10 October 1665, TNA SP 89/7, f. 82; *Oxford Gazette,* 14–18 December 1665.

23 Dumouriez, p. 83; d'Ablancourt, p. 180.

24 H.M.C. Heathcote MSS, p. 226.

25 Southwell to Ormond, 10 June 1667, cited in Carte, p. 187.

26 *Memoirs of Ann Lady Fanshawe,* p. 182.

27 Ibid., p. 194.

CHAPTER 11

1   Michael Howard and Peter Paret (eds.), Karl-Maria von Clausewitz, *On War* (Princeton, 1976), pp. 87–8, 603, 605–7.

2   Pepys, *Diary,* p. 122.

3   2 April 1666, TNA S.P. 89/7, f. 156.

4   H.M.C. Heathcote MSS, p. 223.

5   *London Gazette,* 26 February–1 March 1666.

6   D'Ablancourt, p. 181.

7   Dumouriez, p. 83.

8   Ibid.

9   D'Ablancourt, p. 182.

10 Ibid., p. 188.

11 Ibid.

12 Dumouriez, p. 86.

13 D'Ablancourt, p. 189.

14 For a detailed account see Sir Robert Southwell's letters in Carte.

15 15 January 1666/7 and 3, 20 January 1667, TNA SP 89/8.

16 Southwell to Arlington, 26 January 1667, TNA SP 89/8, f. 39.

17 Southwell to Joseph Williamson, 14 March 1667, TNA SP 89/8, f. 97.

18 The descriptions of the terrain are drawn from the author's detailed reconnaissance on foot in January 2012.

19 Melendez, 'The Recovery of Extremadura and Spanish Military Memory'.

20 Jennings, pp. 371, 622, 465; Wienand Drenth, *Regiments of the Modern British Army 1660–1714* [unpublished].
21 Southwell to Joseph Williamson, 14 March 1667, TNA SP 89/8, f. 97.
22 Maynard to Clarendon, 12 March 1667, SP 89/8, f. 95.
23 14 March 1667, TNA SP 89/8, f. 97; Dumouriez, p. 89.
24 Maynard to Clarendon, 12 March 1667, SP 89/8, f. 95.
25 Southwell to Joseph Williamson, 13 March 1667, TNA SP 89/8, f. 84.
26 Southwell to Joseph Williamson, 14 March 1667, TNA SP 89/8, f. 98.
27 Southwell to Joseph Williamson, 14 March 1667, TNA SP 89/8, f. 97; D'Ablancourt, pp. 203–204.
28 Maynard to Arlington, 5 March 1667, TNA SP 89/8, f. 86.
29 Maynard to Arlington, 15 March 1667, TNA SP 89/8, f. 86.
30 Southwell to Arlington, 4 February 1667, TNA SP 89/8, f.39.

CHAPTER 12

1   Chalmers, vol. II.
2   Southwell to Ormond, 5 November 1667 cited in Carte, pp. 284–285.
3   D'Ablancourt, p. 234.
4   Southwell to Arlington, 5 November 1667 cited in Carte, pp. 339–340.
5   Southwell to Ormond, 5 November 1667 cited in Carte, pp. 294–295.
6   Maynard to Arlington, 22 July 1667, TNA SP 89/8, f. 189.
7   D'Ablancourt, p. 134.
8   Maynard to Arlington 8 June 1667, TNA SP 89/8, f. 157.
9   Treaty Paper Spain, TNA SP Foreign 103/16, f.16.
10 *Arlington's Letters*, ed. T. Bebington, (London, 1701), vol. II, pp. 254–256.
11 Southwell to Arlington, 21 March 1667, TNA SP 89/8, f. 108.
12 6 April 1667, TNA SP 89/8, f. 132; Southwell to Arlington, 10 May 1667, *Arlington's Letters*, vol. I, p. 70.
13 For the terms of the treaty see Frances Gardiner Davenport, *European Treaties Bearing on the History of the United States and Its Dependencies to 1658* (New York, 2007), p. 361 *et seq.*
14 Maynard to Arlington, 5 February 1667/8, TNA SP 89/9, f. 28.
15 Pepys, *Diary*, 19 February 1667/8, p. 487; D'Ablancourt, pp. 241–253.
16 Maynard to Arlington, 19 May 1668, TNA SP 89/9, f. 66; Southwell to Williamson, 7 June 1668, TNA SP 89/9, f. 76.
17 Southwell to Williamson, 7 June 1668, TNA SP 89/9, f. 76.
18 Maynard to Arlington, 5 February 1668, TNA SP 89/9, f. 28.
19 Dalton, vol. I, p. 81.
20 Maynard to Arlington, 5 February 1668, TNA SP 89/9, f. 28.
21 Carl A. Hanson, *Economy and Society in Baroque Portugal 1668–1703* (London, 1981), p. 144.
22 8 November 1667, TNA SP 89/8, f. 241.
23 31 May 1668, TNA SP 89/9, f. 68.
24 Arlington to Southwell, 28 June 1667, *Arlington's Letters*, vol. I, p. 74.
25 Southwell to Joseph Williamson, 14 June 1668, TNA SP 89/9, f. 75.
26 31 May 1668, TNA SP 89/9, f. 68.
27 Schomberg, Dempsey and Trelawney to Arlington, 8 February 1668, TNA SP 89/9, f. 15.
28 Maynard to Arlington, 10 March 1667/8, TNA SP 89/9, f. 40.
29 Maynard to Arlington, 19 May 1668, TNA SP 89/9, f. 66.
30 Maynard to Arlington, 7 May 1668, TNA SP 89/9, f. 40.
31 Southwell to Joseph Williamson, 20 July 1668, TNA SP 89/9 f. 87; Southwell to Joseph Williamson, 7 August 1668, TNA SP 89/9, f. 97.
32 Southwell to Joseph Williamson, 5 September 1668, TNA SP 89/9, f. 106.

33 Parry to Williamson, 18 September 1668, TNA SP 89/9, f. 110.
34 'The Collection of Autograph Letters … formed by Alfred Morrison', 2nd series, The Bulstrode Papers, (London, 1897), vol. I, p.29.
35 Ibid., p. 42; Routh, *Tangier*, p. 315.
36 Davis, vol. I, p. 93.
37 Ibid.; Riley, 'English Army 1658–1668', p. 89.
38 31 May 1668, TNA 89/9, f. 112.
39 Rumsey to Williamson, 15 September 1668, TNA SP 89/9, f. 113.
40 Southwell to Williamson, 14 June 1668, TNA SP 89/9, f. 75.
41 Routh, *Tangier*, pp. 78–79.
42 Davis, vol. I, p. 95.
43 For more details see Riley, 'English Army 1658–1668'; Dalton, vol. I and Routh, *Tangier*.
44 Riley, 'English Army 1658–1668', p. 74.
45 Southwell to Arlington, 17 September 1668, TNA 89/9, ff. 108, 109; for details of the shipping see TNA 89/9, f. 90 (undated).
46 Norwood to Arlington, 24 September 1668, TNA CO 279/10.
47 Davis, vol. I, p. 95; Childs, *Army of Charles II*, p. 126.
48 28 February 1665, CO 279/4, f. 53.
49 *London Gazette*, 15–19 October 1668.
50 Dalton, vol. I, p. 92.
51 15 February 1667/8, TNA SP 89/9, f. 32.
52 8 February 1667/8, TNA SP 89/9, f. 33.
53 29 January 1667/8, TNA SP 89/9, f. 26.
54 TNA SP 29/233, ff. 180–181; SP 29/233 f. 29; Miller, p. 43.
55 TNA SP 29/75, f. 294.
56 TNA SP 29/225, f. 243; TNA SP 29/250, f. 25; TNA SP 29/251, f. 108.
57 TNA SP 29/75, f.149.
58 Riley, 'English Army 1658–1668', p. 74.
59 Southwell to Arlington, 10 September 1668, TNA 89/9, f. 112.
60 TNA SP 29/75, ff. 150–151.
61 C.S.P.D., 1668–1669, p. 90; H.M.C. Montagu of Beaulieu MSS (London, 1900), p. 169.
62 TNA SP 29/251, f. 148.
63 TNA PC 2/62, f. 21; C.S.P.D., 1668–1669, pp. 542, 561.
64 Dalton, vol. I, pp. 82, 219.
65 Ibid., p. 207.
66 Hardacre, p. 123.
67 Dalton, vol. I, p. 130.
68 Ibid., pp. 147, 202.
69 Ibid., pp. 80, 134.
70 Ibid., p. 201.
71 Ibid., p. 226.
72 Ibid., p. 119.
73 Ibid., p. 129.
74 Ibid., p. 241.
75 Ibid., p. 134.
76 C.S.P.D., Addenda 1660–1685, p. 461; TNA SP 29/442, f. 301.
77 Dalton, vol. I, p. 206.
78 Ibid., p. 135.
79 Ibid., pp. 133, 198, 322.
80 Ibid., p. 135.

81 Ibid., pp. 163, 171.
82 Ibid., p. 213.
83 Ibid., pp. 203, 256, 313; Dalton, vol. III, p. 99.
84 Dalton, vol. I, p. 209.
85 C.S.P.I., 1660–1662, p. 51; H.M.C. Heathcote MSS, pp. 55–56, 106, 112, 114, 122; Dalton, vol. I, p. 209; H.M.C. Tenth Report (Appendix), Part V (London, 1885), p. 131; D'Alton, p. 108.
86 Pepys, *Diary*, 30 June, 4 July 1663; Hardacre, p. 125.
87 Croke, p. 53.
88 D'Ablancourt, Introduction.
89 Dumouriez, p. 46.
90 Rev. Thomas Gumble, *The Life of General Monck, Duke of Albermarle* (London, 1671); Firth and Davis, p. 500.

Bibliography and Sources

PRIMARY SOURCES

The National Archive, Kew
Calendar of State Papers Domestic, Charles II, ed. F.H. Blackburne Daniell (London, 1939): 1660–1661, pp. 87, 151, 303, 320, 347, 445; 1661–1662, pp. 335, 344, 508, 577; 1663–1664, pp. 315, 553; 1664–1665, p. 199; 1666–1667, p. 403; 1668–1669 pp. 90, 542, 561; Addenda 1660–1685 p. 461.

Calendar of State Papers, Ireland, 1660–1662 p. 51; 1663–1665, pp. 362–363, 366–368, 382.

Calendar of State Papers, Venice, 1661–1664.

State Papers Domestic, Charles II:
    SP 29/75; 29/186; 29/225; 29/250; 29/251; 29/442.
    SP 44/2.

State Papers, Portugal, 1660–1668:
    SP 89/5, ff. 159, 162; SP 89/6, ff. 7–10, 23, 44, 257–258, 293; 89/7, ff. 46, 48–52, 63, 156; 89/8, ff. 1, 3, 15, 38, 39, 66, 84, 86, 97, 140, 157, 189, 197, 223, 312; 89/9, ff. 22, 28, 32, 40, 42, 53, 68, 75, 87, 90, 92, 97, 99, 106, 108, 109, 110, 112, 113.

State Papers Foreign, Charles II:
    Treaty Paper Spain 103/16, f.16.

Colonial Office Papers for Tangier:
    CO 279/10, f. 3.

Privy Council Papers:
    PC 2/62.

Exchequer Declared Accounts for Tangier 1660–1661:
    E351/344.

National Library of Spain
MS 2391, 'Defense of the town of Alcantara'.

Historical Manuscripts Commission
Heathcote Manuscripts, Series 50 (Norwich, 1899).
Montagu of Beaulieu MSS (London, 1900).
Portland MSS (London, 1894), vol. III.
Seventh Report (London, 1879).
Tenth Report (Appendix), Part V (London, 1885).

Portuguese Commission for Military History, Lisbon
Cartas do marquis de Castelo Melhor para Roberto Southwell e para Antonio Soares da Costa, vol. X, ff. 126–127.
Cartas patentes, vol. X, ff. 47–125.
Cartas Régias, vol. X, ff. 3–29.

De Freitas, Jorge Penim, *A Cavalaria na Guerra da Restauração: Reconstrução e evolução de una força militar, 1641–1668* (2005).

De Freitas, Jorge Penim, *O Combatente Durante a Guerra da Restauração, 1640–1668* (2007). Documentos existentes no Arquio Histórico Militar, vol. X, ff. 1–147.

Espírito Santo, Gabriel, *A Grande Estratégia de Portugal na Restauração, 1640– 1668* (2009).

Espírito Santo, Gabriel, *Montes Claros 1665: A Vitória Decisiva* (2005).

Nunes, António Lopes Pires, *Dictionário de Arquitectura Militar* (2005).

Bodleian Library

Calendar of Clarendon State Papers, 1660–1726, vol. V, ed. F.J. Routledge (Oxford, 1974).

Clarendon MS 76, ff. 361–362; 77 ff. 31–32; 90a–91; 82 ff. 61–62; 83 ff. 48, 59–60.

Harleian Miscellany, vol. III, Major General Morgan's *Memoirs*, 1657–1658.

Rawlinson MSS C. 808, 'Militarie Occurrences in Portugal: The Spring Campaign A.D. 1663'.

Sir William Clarke MSS, 1662–1664.

Thurloe Manuscripts (Rawlinson A Volumes 1–67).

Regulations

Articles and Ordinances of War established for the better conduct of the Army (1642).

Gheyn, Jacob De, *Die Drillkunst: das ist Kriegubliche affenhandlung der Musqueten und Pique* (1664), illustrated by reduced re-engravings of the 1608 Drill Instructions by De Gheyn, with instructions in French and German copied from the 1619 edition.

Hexham, Henry, *The First Part of the Principles of the Art Military, practised in the warres of the United Netherlands. Second Edition, newly corrected and amended.* (Delft, 1642).

Hexham, Henry, *The Second Part of the Principles of the Art Military, practised in the warres of the United Netherlands. Second Edition, newly corrected and amended.* (Delft, 1642).

Hexham, Henry, *The Third Part of the Principles of the Art Military, practised in the warres of the United Netherlands. Second Edition, newly corrected and amended.* (Rotterdam, 1643).

Contemporary Accounts

'A List of Officers Claiming to the £60,000' (London, 1663).

A True Relation of the Manner of the dangerous dispute and bloody conflict between the Spaniards and the French, etc (London, 1661).

Arlington's Letters, ed. T. Bebington, (2 vols., London, 1701).

Bishop Burnet, *A History of His Own Time* (London, 1906).

Brown, Tom, (ed.), *Miscellanea Aulica* (London, 1702).

Carte, Thomas, *The History of the Revolutions of Portugal, From the Foundation of that Kingdom to the year MDCLXVII: With Letters of Sir Robert Southwell, During his Embassy there, to the Duke of Ormond; Giving a particular Account of the deposing of Alfonso, and placing Don Pedro on the Throne* (London, 1760).

Clonard, Conde de, *Historia Orgánica de las Armas de Infantería y Caballería* (Madrid, 1851–1862) vol. VIII.

Colbatch, John, *An Account of the Court of Portugal* (London, 1700).

Croce, Flaminio della, *L'essercito della cavalleria et d'altre materiel* (Henrico Aertsio, 1628).

Croke, Charles, *Fortune's Uncertainty, or Youth's Unconstancy* (London, 1667; reprinted Oxford, 1959).

Gumble, Rev. Thomas, *The Life of General Monck, Duke of Albermarle* (London, 1671).

Mallet, Allain Manesson, *Les traveaux de Mars, ou L'art de la guerre* (2nd edn, Paris, 1684).

Melzo, Fr Lodovico, *Regole militari sopra il governo e servitio particolare della cavalleria* (Gioachimo Trognaesio, 1611).

Memoirs of the Sieur d'Ablancourt: Containing a general history of the court and kingdom of Portugal (Translated from the French, London, 1703).

Monck, George, *Observations upon Military and Political Affairs* (London, 1671).

Original Letters and Negotiations of Sir Richard Fanshawe (London, 1724), vol. I.

Pepys, Samuel, *The Diary of Samuel Pepys*, ed. H.B. Wheatley, (8 vols., London, 1904–1905).

Ribiero, Ângelo, *História de Portugal: A Restauração da Independência – O início da Dinastia de Bragança* (Lisbon, 2004).

Shipman, Thomas, *Carolina: or Loyal Poems* (London, 1683).

'The Collection of Autograph Letters … formed by Alfred Morrison', 2nd series, The Bulstrode Papers, (London, 1897), vol. I.

The Memoirs of Ann Lady Fanshawe (London, 1908).

Vila Flor, Sancho Manuel de Vilhena, Conde de, *A relation of the great success the King of Portugal's army had upon the Spaniards, the 29th of May Engl. stile 1663* (London: Printed by Alice Warren, for William Garrett, 1663).

Whitelocke, Bulstrode, *Memorials* (Oxford, 1853), vol. III.

Williams, Sir Roger, *The Actions of the Low Countries* (New York, 1985).

Newspapers

London Gazette, 26 February–1 March, 1665–1666; 15–19 October, 1668.

Mercurius Publicus, 31 July–7 August 1662; 21–28 August 1662; 31 July–7 August 1662; 2–9 July 1663.

Mercurius Scoticus, 18–21 February 1651.

The Kingdom's Intelligencer, 5–12 May 1662; 26 May–2 June 1662; 2–9 June 1662; 23–30 June 1662; 25 August–1 September 1662; 16 May 1664; 8 August 1664; 16 August 1664; 17 July 1665; 13 November 1665.

The Newes, 20 June 1664.

Oxford Gazette, 14–18 December 1665.

Parliamentary Publications

Grey, Antichel, *Debates of the House of Commons* (9 vols., London, 1769).

Journals of the House of Lords, vol. II.

Journals of the House of Commons, vol. VII.

Reference Works

An Historical Account of the British Regiments employed since the Reign of Queen Elizabeth and King James I in the formation and defence of the Dutch Republic, particularly of the Scotch Brigade (London, 1795).

Aubrey, John, *Brief Lives*, ed. Richard Barber, (Woodbridge and New York, 1975).

Bagwell, Richard, *Dictionary of National Biography* (London, 1961), vol. XV.

Chalmers, George, *A Collection of Treaties Between Great Britain and Other Powers* (2 vols., London, 1790).

D'Alton, John, *Illustrations, Historical and Genealogical: Of King James's Irish Army List (1689)* (Dublin, 1855).

Dalton, Charles, *English Army Lists and Commission Registers, 1661–1714* (6 vols., London, 1894–1904).

Dalton, Charles, *Irish Army Lists, 1661–1685* (London, 1907).

Dalton, Charles, *The Scots Army, 1661–1688* (London, 1909).

Davenport, Frances Gardiner, *European Treaties Bearing on the History of the United States and Its Dependencies to 1658* (New York, 2007).

Drenth, Wienand, *The Regiments of the Modern British Army 1660–1714: From the Beginnings through the end of the War of the Spanish Succession* [unpublished].

Firth, Sir Charles, and Davies, G., *The Regimental History of Cromwell's Army* (2 vols., Oxford, 1940).

Howard, Michael and Peter Paret (eds.), Karl-Maria von Clausewitz, *On War* (Princeton, 1976).

Notes which Passed at Meetings of the Privy Council between Charles II and the Earl of Clarendon, ed. W. D. Macray (London, 1896).

Original Letters and Negotiations of Sir Richard Fanshawe (London, 1724), vol. I.

Shaw, William A., *Calendar of Treasury Books, 1661–1668* (Institute of Historical Research, 1916), vol. VII.

The Journals of Sir Thomas Allin, 1660–1678, ed. R.C. Anderson, (Navy Records Society, 1939–1940), vol. I, pp. 76–85.

Woodhouse, A.S.P., *Puritanism and Liberty: Being the Army Debates (1647–9) from the Clarke Manuscripts with Supplementary Documents* (London, 1938).

MODERN SECONDARY SOURCES

Books

Alden, Dauril, *The Making of an Enterprise*: *The Society of Jesus in Portugal, Its Empire, and Beyond, 1540–1750* (Stanford, USA, 1996). Anderson, James Maxwell, *The History of Portugal* (London, 2000).

Atkinson, William C., *A History of Spain and Portugal* (London, 1961).

Birmingham, David, *A Concise History of Portugal* (London, 2003).

Brauer, Jurgen, & Van Tuyll, Hubert, *Castles, Battles & Bombs: How Economics Explains Military History* (London, 2008).

Childs, John *The Army of Charles II* (London and Toronto, 1976).

Childs, John, 'Huguenots and Huguenot Regiments in the British Army, 1660–1702: "Cometh the moment, cometh the men"', Matthew Glozier (ed.), *War, Religion and Service: Huguenot Soldiering, 1685–1713* (Aldershot, 2007).

Childs, John, *Warfare in the Seventeenth Century* (London, 2003).

Clark, G.N., *War and Society in the Seventeenth Century* (Cambridge, 1958).

Cotton, Richard W., *Barnstaple and the Northern Part of Devonshire during the Great Civil War, 1642–46* (London, 1889).

Davis, Colonel John, *History of the Second Queen's, now the Royal West Surrey Regiment* (London, 1887), vol. I.

Duffy, Christopher, *Fire and Stone: The Science of Fortress Warfare 1660–1860* (New Jersey, USA, 1975).

Dumouriez, C.F.D., *Campagnes de Maréchal Schomberg en Portugal, 1662–1668* (London, 1807).

Elliott, J.H., *The Revolt of the Catalans: A Study in the Decline of Spain 1598–1640* (CUP, 1984).

Feiling, Keith, *British Foreign Policy 1660–1672* (London, 1972).

Firth, C.H., *Cromwell's Army* (London, 1921).

Gamazo, Gabriel Maura, *Carlos II y su corte* (Madrid, 1911), vol. I.

Glozier, Matthew, *Marshal Schomberg 1615–1690* (Brighton, 2005).

Glozier, Matthew, *Scottish Soldiers in France in the Reign of the Sun King: Nursery for Men of Honour* (Leiden, 2004).

Grose, Francis, *Military Antiquities respecting a history of the English Army* (London, 1786–1788), vol. II.

Guizot, F.P.G., *History of Richard Cromwell and the Restoration*, tr. A. R. Scoble, (London, 1854).

Hanson, Carl A., *Economy and Society in Baroque Portugal 1668–1703* (London, 1981).

Henry, Gráinne, *The Irish Military Community in Spanish Flanders, 1586–1612* (Irish Academic Press, 1992).

Hutton, Ronald, *The Restoration, 1658–1667* (Oxford, 1987).

Hyde, Edward, Earl of Clarendon, *The Life of Edward, Earl of Clarendon* (London, 1857), vol. I.

Jennings, Brendan, *Wild Geese in Spanish Flanders, 1582–1700* (Dublin, 1964).

Kiernan, V., 'Foreign Mercenaries and Absolute Monarchy', T. Aston (ed.), *Crisis in Europe 1560–1660* (London, 1965).

Lister, T.H., *Life and Administration of Edward, First Earl of Clarendon* (London, 1837), vol. III.

Livermore, H.V., *A New History of Portugal* (CUP, 1969).

Macaulay, Thomas Babington, 1st Baron, *The History of England from the Accession of James II* (5 vols., 1848).

Maland, David, *Europe in the Seventeenth Century* (London, 1991).

Mallett, Michael, *Mercenaries and their Masters: Warfare in Renaissance Italy* (Totowa, NJ, 2009).

McGurk, John, 'Wild Geese: the Irish in European armies (sixteenth to eighteenth centuries)', P. O'Sullivan (ed.), *The Irish World Wide: Patterns of Migration* (Leicester, 1992).

McMurdo, Edward, *The History of Portugal: From the Reign of D. Joao II to the Reign of D. Joao V*, Vol. III (London, 1889; facsimile reprint London, 2010).

Murtagh, Harman, 'Irish soldiers abroad, 1600–1800', T. Bartlett (ed.), *A Military History of Ireland* (CUP, 1996).

Newman, P.R., *The Old Service: Royalist regimental colonels and the Civil War, 1642–1646* (London, 1993).

Parker, Geoffrey, *The Army of Flanders and the Spanish Road, 1567–1659* (CUP, 1972).

Reese, Peter, *The Life of General George Monck: For King and Cromwell* (Barnsley, 2008).

Riley, Jonathon, *Decisive Battles* (London, 2010).

Riley, Jonathon, *Napoleon as a General* (London, 2007).

Routh, E.M.G., *Tangier: England's Lost Atlantic Outpost 1661–1684* (London, 1912).

Sagnac, P., and A. De Saint-Léger, *La Prépondérance française: Louis XIV (1661–1715)* (2nd edn, Paris, 1944).

Sepulveda, Christovan Ayres de Margalhäes, *Um capitulo da Guerra da restauração, 1660 a 1668: O Conde de Schönberg em Portugal* (Lisbon, 1897).

Stradling, R.A., *The Spanish Monarchy and Irish Mercenaries: The Wild Geese in Spain, 1618–1668* (Irish Academic Press, 1994).

Trim, D. J. B., 'The Huguenots and the European wars of religion, c.1560-1697: soldiering in national and transnational context', Trim (ed.), *The Huguenots: History and Memory in Transnational Context: Essays in Honour and Memory of Walter C. Utt.* (Leiden, 2011).

Van Creveld, Martin, *Supplying War* (CUP, 1977).

Wilson, Peter H., *German Armies: War and German Politics, 1648–1806* (London, 1998).

Wilson, Peter H., *War, State and Society in Württemberg, 1677–1783* (CUP, 1995).

Winstock, Lewis, *Songs & Music of the Redcoats: A History of the War Music of the British Army 1642–1902* (London, 1970).

Articles in Journals

Ames, Glenn Joseph, 'Renascent Empire?: the House of Braganza and the Quest for Stability in Portuguese Monsoon Asia c.1640–1683', *The International History Review*, 23:3 (September 2001).

Appleby, David J., '"God forbid it should come to that": the feud between Colonel Molesworth and Major-General O'Brien in Portugal, 1663', review by M. N. Pearson., *The Seventeenth Century*, 26:2 (2011), pp. 346–367.

Atkinson, C.T., 'Charles II's Regiments in France, 1672–1678', *Journal of the Society for Army Historical Research*, XXIV (1946).

Boxer, C.R., 'Marshal Schomberg in Portugal, 1660–1668', *History Today*, 26:10 (October 1976), pp. 653–663.

Grose, Clyde L., 'The Anglo-Portuguese Marriage of 1662', *The Hispanic American Historical Review*, 10:3 (August 1930), pp. 313–352.

Hardacre, Paul, 'The English Contingent in Portugal, 1662–1668', *Journal of the Society for Army Historical Research*, 38 (1960), pp. 112–125.

Lynn, John, 'The Evolution of Army Style in the Modern West, 800-2000', *The International History Review*, 18:3 (1996), pp. 505–545.

Miller, John, 'Catholic officers in the later Stuart Army', *English Historical Review*, LXXXVIII:CCCXLVI (January 1973), pp. 35–53.

Planchuelo, Sebastian Alonso, 'Journal of the Defense of the town of Alcantara, armed siege of the rebel army, 13 to June 25, 1664', *Historical Issues of Alcantara*, (1) (1986).

Potter, David, 'The international mercenary market in the XVIth century: Anglo-French competition in Germany (1543–50)', *English Historical Review*, 111:440 (1996), pp. 24–58.

Rowlands, Guy, 'Foreign Service in the Age of Absolute Monarchy: Louis XIV and His Forces Étrangères', *War in History*, 17:2 (2010), pp. 141–165.

Shillington, Violet, 'The Beginnings of the Anglo-Portuguese Alliance', *Transactions of the Royal Historical Society*, New Series, XX (London, 1906), pp. 109–132.

Stüssi-Lauterburg, Jürg, 'Swiss Military System and Neutrality in the Seventeenth century as seen by contemporary Europe', *War and Society*, 2:2 (1984), pp. 19–26.

Virginia Magazine of History and Biography, XII (1904).

White, Lorraine 'The Experience of Spain's Early Modern Soldiers: Combat, Welfare and Violence', *War in History*, 9:1 (January 2002), pp. 1–38.

White, Lorraine, 'Strategic Geography and the Spanish Habsburg Monarchy's Failure to Recover Portugal, 1640–1668', *The Journal of Military History*, 71:2 (April 2007), pp. 373–409.

Wilson, Peter H., 'The German Soldier Trade of 17th and 18th Centuries: A Reassessment', *International History Review*, 18:4 (1996), pp. 757–792.

Unpublished Academic Theses

Riley, J.P., 'Continuity in the English Army, 1658–1668' (M.A. Thesis, Leeds University, 1989).

Internet

Alvaro Melendez, 'The Recovery of Extremadura and Spanish Military Memory' [online] (2011).

Conversion rates of money from 1660 to modern day have been worked out using <www. eh.net/ehresources/howmuch/poundq.php> (accessed 2011).

Guisantes, José Antonio Uris, 'Castelo de Santa Cruz' [online], A Guarda-Foros, <https:// www.xenealoxia.org> (accessed 2011).

The History of Parliament: British Political, Social and Local History [online], <http://www. historyof parliament.org.uk> (accessed 2011).

Maps

Instituto Geografico e Cadastral, Carta Geographica de Portugal, 1:50,000 Series M 7810 Edition 2-IGCP (1971), Sheets 29A, 29C, 36A, 36B, 36C, 36D, 37A, 37C, 40A.

Lopez, Tomàs, *Mapa de la Provincia de Extremadura* (1798).

Philip's *University Atlas.*

Turinta Maps *Alentejo*, 1:300,000 (1cm = 3km). Regional Series, 2nd Edition.

Index